D1538796

The Ostpolitik of the
Federal Republic of Germany

Center for International Studies, Massachusetts Institute of Technology

Studies in Communism, Revisionism, and Revolution (formerly Studies in International Communism), William E. Griffith, general editor

1. Albania and the Sino-Soviet Rift, William E. Griffith (1963)
2. Communism in North Vietnam, P. J. Honey (1964)
3. The Sino-Soviet Rift, William E. Griffith (1964)
4. Communism in Europe, Vol. 1, William E. Griffith, ed. (1964)
5. Nationalism and Communism in Chile, Ernst Halperin (1965)
6. Communism in Europe, Vol. 2, William E. Griffith, ed. (1966)
7. Viet Cong: The Organization and Techniques of the National Liberation Front of South Vietnam, Douglas Pike (1966)
8. Sino-Soviet Relations, 1964–1965, William E. Griffith (1967)
9. The French Communist Party and the Crisis of International Communism, François Fejtö (1967)
10. The New Rumania: From People's Democracy to Socialist Republic, Stephen Fischer-Galati (1967)
11. Economic Development in Communist Rumania, John Michael Montias (1967)
12. Cuba: Castroism and Communism, 1959–1966, Andrés Suárez (1967)
13. Unity in Diversity: Italian Communism and the Communist World, Donald L. M. Blackmer (1967)
14. Winter in Prague: Documents on Czechoslovak Communism in Crisis, Robin Alison Remington, ed. (1969)
15. The Angolan Revolution, Vol. 1: The Anatomy of an Explosion 1950–1962), John A. Marcum (1969)
16. Radical Politics in West Bengal, Marcus F. Franda (1971)
17. The Warsaw Pact: Case Studies in Communist Conflict Resolution, Robin Alison Remington (1971)
18. The Transformation of Communist Ideology: The Yugoslav Case, 1945–1953, A. Ross Johnson (1972)
19. Radical Politics in South Asia, Paul R. Brass and Marcus F. Franda, eds. (1973)
20. The Canal War: Four-Power Conflict in the Middle East, Lawrence L. Whetten (1974)
21. The World and the Great Power Triangles, William E. Griffith, ed. (1975)
22. The Angolan Revolution, Vol. 2: Exile Politics and Guerrilla Warfare (1962–1976), John A. Marcum (1978)
23. Socialist Albania since 1944: Domestic and Foreign Developments, Peter R. Prifti (1978)
24. The Ostpolitik of the Federal Republic of Germany, William E. Griffith (1978)

The Ostpolitik of the
Federal Republic of Germany

William E. Griffith

The MIT Press
Cambridge, Massachusetts, and London, England

Copyright © 1978 by The Massachusetts Institute of Technology

This book was set in IBM Composer Baskerville by To the Lighthouse
Press, printed and bound by Murray Printing Company in the United
States of America.

Library of Congress Cataloging in Publication Data

Griffith, William E
    The Ostpolitik of the Federal Republic of Germany.

    (Studies in communism, revisionism, and revolution; 24)
    Includes bibliographical references and index.
    1. Europe, Eastern—Foreign relations—Germany, West.   2. Germany,
West—Foreign relations—Europe, Eastern. I. Title. II. Series.
DJK45.G3G74   327.43′047   78-17939
ISBN 0-262-07072-3

Contents

Preface

This is a study in contemporary history, not in political science or sociology. I neither hypothesize, test, nor predict; rather, I have tried, while knowing that I could not wholly succeed, to "tell it as it really was." After giving some historical background about the eastern policies of previous German governments, I have concentrated on the policy toward the east of the Federal Republic of Germany. I have also tried to give enough background on the policies of the various other eastern and western states toward the Federal Republic to make their and the latter's policies toward them more understandable.

Although this study is primarily based on original documentation and secondary analysis, I have also had the benefit of many discussions with many participants and observers over the more than a decade during which I have been writing this book and in more than the two decades before that which I spent either in West Germany or the United States or in traveling in the Soviet Union and Eastern Europe. I am most grateful to all those who were so willing to talk with me, but their number, and often the confidentiality of the discussions, preclude me from acknowledging them here. I would, however, like to record my particular gratitude to three friends who read an earlier draft of the manuscript of this book and made illuminating comments on it: Klaus Harpprecht, Andreas Meyer-Landrut, and Eberhard Schulz. It has greatly profited from their wisdom.

I could not have begun and completed this book without the generous support, for a year's research leave in 1966-67, of the Ford Foundation, for which I thank the then director of its international division, Shepard Stone, and the Fletcher School of Law and Diplomacy, Tufts University, and its Dean, Edmund Gullion, as well as of the Munich Institute für Zeitgeschichte and Radio Free Europe, Munich, which gave me the use of their research facilities during that year. Its completion was made possible by grants from the Earhart and Carthage Foundations, for which I thank Richard Ware and R. Daniel McMichael respectively, and by a generous invitation from the Rockefeller Foundation to spend a month at their Villa Serbellione, Bellagio (Como), Italy, for which I should like to thank the foundation and especially Dr. and Mrs. William Olsen, who made my stay there so pleasant as well as so productive.

I have also to thank my research assistants during the long gestation of the book: László Urban, Paul Walker, James Cooney, N. Edwina Moreton, and Rada Vlajinac, and my secretaries, Nancy Hearst, Edna Rindner, and Kathleen Sato. Finally, last but certainly not least, I am grateful to my wife, herself a daughter of the Rhineland, from whom I have learned so much about Germany and Germans.

The Ostpolitik of the
Federal Republic of Germany

Unlike the British and French, but like the Russians, Poles, and Hungarians, the medieval and modern Germans expanded primarily to the east. German merchants and artisans settled towns and German landlords ruled over Polish and Czech peasants, sometimes by conquest but more often by invitation of their eastern neighbors, to whom the Germans brought words, skills, and technology.

Thus most Germans believed that they had a *mission civilisatrice* toward the east. But German methods differed. The Catholic Germans from the Rhineland, Bavaria, and Austria usually had better relations with the largely Catholic Hungarians and Czechs than did the Protestant Germans and especially the Prussians. Bismarck's and Bülow's anti-Polish policies were neither the direct forerunners of Hitler's nor qualitatively similar to them, and Frederick Wilhelm I's and Frederick the Great's were even less so. Yet by the eighteenth century Prussian rule over its non-German subjects was diverging from general European practices. Prussia was becoming increasingly anti-Polish and the Poles anti-Prussian.

Prussia acquired Polish territories whose cities were already largely German. The countryside, still Polish, was gradually colonized or ruled over by Prussians. Prussian Protestantism did not mix with Polish Catholicism and modernizing Prussians increasingly despised the underdeveloped Poles. Prussian efficiency favored domination and eventually assimilation of Prussia's non-German subjects. The partitions of Poland intensified Prussian feeling of superiority and contempt for the Poles. Conversely, because Prussia and Poland had no religious and little common political or cultural heritage, Prussia's annexation of Polish territory seemed to the Polish gentry worse than its loss to Austria or even to Russia. The Habsburgs' attitude to the Poles was more liberal than the Prussians'. Catholic heads of a multinational state, they were so occupied with the Turks and their French allies, that they were less repressive over their Polish subjects.[1]

Early German relations with Russia were ambivalent. Germans largely introduced Western commerce and technology into Russia, Baltic Germans were prominent in the tsarist bureaucracy, German idealist philosophy and Marxism influenced Russian thought, and Russo-German cultural relations initially developed to Russia's advantage. Yet the Russian populists and Slavophiles revolted against both and the Russian aristocracy fell under French cultural influence.

The Worsening of German-Polish Relations

The three partitions of Poland, in 1772, 1793, and 1795, took place as modern nationalism was taking shape. Frederick the Great originated them; Catherine the Great of Russia—not for the last time in Russian history—preferred a united Polish state under Russian influence; and Maria Theresa opposed them. All three states became determined to keep Poland partitioned, the more so because of the rising Polish sympathy with revolutionary France and later with Napoleon.[2]

German (and Russian) hostility to Poland was further intensified by their rising nationalism, the product of modernization and industrialization. Germany began to overshadow Russia and Eastern Europe in industrial and military power. All three countries, however, contrary to Western Europe, kept traditional, essentially aristocratic value systems, which impeded democratization and the rise of a less nationalist political Left.

The ascetic devotion to duty characteristic of traditional Prussia was gradually corrupted by wealth, militarism, and imperialism. Even the 1848 German liberals were divided on restoring a Polish state. Thereafter, although some declining, sentimental pro-Polish feelings, furthered by the nineteenth-century Polish risings, remained, particularly in southwest Germany, Bismarck's successful unification of Germany by "blood and iron," dominated by Prussia, made German imperial policy more anti-Polish. Moreover, by separating Austria from Germany and thus preventing a national state of all Germans, it sowed the seeds of pan-Germanism in Austria as well. Dazzled by Bismarck's success, most Protestant German liberals became so nationalist and anti-Catholic that they supported the empire's Germanization and anti-Catholic policies toward Poland, including the forced use of German in the schools and in all governmental activity and the compulsory purchase of large estates for German settlers. The rising German Social Democratic Party (SPD) was not anti-Polish, but as internationalists they disliked Polish nationalism.[3]

In the late nineteenth and early twentieth centuries Polish nationalism became more anti-German, even more than it was anti-Russian in Congress Poland, where oppression and Russification had followed the unsuccessful 1863 Polish rising, and much more than it was anti-Austrian in Galicia, whose Polish elite shared with Vienna Catholicism and a common desire to dominate their Ruthenian peasantry and who after 1867 enjoyed cultural and considerable political autonomy. Industrialization and literacy, introduced by Prussia into its Polish provinces, provided more potential for the rise of Polish nationalism among the Polish bourgeoisie and peasantry. Unlike the Polish gentry and the rising Polish socialists, the anti-German Polish National Democrats abandoned the idea of the multinational Polish "commonwealth" (*Rzeczpospolita*) in favor of an ethnically Polish state, anti-German, anti-Semitic, and Roman Catholic, allied with and if necessary under the suzerainty of the Russian tsars.

There were anti-Russian elements in Imperial Germany: the SPD, opposed to tsarist absolutism, and some pan-Germans who wanted to conquer and colonize the East; but they had no serious influence on Bismarck's pro-Russian policy. The impact in Russia of nationalism led to anti-Russian sentiment in Germany. Yet Bismarck's "reinsurance policy" with St. Petersburg collapsed after he fell in 1890 for other reasons: Wilhelm II's opposition to it; Austro-Russian (and thereby Russo-German) rivalry; the desire of many Germans to become a global power; the struggle over the heritage of the declining Ottoman Empire; and the rising ethnic nationalisms that rose in Austria-Hungary, Germany's only remaining major ally.

The Crisis of Austria-Hungary and World War I

The increasing rivalry between Germans (plus Magyars) and Slavs in Austria-Hungary was another part of the historical heritage of post-1945 Ostpolitik. It began, like German nationalism, in the Paulskirche in 1848, where the Czechs, refused autonomy, began their long struggle for their national identity. The attraction of the German Empire and Czech nationalism engendered pan-German sentiment among the ethnic Germans in Bohemia, Moravia, and Austria. Meanwhile, the 1866 defeat of Austria by Prussia, which restored Hungarian autonomy, enabled Budapest to try to Magyarize its subject Slovaks and Rumanians. Thus Austria-Hungary was increasingly polarized and weakened. All this, plus Russian support of Serbian territorial revisionism, led to Russo-German rivalry for influence over Austria-Hungary as well as the Ottoman Empire and thus further worsened Russo-German relations.

The great powers slid into World War I more by accident, foolhardiness, and incompetence than by design. But potentially from 1871, and actually from 1914 until the battle of Stalingrad in 1943, only the intervention of a non-European power, the United States, twice prevented German domination of Europe.

German Ostpolitik in World War I

German relations with the Slavs were further worsened by World War I. German war aims in it have recently again become controversial.[4] In my view, what before 1914 had been explicit only in limited, pan-German circles became during the war increasingly the maximum aim of the German government and even more of the high command: the formation of a very large area of economic and political German predominance (*Mitteleuropa*),[5] including Eastern Europe, the Balkans, Belgium, and much of Russia, plus overseas colonies and bases, in order to make Germany the dominating power in Europe and globally equal to Great Britain and the United States—an attempt historically comparable to earlier British and French expansionism and to Soviet policy after 1945. It was not the ancestor or the equivalent of Nazi mass murder and enslavement. Nor did the other imperial powers—Great Britain, France, Italy, and Russia—intend during or after the war to give up their own colonial possessions or their economic exploitation and political domination of them.

But this German "grasp for world power" was historically out of phase, particularly in the east. Germany could only keep Central and Eastern European nationalisms suppressed by military and police repression, which in Europe was going out of fashion. It was contrary to, while Allied plans were generally in accord with, the rising principle of self-determination. It would have destroyed the European balance of power. It absurdly underestimated United States power.

During World War I German imperialism wanted eastern satellite states, including the Ukraine, to give it the economic and raw-material base for world-power status and to assure that Russia could no longer menace German hegemony in Europe. Moreover, German policies toward Poland, although modified toward the end of the war to compete with Russia (and Austria) for Polish support and Polish troops, had been extreme before. The wartime German government seriously considered the annexation of more Polish territory and even the transfer of some Poles to the East, to be replaced by German settlers.[6]

Germany's defeat and the failure of the Western intervention made possible the survival and consolidation of Lenin's Bolshevik regime, whose concentration on modernization and industrialization, at the cost of millions of lives, began to make Russia a great industrial and military power. The tier of new Eastern states between Germany and the Soviet Union became independent only because Russia, Germany, and Austria-Hungary were defeated. Their nationalist passions made their foreign policies primarily determined by ethnic and border disputes. Those new or enlarged countries that had acquired territories and national minorities from Germany, Hungary, or Russia—Poland, Czechoslovakia, Rumania, and Yugoslavia—were hostile to the territorially revisionist states—Germany, Hungary, Bulgaria, and (except for Czechoslovakia) the Soviet Union. Their independence depended on France and Great Britain's support and on Germany and Russia remaining weak or hostile to each other or both. Britain refused to accept French hegemony over the continent, encouraged the return of Germany to the European concert, and refused to guarantee the Eastern European states. France was determined to maintain French hegemony in Europe, but its war losses in men, materials, and *élan vital* and its lack of support from London (and Washington) increasingly limited its ability to do so.

Germany and Russia recovered. Neither would accept the 1920 boundaries, particularly those of Poland. Thus genuine reconciliation between Poland and Germany (or Poland and Russia) was impossible. The Eastern European states could not even unite to defend themselves. Thus their independence was doomed.[7]

Weimar Ostpolitik

The overwhelming majority of Germans, including the Social Democrats and the Communists, refused to accept the 1919 German-Polish border and were determined to recover at least Danzig, the Polish Corridor, and Upper Silesia.[8] Thus German-Polish relations could not basically improve. Relations with the Soviet Union, however, could and did. This inevitably meant an anti-Polish German policy and good relations with Moscow in order to put pressure on Poland (*Russlandpolitik*.) Only such extreme nationalists as Hitler continued to advocate the pan-German program of conquest and colonization of Eastern Europe and the Soviet Union. Less extreme ones, such as Reichswehr head General Hans von Seeckt, wanted to cooperate with Moscow in a fourth partition of Poland. More moderate conservatives, such as the longtime Weimar Foreign Minister Gustav Stresemann, favored the continued existence of, and good German relations with, a smaller Poland and the other Eastern European states, out of anti-Bolshevism and the belief that France (and Great Britain) would prevent another partition of Poland.

They were strongly anti-Polish: It seemed to them right and proper that Germans should rule over Poles but degrading, indeed unthinkable, that Poles should rule over Germans. Only intellectual prudence, not emotional preference, made them reject a fourth partition of Poland. Their priority for reconciliation with France, directly or via Great Britain, was largely to make easier peaceful revision of the Polish-German boundary. However, as they realized this was unrealistic, for some of them, probably including Stresemann, reconciliation with France became an end in itself. A few Catholics and most of the Social Democrats and "independent leftists" genuinely wanted reconciliation with Poland as well as with France, but with very few exceptions even they refused to recognize the 1919 German-Polish boundary.

The Weimar leaders differed on the tacts of Ostpolitik, often more for emotional and bureaucratic than for policy reasons. Stresemann opposed a pro-Russian orientation in part because he was strongly anticommunist. Brockdorff-Rantzau, however, the German ambassador in Moscow, violently anti-French and therefore susceptible to Soviet hints that Moscow would come to terms with Paris, or Warsaw, or both unless it could do so with Berlin, favored a pro-Russian course. Bureaucratically, the Foreign Office was jealous of the Reichswehr's secret operations in the Soviet Union (see below) without Foreign Office control or interference. Stresemann and von Seeckt were personal enemies.

The most important and the most difficult for the historian to judge, the more so because his views changed rapidly and he died prematurely, is Stresemann. Was he a "good European," indeed the forerunner of Bonn's new Ostpolitik? Or was he only tactically, indeed deceptively, a European and underneath only a more sophisticated German nationalist?

Stresemann had some persistent traits: strong, emotional German nationalism, a determination that Germany should again become a great power and that this required revision of the German-Polish boundary, intellectually democratic but emotionally authoritarian convictions, contempt for Poles, strong anti-Sovietism, pragmatism, and realism. He matured rapidly from the nationalist expansionist of World War I to the cautious, conciliatory statesman of Locarno. Unlike the extreme nationalists, Stresemann soon realized that Germany's military weakness required European reconciliation if it were again to be a great power and revise the German-Polish frontier.

Stresemann's policy of conciliation with France aimed to restore Germany's sovereignty, end reparations and the occupation of the Rhineland, and get security in the west so that he could more easily pressure Poland. When after 1936 Poland became stronger, he postponed but did not abandon frontier revision. We cannot know whether he would have changed his policy again if Germany had become militarily strong. But he became more of a European as time went on, and had he not died and had the Great Depression not occurred, he might have become more so still.[9]

Brockdorff-Rantzau was profoundly anti-French, favored reconciliation with Great Britain, distrusted the Soviet Union but advocated normalization of relations with it, and favored a balancing position (*Schaukelpolitik*): For him Stresemann's Locarno policy leaned too far to the West. Von Maltzan, the originator of Rapallo, first head of the Eastern Department of the Foreign Office and then state secretary, was not one-sidedly pro-Russian and favored reconciliation with the West. His differences with Stresemann were tactical, not basic.[10] His successor as state secretary, von Schubert, contrary to what his enemies maintained, was only tactically pro-Western. The Social Democratic ambassador to Warsaw, Ulrich Rauscher, was the most conciliatory toward Poland, but he also wanted Franco-German reconciliation and normalization with Moscow in order to achieve peaceful revision of the German-Polish border.

Weimar Ostpolitik centered on the Polish question. It was relatively indifferent to the other Eastern European states, once the Western powers vetoed the *Anschluss* of Austira to Germany; and although primarily concerned with Western Europe and domestically anticommunist, it wanted good relations with the Soviet Union. After Moscow had lost hope of Germany going communist, it tried to block the establishment of an anticommunist coalition, including Germany, against the Soviet Union and to obtain Western aid and trade for Soviet economic development. Moscow thus had (temporary) common interests with Berlin: Both resented their frontiers with Poland, their exclusion from international politics, and their economic and military inferiority vis-à-vis the Western powers: and both were economically and militarily complementary.

German relations with the Eastern European states were more complex. German-Polish hostility continued. Hungary, because of its territorial revisionism, was hostile to Czechoslovakia, Rumania, and Yugoslavia, who composed the "Little Entente" formed under French protection against Magyar revisionism and all of whom had acquired Hungarian territory, and it was therefore pro-German for irredentist as well as traditional reasons.[11] Bulgaria, potentially the same, for historical reasons could not be anti-Russian; and therefore it tried to keep on good terms with both.[12] Rumania was anti-Soviet for territorial, cultural, and traditional reasons; but until Hitler's successes it was not particularly pro-German because of German sympathies for Bucharest's main enemy, Hungary. Yugoslavia was pro-French and anti-German for the same reasons.[13] Czechoslovakia was pro-French for security, cultural, and anti-German reasons but not anti-Russian.[14]

German-Soviet Cooperation

The secret cooperation between the Reichswehr and the Red Army involved several German air and land force bases on Soviet soil, including armored and air force training facilities, and extensive German technical assistance to the Red Army, financed by secret German funds and contrary to the Versailles treaty.[15] The Reichswehr's purpose was to further its clandestine rearmament, thus help to make Germany again a great power, and also, in the view of von Seeckt and his associates who favored a pro-Russian orientation, to work toward a Soviet-German fourth partition of Poland. The Soviets got valuable military assistance and hoped to influence German policy in a pro-Soviet direction. German-Soviet cooperation began, at the initiative of von Seeckt, at the latest in 1921 and continued until 1933. It was not significantly interfered with by the Locarno treaties, the fall of von Seeckt, the publicity given to it by the German Social Democrats in 1926, or the knowledge of it by French and Polish intelligence. The German Foreign Office documents demonstrate that Stresemann, all other Weimar Chancellors and foreign ministers, and all the major parties, including most of the SPD leaders, knew of and endorsed it. However, neither Stresemann nor the other Weimar politicians, who feared and mistrusted communism in general and the Soviet Union in particular, were its main initiators or proponents; and in 1926 Stresemann did not react to a Soviet proposal to expand it greatly. Moreover, they feared that it might drag Germany into a Soviet war with Poland, in which they believed that Germany would be defeated by France. The Foreign Office and the German ambassador in Moscow, in view of its momentum and Reichswehr support, never made any decisive moves to end it but did eventually bring it under some political control.

The 1922 German-Soviet Treaty of Rapallo reflected the determination of Berlin and Moscow to change the Versailles status quo, in particular the boundaries, if not the existence, of Poland. The German negotiations were directed by Chancellor Wirth, who strongly favored Poland's destruction, and by von Maltzan, who then opposed rapprochement with Britain and France via a policy of fulfillment *(Erfüllungspolitik)*, both with the aim to recover Germany's pre-1914 role: an independent and eventually dominant power in Europe. (Foreign Minister Rathenau was less enthusiastic about it but did not oppose it. Stresemann was also unenthusiastic.) Rapallo signaled Berlin's rejection of Lloyd George's plan for a concert of Europe including Germany but excluding the Soviet Union. It strengthened the France-British entente and encouraged Poincaré to occupy the Rhineland. It also ensured increased German-Soviet secret military cooperation and trade. Rapallo gave Germany and Russia more freedom of maneuver and something close to a revisionist alliance in the east. By keeping open the Polish boundary issue, it rejected the kind of Western European comity that developed after World War II.[16]

The great interwar victory of Stresemann's policy of fulfillment was the 1925 Locarno treaties. Stresemann at Locarno wanted to recover German sovereignty, end reparations, end the

Allied occupation of the Rhineland, keep a free hand vis-à-vis Poland, and lower the credibility of the French guarantee to Warsaw. The Soviets, who wanted to keep up German pressure on Poland and to prevent Germany from joining the League of Nations, or at least to ensure that Germany would not participate in league sanctions against the Soviet Union, tried hard but unsuccessfully to prevent Stresemann from signing the treaties. Moscow hinted that it would then move toward Poland and France but that if Stresemann desisted it might help Berlin to drive Poland back to her "ethnographic frontiers" or even make possible a Russo-German military alliance. ("Coming events cast their shadows before . . . .") The treaties provided for guarantee by Germany, reinforced by France, Great Britain, and Italy, of the Franco-German frontier in return for a general guarantee against aggression, French evacuation of the Rhineland, the prospect of American credits for the German economy (one of Stresemann's main objectives), and Germany's entry into the League of Nations.

Stresemann's greatest achievements at Locarno were his refusal to guarantee automatic German support to any future League sanctions against the Soviet Union and to sign an "Eastern Locarno," that is, to guarantee the Polish western frontier. (He did sign arbitration treaties with Poland and Czechoslovakia.) He thereby continued his balancing position because the West feared that the alternative would be a German alliance with Russia. London wanted a balanced concert of powers in Europe, and the failure of Poincaré's occupation of the Rhineland had led in late 1924 to a victory of the less anti-German Left in France.

The Soviet Union was very alarmed by it and only partially reassured by Stresemann's rejection of an "Eastern Locarno." Stresemann tried to reassure the Soviets by signing with them the 1925 Treaty of Berlin, little more than a reaffirmation of the Treaty of Rapallo.[17]

Weimar and Poland

Poland (and Czechoslovakia) were weakened and humiliated by Locarno's discriminatory provisions against them, that is, the lack of an "Eastern Locarno." Warsaw was the more disturbed when Berlin thereafter intensified economic warfare against Poland to try to get Warsaw to agree to border revisions and continued its propaganda for territorial revisionism. German hopes for it fed on the illusion of Western support for its claims, underestimation of and lack of knowledge about the fierce Polish determination never to make territorial concessions, and arrogance toward the despised Poles.

Berlin's hopes were doomed in the short run by the political and economic consolidation of Poland after Marshal Piłsudski's coup d' état in 1926. Although the coup had primarily internal causes, Piłsudski also acted in response to Polish foreign policy malaise.[18] Because he knew that Locarno demonstrated rising French (and even more British) disinterest in Eastern Europe, he began a more independent Polish foreign policy. Born in eastern Poland, profoundly anti-Russian, having fought with Germany during World War I, and admiring Germany's military and economic efficiency although distrusting its political aims, Piłsudski wanted to improve relations with Berlin, but only on the basis of equality and the territorial status quo. He was one of the few Poles who ever impressed Stresemann, who, adjusting pragmatically to the necessary postponement of hope of territorial revision reciprocated Piłsudski's desires. This, plus those few elements in German public opinion who favored genuine reconciliation with Poland, German economic interests, and the patient efforts of German Ambassador Reuscher in Warsaw, led to a tenuous, brief improvement in relations that culminated in the Polish-German economic agreement of 1930. Thereafter the worsening world economic situation and the move toward the right in their domestic politics made German-Polish relations deteriorate rapidly in 1933.[19]

German-Czechoslovak Relations

Czechoslovak Foreign Minister Beneš intimated that he would like to improve relations with Berlin and would disassociate Prague from the 1919 German-Polish frontier.[20] But this had only a temporary effect and did not help him with his main potential problem with a reviving Germany: the several million ethnic Sudeten Germans in Bohemia and Moravia, near the German and Austrian borders. The establishment of the state of Czechoslovakia seemed to the Sudeten Germans a political catastrophe, for to them it was an intolerable humiliation that they should be ruled by the Czechs, whom they so despised. However, interwar Austria, denied union with Germany, was too weak to help them; and Weimar Germany gave priority to relations with the Soviet Union and Poland.

The Czechs were relatively moderate in their treatment of the Sudeten Germans. But even if, which is unlikely, the Sudeten Germans could have been reconciled to majority (Czech) rule, Czech psychological blunders would have made that even more difficult. However, after an initial period of near-unanimous defiance, the more moderate Sudeten German parties decided in 1926 to enter Czechoslovak politics. Conversely, Beneš tried, with considerable success, to keep on good terms with Weimar. But the world depression and the rise of nazism radicalized the great majority of Sudetens to the right, and Hitler used them to destroy Czechoslovakia.[21]

Soviet-German Relations After 1926

The 1927 Anglo-Soviet diplomatic break forced Stresemann to balance carefully between the two, thus further increasing Soviet suspicions of Germany. Moscow's worsening economic situation and increasing international tension made it a less interesting partner for Berlin, especially against Poland.

Stalin's 1928 turn to extremism plus the 1929 depression in Germany led to a much more militant German Communist Party (KPD) line and thus to increased disquiet in Berlin, the more so because post-Rapallo high hopes for trade with the USSR had been rapidly disillusioned. Even so, German-Soviet relations did not drastically worsen. Indeed, in late 1928 and early 1929 they improved, especially in the military field, only to worsen again because of Germany's preoccupation with the Young Plan, rising KPD agitation, and public concern about the fate of ethnic German peasants in the USSR during the forced collectivization campaign. They improved again in 1930 because Soviet policy became more anti-French, anti-Polish, and internally more stabilized and because the 1929 depression made Germany need more export markets.

The 1930 Nazi electoral victory and the subsequent rapid radicalization of German politics caused increasing concern in Moscow. Initially, however, because this led to much stronger anti-Polish sentiment in Germany, the Treaty of Berlin was renewed indefinitely in 1931. But rising Soviet (and French) fears of German revanchism led in the same year to a Soviet-French non-aggression pact, and in January 1932, since the Soviets were increasingly involved with Japan in Manchuria and Piłsudski had come to fear Germany more and value France less, to a Soviet-Polish one, which Berlin vainly attempted to prevent. Thereafter, until Hitler's accession to power in early 1933, the confusion in Berlin was so great that no significant developments in Soviet-German relations occurred, except for Stalin's insistence on the KPD continuing to attack the SPD—a blunder that contributed considerably to the Nazi victory.[22]

Adenauer and Stresemann

Stresemann was ambivalent toward Western Europe. For him Germany was still *das Reich der Mitte,* whose *raison d'état,* like that of Bismarck's Reich, required in the long run a balancing policy (*Schaukelpolitik*) between the West and Russia. The alternative, a policy centered on Western Europe, was outlined in the early 1920s by Konrad Adenauer, the lord mayor of Cologne, then relatively unknown abroad, who was two years older than Stresemann. Above all else a Rhineland Catholic, Adenauer had never liked Prussia or the Bismarck Reich. Confronted after 1918 with the prospect of French domination or even annexation of his beloved Rhineland and aware that the French conception of security was profoundly anti-Prussian, he advocated a compromise between Rhineland separatism and "Prussian centralism": a Rhineland state still in the German Reich but with close economic ties between French and Rhineland industry. He favored a majority Christian party of Protestants and Catholics and opposed *Schaukelpolitik* in favor of reconciliation and alliance with Western Europe, notably France. German nationalism and French lack of persistence made these policies premature—until 1945, when he resumed them essentially unchanged.[23]

Stresemann and Adenauer had many similarities. Both were democrats by intellect, authoritarian by temperament, realistic, conciliatory, and pragmatic. Both saw as the priorities for a defeated Germany the recovery of sovereignty, security, and equality with other European powers. But their differences were greater and more important. Stresemann remained a Protestant, north German nationalist, a territorial revisionist toward the Poland he despised, and a firm believer that German foreign policy must balance between West and East. Adenauer was always a Rhineland Catholic, German and European, a firm believer in European unity centering on Franco-German reconciliation, and a man who deeply distrusted German nationalism.

Nazi Eastern Policy

Hitler's policy was qualitatively far different from his predecessors', most of all toward the East, and it drastically worsened German-Slav relations.[24] He would not have come to power without the economic depression or had his opponents been less disunited and blind to his true aims. He was not the logical consequence of German or even of Weimar history, but he was a malignant, maniacal fanatic, driven by overpowering lust for power and by an ideology that combined social Darwinism, the Germanic superrace, the selection by conflict of the fittest to rule, and a limitless, long-term aim of world conquest. These aims primarily required, in his view, the destruction of the Jews and the Bolsheviks, for him a vast joint international conspiracy centering in Moscow, and the conquest of Russia to get new *Lebensraum*. In Western Europe he saw the French as his main enemy and the British as potential but temporary allies.

The ruthless conquest, colonization, and domination of the Slav East was one of Hitler's main guiding principles. His lust for *Lebensraum* in the East was qualitatively different from

Prussian expansionism and the pan-German dreams of World War I. For unlike them it was organically linked with racism and particularly with anti-Semitism; it replaced the German "civilizing mission" for the enslavement of the Slavs; and it glorified war, murder, and slavery as the highest form of German patriotism.[25]

Nazi-Soviet Relations

In 1933, overruling objections by the Red Army (and the Reichswehr), Stalin ended the secret German-Soviet military cooperation.[26] It was already less important to Moscow because new Red Army cadres had been trained and because German rearmament would make Berlin less interested in it.

Determined to conquer the Soviet Union, Hitler felt that he could afford to wait while he consolidated his domestic position and then turned to Austria and Czechoslovakia. He was thus at first relatively unconcerned about German-Soviet relations and wanted them neither too good nor too bad. Anti-Bolshevik Nazi polemics did not interfere with German-Soviet trade.[27]

Stalin knew that he could not stand alone against Hitler, and he feared an alliance between Germany and the West against him. He therefore in 1935 began his popular front policy, signed an alliance with France, supported Czechoslovakia, aided the Spanish Loyalists against Franco's German- and Italian-supported rebellion, and prepared for a German attack. He hoped to postpone it, to acquire buffer territory against it, and to turn Hitler first against the West. British and French support of Poland's defiance of Hitler made this possible. Thus in 1939 Stalin could feel that he had scored a double victory, for communism and Russian nationalism. But while Stalin's ambitions went far beyond eastern Poland, Hitler's involved the conquest and subjugation of the Soviet Union.

Nazi-Polish Relations

Hitler's pre-1938 policy toward Poland was remarkably conciliatory.[28] He was impressed by the rumors, perhaps deliberately launched by Piłsudski, of a preventive war by Poland against

Germany.[29] He wanted to bring Germany out of its isolation and to weaken French influence in Eastern Europe. He may well for a time have contemplated moving against the Soviet Union with Poland as a junior partner. In any case, because his ultimate aims in the east were so limitless, Hitler was less concerned than his diplomats about immediate, partial revision of the German-Polish boundary. Piłsudski, on the other hand, because of the decline of French influence and the relative weakness of the post-1929 Soviet Union, wanted a more independent foreign policy. In 1934, Hitler signed a nonuse of force pact with Poland and German-Polish relations improved considerably.[30] He tried to persuade Poland to join with him to attack the Soviets, and he ordered the German minority in Poland and the Nazi rulers of Danzig to stop opposing Warsaw. Finally, he supported Poland's use of the 1938 Munich crisis to force Prague to cede Těšín (Teschen), although he did not support Poland's attempt before March 1939 to gain primary influence in Slovakia.

Hitler's demands on Poland in early 1939 (the return of Danzig to Germany and an extraterritorial German railroad and highway through the Polish Corridor to east Prussia) were neither as extreme as Stresemann's nor necessarily intended only as the first step toward the conquest of Poland. Their relative moderation was probably in part due to Hitler's wish not to provoke France or England. Hitler seems genuinely to have thought that he could obtain them and that Poland would thereafter become a reliable albeit a subordinate and probably only a temporary ally in conquering the Soviet Union.[31]

To accept Hitler's demands and a German-Polish alliance against the Soviet Union would have made Poland a satellite of Germany, which Warsaw would not accept. Piłsudski's epigones were as determined as the marshal himself not to surrender an inch of Polish territory. Poland's response to the decline of French influence in Eastern Europe had been only secondarily a limited rapprochement with Germany. Its primary policy, doomed to failure by Polish weakness, Czechoslovak hostility, and German power, had been the creation of an Eastern European "third force" under Polish leadership. When Hitler's demands on Warsaw came, in early 1939, his occupation of Prague in March enabled Beck to get a British guarantee and therefore to reject them. Hitler determined to crush Poland even at the cost of a temporary alliance with the Soviet Union.

Nazi Occupation of Poland

Hitler's occupation aims in Poland were to slaughter the Polish intelligentsia; enslave the Polish workers and peasants; colonize the country, particularly western Poland, with German colonists; use the enslaved Polish population as a captive labor force; and destroy the Polish state and Polish culture. He had Himmler's SS begin the slaughter of the Polish educated classes; he annexed western Poland to the Reich and ruled directly what was left of the German-occupied part of Poland; and he rejected the attempts of the very few Germanophile Poles to set up some kind of Polish government. Murder, terror, and enslavement, Hitler's only policies for Poland, were made worse by the growing underground Polish Resistance that they helped to generate. Nor were they equaled by Stalin's policies in eastern Poland, where he imposed communist rule and deported up to one million ethnic Poles, largely the intelligentsia, to Siberia and the Arctic north of Russia.

Hitler and the Rest of Eastern Europe

Hitler's policies in the rest of Central and Eastern Europe varied considerably. He began with the annexation of Austria[32] and continued with the isolation, disruption, and conquest of Czechoslovakia.[33] He was at first favorably disposed toward Rumania, because of its natural resources, toward Yugoslavia, because of what he (incorrectly) thought to be its strong army, and because both shared his hostility to a reconstituted Habsburg Empire. He was little interested in Hungary, which he regarded as poor, for which—as for Czechs—he retained a Viennese disdain, and which he felt, like Bulgaria, had no alternative, because of its territorial irredentism, but alliance with Germany.

Hitler had three great weapons toward the Balkans: military

successes, economic penetration, and the subversive activities of the ethnic German minorities. German economic penetration of the Balkans expanded rapidly after 1933, primarily because Berlin used its reflationary economic recovery to buy Balkan agricultural surpluses in return for Balkan purchases of German manufactured goods. By 1938, Balkan imports and exports were almost one-half to and from Germany, twice as much as in 1933.

The largest and most important German minority was in Czechoslovakia. In Rumania, Poland, Yugoslavia, and Hungary Hitler also manipulated them for his purposes. The rise of nationalism had already replaced the old conservative, oligarchic, ethnic German elites by younger, more radical leaders (the *Erneuerungsbewegung*). Hitler sacrificed them when he deemed it desirable, as when he abandoned the ethnic Germans of south Tirol to Mussolini; but elsewhere he used them far more effectively than Weimar ever did.[34]

The Nazi Attack on the Soviet Union

Hitler had always intended to attack Russia after he had conquered the rest of Europe. He had hoped to undertake it in an alliance with Great Britain, to whom he was ready to leave a diminished empire, at least for a transitional period, before, if possible again in alliance with London, he undertook the final struggle with the United States for the domination of the world.[35]

But in 1939, unwillingly and unexpectedly, he was forced to fight Great Britain and therefore to become partially dependent on Stalin. When, again totally contrary to his expectations, Churchill in the summer of 1940, after the German conquest of France, refused to make peace, which would have given Hitler a free hand for his more important objective, the conquest of the Soviet Union, Hitler reluctantly decided to attack the Soviet Union before the British were defeated. Moreover, he was convinced that Germany would rapidly defeat the Soviet Union, which, he felt, would free Japan to put enough pressure on the United States (whose aid to Great Britain, he realized, was a mortal danger to his objectives) so that Germany could crush

Britain despite American aid. Thus as early as summer 1940 Asia and North America had become essential, if only still potential, factors in European politics.

Later that year, however, Hitler tried out Joachim von Ribbentrop's plan for a "Continental bloc," including the Soviet Union as well as Italy, France, and Spain. He hoped that this would persuade the Japanese, who wanted a neutral Soviet Union so that they could conquer China and southeast Asia, to finish off Chiang Kai-shek and thus to force the United States to accept Japanese hegemony in east and southeast Asia and thereby move U.S. policy toward less aid to Great Britain. But the Italian defeats in the autumn of 1940 in Greece and the Mediterranean finished Mussolini as an independent actor. The wily Franco and the indecisive and reluctant Pétain would not play. Continued Soviet (and American) aid to Chiang made such a bloc no longer interesting to Japan. Above all, Stalin's terms proved too high for Hitler—and foreshadowed Soviet postwar aims in Central and Eastern Europe.

By autumn 1940, Stalin was in his preferred position: He was being wooed by Italy, Japan, Germany, the United States, and Great Britain. He realized that U.S. rising power and engagement against Germany lowered Hitler's bargaining power and raised his. But he did not understand how weak Hitler (unrealistically) thought the Soviet Union was and thus how inclined he was to attack it. Stalin therefore unwisely revealed to Hitler the full extent of his ambitions: He demanded immediate hegemony over Finland, southern Bukovina, and Bulgaria, plus Soviet bases on the Dardanelles; and he made clear that his long-range aims included hegemony over Yugoslavia, Hungary, Greece, and western Poland, as well as control over the Danish straits and the mouth of the Danube. These he hoped to get from Hitler, but he certainly intended to get them in the (to him already more probable) event of a Western victory. Not surprisingly, Hitler rejected these Soviet goals; and after his inconclusive November 1940 conversations with Molotov in Berlin, he irrevocably decided to attack the Soviet Union. When in early 1941 Stalin got wind of this, he indicated his willingness to make further concessions to the Germans, but Hitler was no longer interested.

Hitler attacked the Soviet Union in June 1941. He lost the war in six months. His attack on Moscow failed, and even though in 1942 the German army drove far into southern Russia, it never again came as close to defeating the Soviets. Moreover, independent of Hitler and contrary to his desires, the Japanese decided in late 1941 either to get American recognition of their hegemony in east Asia or to attack the United States. Either course doomed Hitler, since either meant U.S. entry into the war.[36]

German Wartime Rule in the Soviet Union

There were three schools of thought in German governing circles about the treatment of the Soviet Union. Hitler, Himmler, and Bormann wanted treatment similar to Poland's (that is, partition, enslavement, and colonization). Rosenberg wanted to favor the non-Great Russians, particularly the Ukrainians, under German hegemony. The more traditional diplomats and the Wehrmacht wanted to ally with all anticommunists in the Soviet Union in order to help win the war and ensure German influence thereafter. Although the third school was eventually helped by German defeats and finally even Himmler came over to their side, notably in supporting the Vlassov movement, Hitler's concept prevailed and thus contributed to catastrophic German defeat and the greatest possible hostility of the Soviets. Meanwhile, British and American desire to keep Russia fighting and their (probably unjustified) fear of a separate peace between Berlin and Moscow, plus Roosevelt's shortsightedness about postwar Soviet aims, sufficiently united the Allied coalition and the Soviet Union so that the end of the war saw the Red Army on the Elbe and in Berlin, Prague, and Vienna. Stalin's fondest dreams of victory had been overfulfilled.[37]

German Relations with Eastern Europe During the War

Hitler's mania for the destruction, colonization, and enslavement of the Soviet Union, Poland, the Czech lands, and Yugoslavia determined his country's relations with Eastern Europe during the war. Although he would have eventually subjugated Hungary, Rumania, and Bulgaria as well, his treatment of them during the war was less extreme, reflecting traditional German attitudes.

Bohemia and Moravia became a German colony. Eventually the more "Nordic" part of the Czech population was to be forcibly Germanized and the rest deported to the East and replaced by German colonists. Much of the Czech intelligentsia was liquidated. The Czech workers and peasants became a captive labor force for Germany, and thereby survived the war with little loss, and indeed contributed to a great increase in Czech industrial capacity. Czech wartime resistance was not great and declined as the war went on. Czech hatred of the Nazis and particularly of the Sudeten Germans who had largely collaborated with them led to the expulsion to Germany of the latter in 1945, thus binding Czechoslovakia to Russia for protection against the danger of German revenge.[38] In "independent" wartime Slovakia, in contrast, German hegemony was relatively mild and anti-Germanism, never strong there, remained relatively low.[39]

Admiral Horthy's Hungary was an irredentist but reluctant German ally and unsuccessfully tried to change sides when the Nazis began to lose the war. Like Slovakia, it remained for most of the war an island of relative quiet, and this, plus the traditional ties of Hungary to Germany, made post-1945 anti-German feeling in Hungary relatively insignificant.[40]

The same was true in Rumania. Its wartime dictator, Marshal Antonescu, Hitler's favorite ally, fought the Soviet Union to get back Bessarabia and Bukovina—and more besides. But unlike Hungary, Rumania managed to switch sides, as it had in World War I, and thus got back from Hungary Transylvania, which Hitler had given to it.[41]

Bulgaria also came out of World War II with little anti-German feeling. Although traditionally Russophile, it was Berlin's ally in both world wars, due to imperial Russia's preference for anti-Bulgarian Serbia and to the Soviet Union's bolshevism; and Hitler gave it part of Yugoslavia and Greece and postwar Bulgaria.

Moreover, Bulgaria was far away from the center of German-Slav conflict.[42]

The contrary was true of Yugoslavia, which like Czechoslovakia had emerged from German and Austro-Hungarian defeat in World War I. In 1941, Hitler defeated and partitioned the country. The Germans ruthlessly occupied Serbia and put Croatia under the Fascist terrorist Ante Pavelić. Bloody Serb-Croat civil war made the anti-Nazi partisan struggle even more ferocious. Postwar Yugoslavia was therefore strongly anti-German.[43]

The Ostpolitik of the German Resistance to Hitler

The ideas on Ostpolitik of the German anti-Nazi Resistance had no decisive immediate effect on postwar West German policy. Adenauer, because he thought the resistance incompetent and unlikely to succeed, did not participate in it and Schumacher, the post-war SPD leader, was in a concentration camp. Nevertheless, its ideas, notably on European unity, did contribute considerably to postwar elite opinion in the Federal Republic.

The Nazi elite argued among itself about Eastern policy, whether Nazi imperialism should be more or less rational or fanatical. Within the Wehrmacht, however, there were many active anti-Nazis. Count Stauffenberg, who on July 20, 1944, nearly assassinated Hitler, and many of his associates were active in German Eastern policy. They advocated better treatment of Soviet prisoners of war and the formation of the Vlassov army.

There were four schools of thought among the civilian anti-Nazi opposition: the conservative nationalists, centering around Gördeler, von Hassell, and Beck; the pro-European internationalists around the Kreisauer Kreis; the Social Democrats, primarily in Western emigration: and the Communists, primarily in Moscow.

The conservative nationalists continued Stresemann's policies, adjusted to the German victories. Because they had never favored Weimar democracy or the abandonment of pre-1914 German claims to great power and if possible world power status, they naturally wanted the latter once it again seemed possible. From 1938 until 1944, when German defeats made it again unrealistic, they considered the 1914 German eastern boundaries, Austria, the Sudetenland, Alsace-Lorraine, south Tirol, and German hegemony over Bohemia, Moravia, and Slovakia as just and proper German claims. This would have meant a revival of Friedreich Naumann's *Mitteleuropa:* German rule over the Bismarck Reich plus the German parts of imperial Austria and thereby what they felt Germany's position, population, and power entitled her to, German hegemony over Central Europe—plus, if possible, the return of the former German colonies.

In sum, the conservative nationalists still thought in the traditional patterns of European great power politics and European rule in the colonial world—as did their British, French, and Italian counterparts. But they felt before 1939 that these aims could probably be achieved only by war and that war must be avoided at all costs, since they were convinced that Germany could not win it and that its result would be the end of the German Reich and of the possibility of territorial revision in Germany's favor.

The conservative nationalists' opposition to Hitler was moral and ethical as well, and Hitler's victories never reconciled them to his aims or methods. Even so, after the fall of France they developed ideas of European unity under German leadership that would have amounted to German hegemony over all of Europe. This was totally unacceptable to the rest of Europe, Britain, the United States, and most of all to the Soviet Union. Soon, however, the entry of the Soviet Union and the United States into the war convinced them that any such German hegemony, and indeed Europe's predominance in world politics, was doomed.

They also changed their views because of their increasing contacts with the second group, the Kreisauer Kreis. This was made up of relatively young, left-wing internationalist aristocrats, bourgeoisie, and Social Democrats, named after the Silesian estate of their main figure, one of the greatest heroes of the German Resistance, Count Hellmuth von Moltke. Their motives were primarily ethical and moral. They rejected Western parliamentary democracy for a "German way," a kind of Christian socialism in an organic, nonconflict model state. They were convinced that the European national states must be replaced by a European confederation or federation. Many of them had endorsed these ideas, including a liberal attitude toward Poland (Moltke in 1928 condemned Berlin's manipulation of the German minority in Poland) and the rejection of German hegemony over *Mitteleuropa,* before Hitler came to power. Unlike the conservative nationalists, the second group was only made more determined in their views by Hitler's victories.

The Kreisauer ideas had increasing influence on Gördeler and his conservative associates, who by 1942–1943 had become more committed to the idea of European unity. They even turned toward the idea of an alliance with a reconstituted Poland against the Soviet Union, including a German military guarantee of the 1939 Polish eastern frontier. Even so, Gördeler still gave priority to great power politics: He proposed to negotiate the Polish frontiers with the British, not with the Poles.

Neither the conservatives nor the Kresauer Kreis supported an "Eastern orientation" or a German-Soviet deal. On the contrary, they wanted to overthrow Hitler, make a separate peace with the Western Allies, and thus prevent the Red Army from overrunning Central Europe. Gördeler and von Moltke made such proposals to the West. But von Moltke also realized that the war was lost and that this plus the guilt the Nazis had brought on the German people would make great losses for Germany inevitable. By 1943, he had resigned himself to the loss of his own province, Silesia. He and many of his associates felt by 1944 that although the attempt to overthrow Hitler would probably fail and they would be executed, it still had to be made to demonstrate to Germany and the world that some Germans were prepared to die for their anti-Nazi moral principles.[44]

Most Social Democratic leaders emigrated after 1933 and thereafter suffered the usual fate of émigrés: splits, intrigues, feuds, and impotence. A few remained in Germany. Leber, Mierendorff, and Leuschner played leading roles in the Kreisauer Kreis, in which they took a more left-wing position than its other members, one more favorable, for example, to Poland but not otherwise decisively different. The Social Democratic emigration was split until 1939. The SPD leadership maintained its traditional reformist, pro-Western, anti-Soviet, anticommunist policies. Some younger left-wing figures formed *Neu Beginnen,* which included such postwar SPD leaders as Willy Brandt, Erwin Schöttle, Fritz Erler, Waldemar von Knöringen, and, as its main theoretician, Richard Löwenthal. Disillusioned with the pro-Nazi sympathies of most Germans, they advocated a Leninist "educational dictatorship of the proletariat" and a popular front with the communists. The Soviet-Nazi Pact ended these ideas.

By 1929, the German communists had been purged and Stalinized.[45] After 1933, their leadership in Moscow, thinned by Stalin's bloody purges of 1937-1938, was headed in fact by Walter Ulbricht. Although not a quisling, as his 1971 opposition to Moscow's policy in the Berlin negotiations would demonstrate, he saw no other way to grasp and keep power but unconditional obedience to Stalin. So did communist émigrés in the West and those in concentration camps or in hiding within the Nazi Reich. All shared a burning hatred for the Nazis and an overriding determination to carry out an economic and social revolution in postwar Germany. Intellectuals in the party were few and disliked by Ulbricht and most of the other leaders.

The popular front policy at the 1935 Seventh Comintern Congress met considerable resistance in the KPD leadership, which reflected communist hostility to the SPD and which Ulbricht and Pieck overcame, with Soviet assistance. After Hitler invaded the Soviet Union in June 1941, Stalin remained determined to keep the territories he had gotten in 1939 and to get more. His strategy ranged from alliance with the West to the hope of peace with Germany without Hitler, or even with him. Stalin's postwar objectives were indicated in a draft treaty that Soviet Ambassador Maisky gave Eden in late 1941: Moscow was to keep the 1941 western boundaries and get bases in Rumania; the Rhineland and perhaps Bavaria were to be separated from Germany; and Britain was to have continental bases—in short, Anglo-Russian *double hégémonie.* The British, however, like the Americans, adopted a policy of delay on postwar arrangement.

This led Stalin in 1942 to reconsider a separate peace with Germany. Japan also tried to mediate between Moscow and Berlin. This failed, as did secret Soviet-German negotiations in 1943–1944. Hitler was ambivalent and skeptical about the negotiations.

Meanwhile, in mid-1942, the Soviets had begun to recruit captured German officers for propaganda purposes, over some KPD reluctance, because they were getting nowhere in negotiations with Berlin and were dissatisfied with the West's failure to start a second front. To the West's dismay, the *Nationalkomitee Freies Deutschland* was formed in July 1943 and the *Bund deutscher Offiziere* was formed in September to propagandize German war prisoners and the German civilian population, dominated by the Soviets and their KPD associates. In August 1943, Maisky again suggested to Eden the division of Europe into spheres of influence, or otherwise the right of East and West to participate in all decisions concerning the Continent, but Eden again delayed.

Thereafter Soviet victories made Moscow less concerned, and London more so, about postwar settlements. Washington, dominated by Roosevelt's aversion to wartime postwar planning, supported democratization and partition for Germany. Moscow agreed in theory but did not commit itself, probably because it hoped to get influence over all of Germany. In that same year, at the Tehran Conference, Roosevelt and Churchill agreed to move Poland's boundaries to the west in return for the Soviet Union retaining its 1939 gains from Poland in the east. However, they did not bind themselves to a specific German-Polish boundary and they rejected Stalin's most extreme proposals for Germany. Thereafter the Americans and British made fairly detailed proposals for postwar Germany but the Soviets only insisted on separate zones. They finally agreed to zonal division because Stalin feared that the Western Allies might reach Berlin before him.

At the beginning of 1944, the KPD leadership in Moscow, under Soviet supervision, began making secret plans for postwar Germany, plans that accurately foreshadowed immediate postwar developments in the Soviet zone. The Soviet role was to be predominant. Socialization was not to begin immediately and the SPD was to be given a more nationalist image, but newly formed parties would operate as a block under KPD leadership. The SPD was to merge rapidly with (placed under the control of) the KPD. Unified trade unions would be controlled by the KPD. Most of industry would be nationalized. A drastic land reform would result in agricultural cooperatives, but no mention was made of collectivization. An extensive denazification program was to be carried out to replace the old elite with a new communist-dominated one. All this was, as Pieck cited from Lenin, the revolutionary dictatorship of the proletariat and the peasantry, as the first stage, under communist leadership, toward socialism.

At the February 1945 Yalta Conference the West was already very disillusioned with the Soviet Union with respect to Eastern Europe. Stalin again raised the issue of German partition. Churchill favored a separate south Germany, including Austria, and Roosevelt favored partition in principle but no decision was reached. The major East-West controversy there was on reparations and level of industry in postwar Germany. Stalin insisted on massive reparations, a low level of industry, and close economic control, to which Churchill refused to agree because this would make it impossible to feed Germany. Churchill and Roosevelt also refused to agree to a final German-Polish boundary on the Oder and western Neisse, but they did agree to Polish occupation "until a peace conference."

This was the last time that Stalin brought up German partition; the idea died a natural death. Once he had gotten Western de facto acceptance of the Oder-Neisse boundary, he may well have felt that Soviet security was sufficiently guaranteed so that he did not also need a divided Germany. Rather, he could support a united Germany in the hope of getting influence over Ruhr industry (instead of the French getting it, if partition had occurred) and, if and when the United States left Europe (and Roosevelt had told him at Yalta that U.S. troops would stay only for two years) of getting predominant influence over all of Germany.

Because compromise with the West on Germany still seemed desirable and because there had been no German rising against the Nazis, the KPD (and the Soviets) had to revise their short-run postwar planning. They postponed the establishment of a central government and therefore of a "bloc of democratic parties" to concentrate on denazification and governmental units, under KPD control, at the local level, as well as ideological and educational activity.

Meanwhile, Churchill's efforts to persuade Truman not to evacuate Thuringia, Saxony, and Mecklenberg (which, it had been agreed, would belong to the Soviet zone but which the Allied armies had initially occupied) until the Soviets agreed to a democratic regime in Poland were of no avail. Moreover, despite Ambassador Murphy's urgings, the United States (and the United Kingdom) did not insist on a detailed agreement on access to their sectors of Berlin.

The Soviet and KPD goal remained the same: total control. As a leading Soviet propaganda official put in in a closed discussion in September 1945, the political situation in the Soviet zone was characterized by "the successful liquidation of fascist elements, the gradual restoration of economic and cultural life, important social structural changes, and the growing political activity of the anti-fascist, democratic strata of the population." As for the Western Allies and the SPD, he added that their arrival in the western sectors of Berlin had increased "the hopes of bourgeois circles and the right-wing of the SPD for the reestablishment of a bourgeois-liberal regime of the Weimar variety" as well as their own "orientation toward the West."[46]

The plans and hopes of the German anti-Nazi opposition were neither known nor taken seriously in the Soviet Union and Eastern Europe—except those of the German communists by the Soviets. Nazi onslaught had kindled in the Slav elites and masses, communists and noncommunists alike, a burning determination for revenge and for preventing Germany from ever again attacking the East. This was the main emotional dynamic behind the Oder-Neisse line, the expulsion of twelve million ethnic Germans to the West, the Red Army rape and pillage, and the partition of Germany.

Thus the heritage of pre-1945 German relations with the East was one of almost steadily increasing hostility. Cultural and technological superiority, conquest, settlement, domination, and eventually terror and mass slaughter on the German side; comity changing to fear, hatred, and eventually fury and horror on the side of the Slavs. Stalin's insistence on the Oder-Neisse line as Poland's western boundary and the Polish and Czechoslovak expulsion, with his full support, of some twelve million ethnic Germans to what remained of Germany tied Poland and Czechoslovakia to the Soviet Union. Germany's total defeat and partition, massive Soviet power, and above all the atomic age, which has frozen international boundaries, fundamentally and permanently changed the German-Russian relationship to Moscow's benefit. Germany's total defeat destroyed all that German settlement and conquest had accomplished in the east since the twelfth century. West Germans said that 1945 was *das Jahr Null* ("Year Zero"); and so it was—nowhere more than in the east. There was political and military impotence; near-universal world hatred; and partition, poverty, and massive destruction. Few then could envisage a postwar German Ostpolitik. The rest of this study tells the story of how it developed.

The International Dimension

1945 was very different from 1918. Eastern Europe was under Soviet control. Western Europe was greatly weakened and dependent on the United States. Neither the Soviet Union nor the Western powers were prepared to evacuate Germany and restore a strong central German government with sufficient military power to protect its own security. Stresemann's policy of balancing between West and East, therefore, was no longer realistic. Germany was too weak, Russia too strong, and Western Europe too anti-German and weak.

Soviet Policy

Despite the view of many revisionist historians that the United States started the cold war, there was in my view never any serious prospect of a postwar Soviet-American global agreement and perhaps least of all of one on Germany.[1]

Russia has always been expansionist with respect to its own subject nationalities and toward Europe wherever it was strong enough, as under Tsar Alexander I after 1815 and Stalin after 1945. After the fearful Russian losses in two world wars, it was unlikely than *any* Russian government would give up East Germany unless it was forced to do so. And Soviet and American intercontinental thermonuclear missiles, *the* major new factor in post-1945 international politics, prevented that. During World War II the United States had rejected a sphere of influence division of Europe without clearly understanding that this would lead to a break with Moscow. In 1945, the not-yet-nuclear Soviet Union was much weaker than the nuclear-armed United States. Stalin was increasingly distrustful of the West. He knew that a strong Western Europe including a strong West Germany allied with the United States would change the European balance to Soviet disadvantage. Stalin's minimal postwar aim with respect to Germany was therefore to keep it weak and divided, to maintain a subservient and thus necessarily a communist government in East Germany, and to keep the territory between it and the Soviet frontier in the hands of "friendly," that is, necessarily communist, governments.

He may well also have had maximal aims: communization *and* Soviet control over all of Germany. But he could not get from the West a Soviet veto over developments in the Western zones, and particularly over the level of Ruhr industry, without them getting a veto right over his zone—that is, preventing its communization. Moreover, he probably feared than any communist Germany might become strong enough (as China did) to challenge Soviet control over it and therefore over the international communist movement. Finally, to make Germany communist would require not only force but also inducements, which would inevitably conflict with the primary Soviet aim of keeping Germany industrially, militarily, and politically weak. When forced to choose, Stalin always gave priority to his minimal goal, German partition and communization of the Soviet zone. He therefore also opposed a united, neutral, militarily weak Germany, for he feared giving up Soviet control over East Germany. He may have considered it in 1952, in order to block West German remilitarization, but he more likely used it as a tactical bait than as a preferred policy. Stalin always chose German partition.

After 1945, Stalin reverted to drastic domestic repression. His suspicions of the West rose with American anticommunism and refusal to accept the legitimacy of Soviet control over Eastern Europe or East Germany and extra-European Soviet-U.S. differences. Conversely, the United States believed, probably correctly, that Stalin would like to get control of West Germany and the rest of Western Europe and, probably incorrectly, that he had firm plans to do so. Conflicts of aims and mutual misperceptions and incomprehension made the cold war inevitable.[2]

There was a fundamental continuity in Soviet policy in Europe from 1939 onward. Stalin and Molotov made clear to Hitler how far their ambitions went. In December 1941, with the Germans at the gates of Moscow, Stalin still insisted on retaining his 1939-1940 gains. However, post-1945 Soviet policy was cautious, primarily because of America's atomic monopoly.

It was therefore not surprising, considering his 1930-1941 policies, that Stalin took over control of as much of Central and

Eastern Europe as the Red Army had occupied. Although Czechoslovakia until 1948 was in theory noncommunist, the Czechoslovak Communists had already in 1945 acquired the commanding heights of power: The 1948 coup confirmed and consolidated it. Stalin did not get complete control of Yugoslavia, and his efforts to do so were the primary cause of the 1948 break between him and Tito. Until 1948, the Soviet zone of Germany was both a part of a still existing if increasingly split Germany and an area in the process of becoming a Soviet satellite.

It is unclear to what extent Stalin wanted from the beginning to sovietize the Soviet zone of Germany. The division of Germany into occupation zones was a compromise based on estimates of where the armies would end up and also on the Western assumption that a democratized, denazified, united German state would emerge. Stalin's minimal objective was an industrially weakened, partitioned Germany with Soviet control complete in its zone or, maximally, united under four-power control with a Soviet veto over Ruhr steel and coal production, leaving open the possibility of ultimate Soviet predominance.

The two primary Soviet postwar objectives were to remove its strategic vulnerability vis-á-vis U.S. atomic weapons and to keep Germany industrially weak and militarily disarmed. It needed massive German reparations to repair Soviet war damage and speed up its atomic research and development programs and to keep German industry weak and controlled. But such a high level of reparations inevitably antagonized the Germans and also the Americans, who realized that they would have to pay for them. Moscow also hoped to use denazification in the Western zones, as it did in its own, to bring about an economic and social transformation that would weaken German nationalism and favor communism. Moreover, since Moscow had given eastern Germany to Poland and was dismantling industry in its zone, Washington rejected a Soviet veto over the Ruhr. France was opposed to *any* united Germany.

The Soviets also feared German partition, for West German industrial potential was much greater than East German and German nationalism was on the Wests's side. Finally, because

Moscow held the key not only to German unity but also to German recovery of its 1937 eastern boundaries in the East, Stalin was probably tempted to use this bait to work toward an all-German government that, if not communist dominated, would at least be favorable to Soviet policy.

Soviet policy toward Germany was thus until 1948 torn between essentially incompatible objectives, ranging from (1) their initial (1944-1945) desire to hold Germany down completely, if possible with the West, through (2) the intermediate (summer 1945-summer 1947) inclination, given Moscow's growing distrust of the West, to work toward a central German government with a low level of industrial production and a Soviet veto over Ruhr industry, with the ultimate objective of undermining and neutralizing or even eventually controlling it, to (3) (1948 onward) partition of Germany, complete sovietization of the Soviet zone, and an attempt to drive the West out of Berlin.

There were probably serious differences of opinion within the Soviet leadership about these variants. Moreover, until the 1948 U.S. stand in Berlin, Stalin and his associates were uncertain how firm the U.S. commitment in Europe was. In any case, the Soviet insistence on massive reparations and communization of their zone precluded coming to terms with the West or with any all-German government. Moreover, Soviet pressure in 1946 and 1947 in the Mediterranean, the Middle East, and Korea (as well as in Germany) to get the United States to withdraw caused greater American commitments. Thus the incompatibility of Soviet objectives pushed the Soviets toward partition and sovietization of their zone because they could only compensate for the uncertainty of attaining their maximum objective, a united, neutralized, industrially weak Germany, by making sure that their minimum objective, a sovietized East Germany, was attained, and the latter precluded the former.

From 1943 to 1946, Roosevelt preferred a "policy of postponement" with respect to Germany, within the context of his general hope for the dissolution of spheres of influence and a worldwide security system. Germany would be an object of European politics, which would be determined primarily by

Moscow and London with minimal American engagement. He underestimated not only Stalin's unwillingness to cooperate in this neo-Wilsonian "grand design" and the weakness of Great Britain and Western Europe but also the readiness, if convinced it were necessary, of U.S. public opinion to remain engaged in Europe and the potential danger to U.S. security from Soviet atomic weapons. Paradoxically, atomic weapons also made war less likely and thus cold war less dangerous.

The initial American policy of keeping Germany down was replaced in 1946-1947 by an intermediate "policy of ambivalance": growing distrust of Stalin and thus greater inclination to deal with some Germans but also to settle if possible with Stalin for a neutralized Germany with a relatively low level of industrial production. By late 1947-early 1948, however, this had given way to complete distrust of the Soviets and to the conviction that the economic recovery of West Germany and of Western Europe and the containment of Soviet power required a trizonal political and economic unit under German administration. This unit would be tied to the West with massive economic aid and a higher level of industrial production and controlled by its integration into a united, economically revived Western Europe.

The new Labour government in London showed some tendencies toward trying to create a socialist Western European "third force," but British economic and financial weakness soon made it so dependent on Washington, whose increasing distrust toward Moscow Attlee and Bevin shared, that it ceased to pursue any independent policy. Postwar Gaullist France initially pursued a maximum policy of partition of Germany, whereby the whole left bank of the Rhine would be under French suzerainty or at least control, the Ruhr coal and steel under international control, the south German states allied to France, and Paris, allied with Washington and London as well as with Moscow, would mediate among them. But French economic weakness, worsening relations with Moscow, and pressure from Washington pushed Paris back, particularly after de Gaulle quit in 1949, to an intermediate, primarily negative policy of preventing the establishment of any central German authorities, either on quadripartite basis or in the three Western zones. In 1946, this French veto contributed toward the Soviet abandonment of their intermediate support of central German authorities in Berlin. After 1947, however, France delayed but eventually gave in to American pressure for the establishment of the Federal Republic, keeping only the Saar (and that temporarily) plus, by means of the Schuman Plan, the incorporation of the Ruhr as well as all other Western European coal and steel into the European Coal and Steel Community.

By 1948, then, the net result was the de facto partition of Germany and the establishment of two German states in West and East, each in tight alliance with its own hegemonic power, the United States and the USSR. Germans, then, if not Germany, became again subjects, after having been since 1945 only objects, of European politicies. In 1946–1948, they played an increasing role in the negotiations leading to the establishment of the Federal Republic and, thereafter, of the German Democratic Republic (DDR).

The SPD-KPD Merger in the Soviet Zone

The first major confrontation between Soviet policy and what was to become West Germany occurred in 1946, when Ulbricht, presumably at Moscow's direction, attempted to bring about a merger between the KPD and the SPD, under KPD control, in all of Germany. The SPD, not the Christian Democratic Union (CDU), and Schumacher, not Adenauer, confronted and defeated Ulbricht and Moscow in the first great test of East-West relations in West Germany.

Despite Stalin's policy toward the KPD, the liquidation of so many KPD leaders in Moscow in 1938, the Soviet-Nazi pact, the wartime and postwar conduct of the Red Army, the postwar Soviet dismantling and reparations program, the Soviet exploitation of the uranium mines, and the arrests and deportations from the Soviet zone after the war were at first still not sufficient to make the Soviet Union appear to German communists as anything less than their liberator, the originator and protector of their power.[3] Nor is there any evidence that any significant elements in the KPD were opposed to a merger, under communist control, with the SPD. Nor were the social democratic leaders in the Soviet zone all opposed. Many who had spent the nazi period in Germany, in concentration camps or in hiding, had concluded that the SPD-KPD split had been one of the major reasons why the Nazis had come to power and that it must be overcome, for only a united workers' movement could prevent the return of nazism and militarism and build socialism in Germany.

Other, more personal factors with respect to the Social Democratic leaders in the Soviet occupation zone favored Soviet and KPD policy, including the merger. They saw no hope of political activity contrary to Soviet orders. They knew that Moscow strongly favored the KPD, but they were confident that most of the population in the Soviet zone supported the SPD and they hoped that Moscow, realizing this, would deal primarily with them rather than with the KPD, to prevent German partition. But they also rapidly realized that the leader of the SPD in the three Western zones, Kurt Schumacher, was strongly anti-communist and would not endorse a procommunist SPD line.

The ironical result was that during the summer and early autumn of 1945 the Social Democratic leadership in the Soviet zone urged the immediate merger of the SPD and the KPD and rapid nationalization of industry, while the KPD leaders and the Soviet Military Administration (SMA) opposed both, authorized the two parties to re-form separately, and delayed nationalization. This strategy was probably intended to gain KPD influence in the Western zones.

By autumn 1945, however, the situation had been reversed. The SPD Soviet zone leadership was better organized and more confident of popular support. Schumacher's anticommunist pressure on them was increasing. The Soviets and the KPD leadership had realized that they could make little political progress in the Western zones against Schumacher's opposition and the rapid formation of a mass Christian Democratic party.

The Soviets and the KPD therefore began pressing the SPD

toward a merger. The SPD leadership shifted to a policy of delay, urging that a KPD–SPD merger take place only on an all-German basis. Thereupon the Soviets and the KPD began to force out local antimerger SPD leaders. This pressure increased and the SPD zonal leadership split: Otto Grotewohl, its head, and Erich Gniffke reluctantly agreed to the merger; and its main opponents, Gustav Dahrendorf and Gustav Klingelhofer, broke with them on the issue. Schumacher unsuccessfully urged them to dissolve the SPD in the Soviet zone instead.

The merger was carried through, under strong Soviet pressure, at the beginning of 1946. Before it, however, antimerger Social Democrats in Berlin had initiated a referendum about the merger, with Schumacher's strong support, which the Soviets forbade in their sector but the three Western powers allowed in theirs. (The Western powers did not take the initiative in or officially support this referendum, although some junior British and American military government officers of anticommunist leftist convictions encouraged the antimerger SPD forces.) The result was a major defeat for the merger in the three Western sectors.

Schumacher rejected the merger and read out of the SPD Social Democrats like Grotewohl who supported it. Thus the anticommunism of Schumacher and his associates in the Western zones made the first major contribution to the beginning of German partition, for it blocked Soviet and KPD hopes of achieving their maximum all-German objective and made them retreat to their minimum one, firm control in the Soviet zone.[4]

Structural instability in Central and Western Europe was the main cause of the East-West split over Germany. Since Moscow could not achieve its maximum aim, a veto over the Ruhr, which in the U.S. view would prevent European economic recovery, it felt compelled to settle for its minimum one, the communization of East Germany, which the United States regarded as a breach of Soviet commitments. Since the United States could not achieve its maximum aim, a united, democratic German state, which would deprive the Soviets of their control of East Germany, it felt compelled to settle for its minimum one, an economically recovered, democratic West Germany, which was bound to tip the balance of power against the Soviet Union. Thus the maximum and minimum objectives of each potentially destabilized both objectives of the other. The result was until 1953 the rigidity of the cold war.

By 1947–1948 any possibility of a Soviet-American agreement on Germany had disappeared. Stalin was convinced that the Marshall Plan was an American attempt to reconstruct an anti-Soviet Western Europe dominated by a new, powerful West Germany, and for this and other reasons he consolidated and greatly intensified his domination of Eastern Europe. Washington was convinced that further negotiations with Stalin were fruitless and that his plan to move into the near–power vacuum in Western Europe must be contained by Western unity and strength. Thus, with the division of Germany firm, Moscow and Washington were each determined to build up its German state.

The great majority of postwar Germans were strongly anti-Russian and pro-Western. Traditional antagonism toward the Slavs; the anticommunism and anti-Russianism instilled into the German people during the twelve years of Nazi rule, confirmed for many German soldiers by the primitiveness they found in occupied Russia; fear of the consequences of the Nazi atrocities in the East; fear and revulsion from the plunder and rape of the Red Army troops as they advanced into Germany and from the horror stories of the expellees and returning prisoners of war; and, finally, the repression in the Soviet zone combined to deprive Soviet policy in postwar Germany of popular support. Indeed, all these, combined with the consciousness of Hitler's total defeat also helped to produce a soundly based democratic Federal Republic. They also produced an oversimplified anticommunism and anti-Russian and anti-Polish feelings, above all among the expellees, which postponed West German popular recognition that the borders of 1937 and the division of Germany were the inevitable consequence of Hitler's crimes and defeat and of the policy of the nuclear superpower to the east.[5]

The Soviets could have drawn upon some support in West Germany—from the ex-military, mindful of the pre-1933 cooperation with the Red Army, and from Christian trade unionists and left Social Democrats who wanted national unity and socialism. Nationalists, left-socialists, and various combinations of the two took over from the Kreisauer Kreis a determination to establish a united Germany cleansed of the errors of capitalism as well as communism. They knew that the Soviet Union would be the most difficult obstacle to its reestablishment, which could only occur with its consent.

But Stalin was never willing to endorse such a policy. He preferred to keep what he had (the Soviet zone) even at the price of thereby sacrificing any significant German popular support for Soviet policies, except among the German communists and their collaborators, for whom Soviet support was the only way to obtain and keep power. Stalin was correctly convinced that Russia could control any part of Germany only by force and that Russia must keep it divided and keep control of East Germany at all costs, for otherwise a reunited Germany would again become strong and expansionist and again endanger Russia's security and very existence. Few Russians probably disagreed with him—then or now.

The two German states, products of the cold war, were set up by the two hegemonic powers and therefore lacked complete national identity. The Federal Republic received its independence, prosperity, and security from the United States. It consolidated all three by its own efforts, however, and its population clearly chose a democratic polity. Its official national goal, reunification, was not attained, not so much because it was opposed by all its neighbors and only moderately supported by its protector, Washington, but because Moscow prevented it. The partition of Germany was the result of Germany's loss of the Second World War, the determination of the Soviet Union to keep Germany weak and divided, and the international consensus that Germany should never again attain the position to which its potential power seemed, at least to many Germans, to entitle it: the dominant power in Europe or, as Hitler had planned, in the world. Moscow and Washington had no need to allow this, since they were far stronger than even a reunited, militarized Germany and since Moscow and to a lesser extent Washington were determined not to allow Germany national nuclear weapons. France's subsequent nuclear capability was intended to prevent itself from being ever again dominated by Germany as well as to protect itself against the Soviet Union and to ensure its great-power status.

The fundamental problem of postwar West German alliance policy was therefore that its Western allies did not regard as their vital national interest what the Federal Republic did: the reunification of Germany. Or, to put it differently, the Federal Republic shared with its allies a vital interest to prevent the Soviet Union from changing the status quo in West Germany to their disadvantage, but its allies did not share the Federal Republic's vital interest to change the status quo in East Germany to its advantage.

This asymmetry was obscured during the height of the cold war. Adenauer and his Western allies could the more easily demand German reunification because none of them either expected or (except Adenauer, and even he only half-heartedly) wanted it. When, after 1953, East-West détente set in, however, Adenauer felt that he had to press even more for reunification, for he feared that any concessions with respect to it (for example, in favor of priority for arms control) would destabilize the Federal Republic and his hold over it and lead to Western concessions to the Soviets that would unfavorably change the status quo in the Federal Republic.[6]

The post-1945 division of Germany affected most Germans somewhat less than it would have most French or Poles, for "Germany" had historically been more of a cultural than a political concept. Bismarck's imperial Germany did not include the Germans in Austria. Genuine voluntary acceptance of Bismarck's Reich and its domination by Prussia was much less widespread in the Catholic Rhineland and Bavaria and even in Baden and Württemberg where the older political cultures lived on underneath the Bismarckian overlay.

Postwar West Germany

The main results of World War II in Germany were the dissolution of Prussia, the loss of the German territories east of the Oder and Neisse to Poland and the expulsion of their inhabitants westward, Soviet control over what had been central Germany, popular discrediting of German nationalism, and the fact that in the Western zones of Germany a near-majority of the population was Catholic and only a minority was both Protestant and Prussian.[7] The new German Federal Republic was thus in one sense a delayed victory, imposed by foreign force, for the Catholic Rhineland and Bavaria over Protestant Prussia—a revival of regional Catholic political culture.

Not that Adenauer's Federal Republic was a total repudiation of Bismarck. True, he, some of the CDU, and more of the Bararian Christian Social Union (CSU), particularly its Catholic wing, felt that Bismarck's Reich had been doomed from the beginning because its challenge to the rest of Europe and to the world had been too great, because it could only have been successfully ruled by a genius like Bismarck, and because it had rejected Catholic Austria and was hostile to Catholic France. Adenauer and the CDU/CSU, like Bismarck, wanted a united German state; but they did not want a Prussian-dominated one.

For the first time in post-Reformation German history, the community of suffering in the antinazi Resistance surmounted the religious division between Protestants and Catholics through the establishment of a mass-based Christian Democratic party in which Catholics predominated. (German nationalists of a Bismarckian persuasion were in it also, as well as in the Free Democratic party, but they were a minority.) Thus during the immediate postwar period traditional German nationalism was submerged in the ruling CDU/CSU. Primarily bourgeois in ethos and Christian and antinazi in ideology, the CDU/CSU was predisposed to be strongly anti-Soviet. So, traditionally, were the Social Democrats.

The fear and hatred of the Soviet Union guaranteed that there would be no significant West German popular support for the traditional Prussian policy of alliance with Russia. On the contrary, historic German anticommunism, the necessity (as after World War I) for American credits for West German economic recovery, and West Germany's vulnerability to Soviet attack made almost all postwar West Germans oriented toward the West.[8] The south and west of Germany had always been pro-Western and particularly pro-French. German Catholicism was pro-Western by definition. The majority tradition of the SPD was firmly pro-Western and anti-Soviet. Moreover, as East-West tension increased, the only realistic way for all or part of Germany to regain equality in Western Europe and thereby both economic prosperity and perhaps even eventually reunification was to join a united Western Europe and thus lessen European and world fears of the revival of German power. Thus the Western orientation became a version of German nationalist strategy—in fact, under Adenauer's leadership, the dominant one.

Another possible German strategy, balancing between East and West, predominated in the resistance. After 1945, it also gained some support from the fact that its abandonment for a Western orientation would cement partition and from the hope among Kreisauer Kreis-influenced groups in the left CDU and left SPD that Germany could be a Social Democratic or Christian Socialist ideological bridge between East and West. The postwar hardening of Soviet foreign policy rapidly weakened the assumptions of this policy and the Berlin Blockade destroyed it for the time being. Nevertheless, it revived after Stalin's death, notably in the Free Democratic Party (FDP), and has never died out since.

American policy, since 1946 increasingly predominant in western Germany, and West German, particularly CDU, policy thus converged. The United States easily agreed with Adenauer's fear of Soviet expansionism, his need for American economic aid, and his willingness to make concessions to France, Great Britain, and the United States.

Konrad Adenauer

As Arnulf Baring has written, "In the beginning there was Adenauer."[9] His postwar West German foreign policy reflected his simplistic, firm convictions and iron determination: priority for integration of West Germany as an equal partner into a united Western Europe and for the Atlantic Alliance over negotiations with Moscow for German reunification.

Adenauer took up after 1945 where he had left off in 1922. He had then, it will be recalled, favored the separation of the Rhineland from Prussia, while keeping it a part of a united Germany, and the establishment of close economic ties between it and France, in order to satisfy the security interests of France, for whom Prussia was anathema, and British balance-of-power policy: in sum, the rejection of traditional German nationalism in favor of Franco-German reconciliation and close alliance with the West.[10] In 1945, he saw much more clearly than his opponents the key factors that would determine postwar West Germany's international situation: Europe had largely destroyed itself and the United States and the Soviet Union would dominate the postwar world; overwhelming Soviet military power and westward push for influence were the greatest dangers to West Germany's security; this and Soviet conflicts of interest with the West would produce the cold war; the long-range unity and determination of the Western democracies was doubtful; Germany would remain divided for the indefinite future; with the Red Army on the Elbe, West Germany was dependent on U.S. military force for its security and on U.S. goodwill to regain and maintain its sovereignty; only thus could it surmount the dangers confronting it and thereafter, with West German political instability contained and West German energy and technological skill unleashed by West European unity, West Germany would become at least an equal partner if not the leader of the united Europe to come. Adenauer feared American isolationism, anti-German French nationalism, and a "return to Potsdam," that is, a revival of Soviet U.S. hegemony over Germany.

One may debate whether Adenauer really wanted reunification[11] or preferred a "Carolingian" West Germany.[12] In the very long run he hoped that a united Western Europe would want reunification not only for German reasons but to compensate for Soviet power. Adenauer was not a theorist but a pragmatist. Since he was convinced that German reunification was not in the cards at any price other than West Germany's political impotence, subservience to foreign powers, low standard of living, and sooner or later, Soviet domination, he saw no reason to choose between it and a united Western Europe.

He also saw that the postwar East-West constellation would enable him to fulfill his policy of the early 1920s; conciliation and economic cooperation with France, led by a Protestant and Catholic Christian mass party. Adenauer's *raison d'état* was much more West German than German. Yet ke knew that the great majority of West Germans, and certainly most of his conservative supporters, shared neither his rejection of modern German nationalism nor his ruthlessly realistic awareness that German partition was there to stay. He therefore made a virtuous myth out of cold necessity: For many years he successfully insisted that only his policy, "positions of strength," would bring reunification and that therefore negotiations or compromise with Moscow or East Berlin were unnecessary as well as immoral. He thus blocked the West German nationalists on the Right and the Left, those in the West who feared another Rapallo, Soviet attempts to use German nationalism, and Western temptations to compromise with the Soviets, and thereby ensured that Bonn and the Western powers would choose each other.

Fearing that German insecurities and identity crises would lead to nationalism or neutralism, Adenauer was convinced that West Germany must be spared the challenge and frustrations of an independent foreign policy. He knew that Germany's neighbors, the United States, or the Soviet Union would never return its independence to a nationalist Germany. Rather, they would keep it dependent on and encircled by them. But West Germany's merger into Western Europe, he believed, would help it to regain and maintain its sovereignty and equality.

Adenauer was above all else a Rhinelander, the heir of its Catholic, conservative, anti-Bismarckian traditions. For him modern Germany's two attempts to dominate Europe and to vaunt itself as different from and superior to the West had been ghastly catastrophes. West Germany, therefore, the heir of Charlemagne and the Holy Roman Empire, with the Rhineland as its center, must become an integral and equal partner in a Christian, democratic Western Europe. He believed that the Soviet Union was not only the center of cummunism but also basically Asiatic and thus the mortal enemy of all that he held dear: Catholicism, the Rhineland, Europe, and the West. And the German Social Democrats were for him the heirs of Protestant Prussia—authoritarian, centralist, and anticapitalist at best, pro-Soviet at worst.

For Adenauer, therefore, postwar West Germany had one overriding historic mission: While still weak, divided, and sharing with the rest of Western Europe an overriding fear of Soviet expansionism, it should submerge itself, on an equal basis, in a politically united Western Europe, Catholic, democratic, and conservative in orientation, allied, also on an equal basis, with the United States and united against the ever-present Soviet threat. Only thus, he believed, could German nationalism be safely and indefinitely submerged in, and West Germany become an equal partner of, an independent Western Europe safe from Soviet domination and American control.

Adenauer was determined that West Germany should recover equal status in Europe. He realized that this could only be achieved rapidly by conciliation and by concessions in advance (*Vorausleistungspolitik*). He correctly calculated that once he had overcome the Western-imposed limits on West German economic recovery and conventional rearmament, and as long as Soviet hostility continued to frighten and unify the West, his concessions would pay off handsomely later.

Adenauer's policy of concillation centered on France. His conbribution to overcoming centuries of Franco-German hostility was one of his greatest achievements. He knew, as he had in 1922, that only Western European multilateralism could blur the tension between French desires for security and West German determination for equality. He traded adherence to the multinational Ruhr Authority for the end of industrial dismantling, adherence to the Schuman Plan for the end of limitations on West German industry, and West European control of West

German coal and steel and West German conventional rearmament for sovereignty and equality.

He was convinced that his principal partner had to be the United States, which alone could deter the Soviet military threat. But he had no intention of accepting indefinite U.S. domination of Western Europe or the Federal Republic. With the exception of Foster Dulles, Clay, McCloy, and a few other Americans, he mistrusted the Americans' constancy, if and when Soviet hostility should subside; and he was determined never to choose between Washington and Paris.

Western unity and strength, therefore, and West Germany as an integrated, equal part of it were Adenauer's foreign policies. All else was tactics. Only thereafter, if indeed at all, he felt, and then within a European, not a German, framework, should Bonn concern itself seriously with the East.

Although Adenauer did not share the Prussian, Bismarckian, Protestant contempt for Poles or the Austrian contempt for Czechs, he was fundamentally uninterested in Eastern Europe, for he saw little chance there for liberalization or decrease of Soviet predominance. He believed that West German Ostpolitik had to center on Moscow. He thus gave Eastern Europe a very low priority in his foreign policy and was prepared to sacrifice any chance of change in it—and he saw none—for Western European integration. For Adenauer anything east of the Elbe had always been foreign: In 1948, he remarked that when before the war he had to go to Berlin, he had always pulled down the curtains of his railway compartment as he crossed the Elbe so that he would not have to see "that Asiatic steppe" (of Prussia).[13]

Adenauer knew what he wanted; he knew what he could get; he knew that they were the same; and he got them. Catholic but not clerical, national but not nationalistic, a "terrible simplifier" and proud of it, autocratic by temperament but democratic by intellectual conviction, like Bismarck successfully determined that foreign policy would be his own exclusive province, determined in disaster and moderate in success, wholly disillusioned and cynical about mankind and especially about his fellow Germans, Adenauer was the greatest son of the Rhineland, a great

European, and the greatest German statesman, as Churchill remarked, since Bismarck. Like Bismarck, he created a partially authoritarian system and a cynical style of rule that without prosperity and firm U.S. support might have become unstable. (But as brilliantly as he rode and channeled the stream of history until the mid-1950s, thereafter, when it turned toward East-West détente, he tried to stop it. The result was foreign policy failure.)

In Adenauer, Stalin and Khrushchev met their match. In 1949, when he became chancellor, West Germany was prostrate and Stalin had just lifted the blockade of Berlin. When he resigned in 1963, the Federal Republic was the third industrial and the second trading nation of the world.[14]

The Western orientation, that is, a policy favoring integration of the Western zones with the rest of Western Europe, was not confined to Adenauer and the CDU/CSU. It had first been expressed, before the end of the war, in a book by a distinguished German economist who had emigrated to Switzerland, Wilhelm Röpke. It was federalist, anti-Prussian, anticollectivist and pro-market economy, pro-American (if only because the United States alone could furnish the credits the German economy would need to revive), anti-Soviet, willing to accept partition, and certainly unwilling to risk any of its other goals in the hope of avoiding it. Its early supporters—the Berlin publicists Erik Reger and Ernst Friedländer and later the Berlin SPD leader and later mayor, Ernst Reuter—saw the establishment of a West German state as inevitable, a necessary precondition for integration into Western Europe, and the necessary base from which reunification could be striven for and obtained. Its anti-Prussian supporters in south and west Germany were the more willing to accept partition because they did not want Berlin to be the capital of a united German state.

Adenauer's Rivals

The views on Eastern policy of Adenauer's two great opponents in the immediate postwar period, Jakob Kaiser and Kurt Schumacher, were minority ones; but they reemerged in the post-Adenauer era. Jakob Kaiser, one of Adenauer's opponents and the first CDU leader in the Soviet zone, was a left-wing trade union Catholic from Berlin. His goal, the same as that of the Kreisauer Kreis, with which Kaiser had been associated, was a left-wing German nationalist one, a new version of Stresemann's policy: a united Christian socialist Germany within its 1937 boundaries. He thought that Stresemann's policy of balancing between East and West was still correct. He wanted negotiations with the Soviets; he believed that a united Christian socialist Germany could be a bridge between East and West; he was not pro-French because Paris was separatist; he suspected the United States because it was capitalist; and he was anti-Polish because he supported the 1937 boundaries. His policy was wrecked by the cold war, by Soviet intransigence in their zone, and by the West Germans' preference for security over unity. Like its right-wing nationalist version,[15] however, it regained strength after Adenauer resigned.[16]

Adenauer's greatest opponent was not Kaiser but Kurt Schumacher, head of the postwar SPD. The party, the only one with firm continuity with pre-1933 Germany, was anticommunist, antimilitarist, anticapitalist, and rather anti-American. It was deeply committed to socialism and German reunification because of its tradition, its concern for the Social Democrats in the Soviet zone, and its realization that in a reunified Germany it, not its conservative opponents, would be in the majority.

Schumacher was a Marxist, indeed a rather dogmatic one. He was also a German nationalist. He was convinced that the SPD had lost to the Nazis in large part because it had not been nationalist enough, and he was determined not to repeat this mistake. In so doing, as it turned out, he was "fighting the last war." The nationalism of most West Germans was still sufficiently numbed by total defeat, and their fear of the Russians and desire for American economic aid so great, that they were prepared to settle for Adenauer's Western integration.

From 1945 onward, Schumacher was strongly anti-KPD and anti-Soviet. In this respect he took up where the SPD leadership left off in Berlin in 1933 and in Prague until 1938. He experienced in concentration camps the ruthless drive of the German Communists for domination over their fellow prisoners. He viewed the Soviet Union as an expansionist, imperialist great power. He totally rejected the Kaiser "bridge" theory. In 1946, as we have seen, he was mainly responsible for preventing the KPD-SPD fusion in the Western zones.

Schumacher was a German nationalist but he was not anti-European. Like the pre-1933 SPD, he looked forward to a democratic socialist Europe. However, conscious that he and the SPD had never collaborated with the Nazis and had suffered for their anti-Nazi resistance, he felt that the SPD had earned a moral claim to leadership in Germany and to treatment as equals by the West. He consequently rejected Adenauer's policy of concessions (*Vorausleistungspolitik*) and of integration into Western Europe before Germany became equal with the other Western European powers, the more so after it became clear that a united Western Europe would be primarily Christian Democratic, capitalist, and conservative.

Schumacher was deeply suspicious of Adenauer and the CDU and of their support by Washington. His fierce demand for German independence and equality and his desire for a more forward strategy against the Soviet zone made him distrust them the more. He depended on support by the British Labour party, but he underestimated its anti-Germanism and Britain's economic weakness. Unlike Adenauer, he underestimated the duration of German partition and therefore refused to exclude the possibility of a united and neutralized Germany—the more so since in it the electoral balance would favor the Protestants and the Social Democrats. Schumacher feared the primacy of the Berlin SPD because he thought it would inevitably be under Soviet influence. He also feared west and south German federalism and particularism and American (capitalist) influence on it. He therefore opposed the 1949 Basic Law. His foreign policy failed because his dream of a socialist Western Europe never materialized. because Labour Britain, its core, was too weak, and because America wanted a Federal Republic to be established without full sovereignty and with a market economy. Adenauer wanted the second as well; and, realistic as ever, he was prepared to accept the first also, correctly confident that it would only be a transitional phase.

Other SPD figures, the ideologist Richard Löwenthal and the south German Carlo Schmid, unrealistically wanted either a socialist Europe as a "third force" between East and West under British leadership (Löwenthal) or a federal Europe with a very provisional German state outside of it (Schmid). The young Willy Brandt had had ideas similar to Löwenthal's during his Norwegian and Swedish exile, going back to his days in the SAP (*Sozialistische Arbeiterpartei*—a left-wing splinter group that left the SPD before 1933). Like other left-wing German socialist émigrés in Scandinavia, he had been skeptical of the capitalist Western powers as well as of the Soviet Union. (Brandt's mid-1930s popular front phase was very brief.) His postwar work with Reuter in Berlin rapidly brought him to a strongly pro-Western position.[17] With the coming of the Berlin blockade, three leading Social Democrats, the city's strongly anticommunist mayor, Ernst Reuter, and the mayors of Bremen and Hamburg, Wilhelm Kaisen and Max Brauer, who led the SPD right-wing, joined Adenauer and the CDU to swing the drafters of the Basic Law toward founding a Western state from which the Soviets could be resisted and reunification striven for.

SPD foreign policy, like Jakob Kaiser's, was defeated by the cold war and West German insecurity and prosperity. Schumacher rejected neutralism and negotiations with Ulbricht, but he proposed an all-European security system that the Soviets would accept only if the SPD negotiated with Ulbricht and that Washington strongly opposed. His opposition to Adenauer's *Vorausleistungspolitik* with France and the United States proved shortsighted. The SPD's socialism ran contrary to West German weariness with the Nazi command economy and post-1948 prosperity. Finally, the cold war, the Berlin Blockade, and the Korean War made the majority of West Germans so fear the Soviets that they would not risk, as the SPD advocated, lessening U.S. military protection in the hope of reunification. Not until the second Berlin crisis and after Adenauer's electoral victories did the SPD accept Adenauer's foreign policy and then, as we shall see, within the context of a fundamentally, but much more realistic, forward Ostpolitik.[18]

One other political grouping in postwar West Germany influenced German foreign policy toward the East: the nearly ten million expellees, primarily from the territories east of the Oder-Neisse line, Pomerania, Silesia, and East Prussia, plus the nearly three million from the Sudetenland. Initially, they were unpopular in West Germany. However, post-1948 prosperity, Bonn's desire to integrate them, and the growing need for their labor absorbed them into West German society; and the passage of time and continuing prosperity weakened their ties with their former homelands. Populist in domestic policy and nationalist in foreign policy, they were initially politically strong within their own party, the *Bund der Heimatlosen und Entrechteten* (BHE), which collapsed in the late 1950s, and within the CDU and SPD. They were organized according to their territorial origins into political pressure groups, the *Landsmannschaften,* largely financed by the Bonn government in order to control as well as to support them. They urged all West German parties to insist on rigid maintenance of the maximum German claims in the East. Party rivalries in West Germany made their negative influence in the 1950s great in this respect, the more so because Adenauer maintained a rigid maximalist legal position vis-à-vis the East for general electoral purposes as well as to conciliate the expellees, to concentrate on Western European integration, and, later, to block East-West détente. The expellees' influence delayed a more flexible West German Ostpolitik; but by the late 1960s, as they became older and more integrated, it became much less important.[19]

While Adenauer, Kaiser, and Schumacher feared the Soviet Union and were determined to ensure West Germany's security, the East saw them all as German nationalists, leaders of a dynamic, disciplined, and technologically highly developed nation that twice had flooded over them and was only defeated after immense losses and the intervention of the United States. Schumacher was the symbol of social democratic challenge in East

Germany. It was Adenauer, ironically, that the East probably misunderstood the most—not his anticommunism, which no one could misunderstand or underestimate, but his lack of German nationalism. For the East the latter was overshadowed, insofar as they understood it at all, by his territorially and ideologically revisionist rhetoric and, as they would put it, by the "objective" nature of his policy: the revival of a strong, revisionist German state in alliance with the United States and, they feared, likely to dominate a united Western Europe.

The First Berlin Blockade

The 1948–1949 first Soviet blockade of West Berlin,[20] the Communist takeover in Czechoslovakia, and the Korean War seemed to most West Germans at best to threaten West German security and at worst to foreshadow a third world war.[21] The blockade demonstrated the structural interaction of Soviet and Western objectives, minimal and maximal. For Stalin it had a minimal, defensive aim: the prevention of the economic unity of the three Western zones of Germany. Yet had the West given up West Berlin, this would have so politically destabilized the Western zones of Germany and the whole East-West relationship that Stalin would have made great progress toward his maximum goal: the expulsion of the United States from Europe and the resultant establishment of Soviet hegemony over it. Conversely, the Western powers, especially the United States, saw West German economic and political unity as a necessary step to save Western Europe from economic collapse and Soviet hegemony and were thus determined to repel the Soviet effort to block it. By so doing and by successfully maintaining their position in West Berlin, they helped to create the Federal Republic and a prosperous Western Europe, which changed the East-West balance of power to the disadvantage of the Soviets. The establishment of NATO and West German rearmament shifted the balance even more.

West German Remilitarization

Stalin precipitated West German remilitarization by his permission to Pyongyang in 1950 to invade South Korea, based on his understandable assumption, judging by its previous statements, that Washington would not resist it militarily. However, Truman not only fought back but he and Acheson decided, as did Adenauer, that the Soviet-sponsored attack in Korea probably presaged one on Western Europe and that West German rearmament was necessary to prevent it. (That they were probably wrong is not the point—only another irony of history.) Adenauer's other main motive was to recover full sovereignty and equality in return for a West German military contribution to NATO within the miltinational European Defense Community (EDC).

Bonn's diplomatic recognition of Belgrade in late 1951 was the first postwar West German step in policy toward the East. For Adenauer it was probably more an adjustment to American support of Tito's move toward the West, his domestic moderation, and Soviet-Yugoslav tension than a conscious major move in West German Ostpolitik. It also showed that Adenauer's anticommunism, like Dulles's, did not stop him from aiding dissident, anti-Soviet Communists. Other West Germans, in the tradition of either *Russland-* or *Randstaatenpolitik,* did urge the improvement of relations with Belgrade as a major Ostpolitik move. One of them, the FDP politician Karl-Georg Pfleiderer, who advocated a neutralized, reunified Germany, became the first West German Ambassador to Yugoslavia; but Adenauer blocked his attempts to make major diplomatic progress there.[22] Although West German-Yugoslav trade and tourism increased after 1954, Bonn's hopes for its new ties with Belgrade fell victim to Khrushchev's détente policies and rapprochement with Tito.

Before Stalin's death in 1953, however, Adenauer's foreign policy seemed triumphant. The early 1950s in East-West relations in Europe were dominated by Stalin's attempts to prevent West German armament. Either directly or via the East Germans, the Soviets made a series of proposals that, as West German rearmament came closer, became ostensibly more attractive and

Western replies to them more negative. In 1950, Moscow proposed the creation of an all-German council (half from each German state) and thereafter free all-German elections. In 1951, after the EDC treaty was signed, the Soviets proposed a neutralized, reunited Germany. In 1952 there were two more extensive Soviet proposals: the first, on March 10, was for a peace treaty with a sovereign, reunited, neutralized Germany with a national army. It included references to Potsdam and to banning organizations "inimical to democracy and . . . peace," that is, it would have meant renewed de facto four-power control. The final and most extensive one, on April 9, added free elections before reunification, controlled by a four-power commission, that is, with a Soviet veto, not by a UN commission, as the West had proposed.

One cannot be certain how genuine these Soviet proposals were. None of them made any concessions to the Western (and West German) proposal of internationally supervised, free, all-German elections—not surprisingly, for such elections would probably have meant the incorporation of the German Democratic Republic into the West German Federal Republic. (Why Stalin or any other strong Russian leader should have agreed to that is very difficult to understand, nor did Adenauer or his allies expect them to.)

Nor was liberalization in East Germany going on at the time: On the contrary, post-Tito purges there were accompanied by increasingly repressive domestic policies. In my view all these Soviet proposals were intended minimally to prevent or slow down West German rearmament and to divide the West within itself and from Bonn. Whether Stalin really then wanted a neutralized, united Germany will probably long remain unclear. If he did, he would have stopped West German rearmament, divided the West, and given Moscow permanent participation in continuing control over a weak, reunited Germany, that is, they would have prevented the balance of power in Europe from tipping against the Soviet Union and indeed tipped it in Moscow's favor. Even so, the East German leadership, understandably fearful then as later of any Soviet willingness to dilute their control over East Germany in order to gain in West Germany, indirectly indicated its distrust of the Soviet proposals.

The Western powers, and particularly the United States understandably skeptical of the Soviet proposals, readily went along with Adenauer's hostility to them. When London and Paris showed signs of hesitation in rejecting them, Adenauer and the Americans pulled them back into line. Washington feared that West German rearmament would be endangered by its postponement or abandonment for the doubtful chance of progress toward German reunification and the instability of a weak, reunified Germany, with no American military presence to control it or check Soviet advances. London and Paris, although much less enthusiastic about West German rearmament, were equally unenthusiastic about German reunification. Adenauer and Schumacher split company on the issue of whether there should even be four-power negotiations to discuss the Soviet proposal. There ensued the first major post-1945 political controversy in the Federal Republic about policy toward the East.

Adenauer and Schumacher agreed that there must be free, internationally supervised all-German elections, that is, that East Germany should be incorporated into the Federal Republic and that Bonn should not negotiate with the East German government. They differed with respect to four-power negotiations about the Soviet proposals. Schumacher believed that these should be undertaken before Bonn finally joined the EDC and NATO in order to carry out the Federal Republic's historic duty to leave no stone unturned in order to get reunification. Adenauer insisted that only if Bonn first joined both could reunification ever occur and that the Soviet proposals were only intended to prevent West German rearmament and entry into NATO and into an integrated Western Europe and to sow disunity and nationalism in the West. Secondly, Schumacher was prepared to accept the neutralization of a reunified Germany; Adenauer was not.

Moreover, they calculated the future policies of the Western powers differently. Adenauer thought that a four-power conference would run the risk of Moscow reestablishing the Old Potsdam framework of four-power control, for him the greatest danger to German sovereignty and security. Schumacher believed that the Federal Republic's integration into NATO and EDC would so seal the partition of Germany that the Western powers would cease to concern themselves with reunification.

The debate was long and fierce. Adenauer won, for he had the parliamentary majority and profited from the West German public's fear for its prosperity and security and its bone-deep distrust of the Soviets. Cynically, for he was anything but a German nationalist, he appealed to West German nationalism and thus blocked Schumacher from using it, by demanding as a precondition for four-power negotiations not only reunification through free elections but also revision of the Oder-Neisse line.

By mid-1952, the NATO treaty was ratified. The Federal Republic had recovered its sovereignty. Stalin had lost his gamble to delay West German reunification and was caught up in the anti-Semitic paranoia of the Slánský trial in Prague and the Doctors Plot in Moscow. Ulbricht stepped up purges and sovietization in East Germany. The cold war had reached its height.

In my view Adenauer's choice was the most prudent one for the Federal Republic and the Western powers. In 1952, the West, the Federal Republic, and the Soviet Union did not feel secure enough to agree to the Central European status quo. West Germany was politically, economically, and militarily too weak to risk the suspicion of Washington for the chance of gain with Moscow. East Germany was also too weak, especially because its inhabitants could still flee through Berlin to the West, as by 1952 they were doing in ever-increasing numbers. The Soviet Union was still militarily far inferior to the United States, although it had tested a thermonuclear weapon, and Stalin was engulfed in paranoic suspicion of enemies at home and abroad. The time for East-West détente and a major new West German Ostpolitik was not yet ripe.

Those who differ will argue that this view is simply historicism—"whatever is, is right." As the reader will see later in this study, I am far from a defender of CDU policy toward the East.

But in my view no serious opportunity for any successful West German Ostpolitik, as either the CDU or the SPD defined it, existed until after Stalin's death.[23]

The Bonn convention of 1952, which with minor changes after the French Assembly rejected the EDC became the Paris agreements of 1954, was the greatest success of Adenauer's holding policy. Like Stresemann at Locarno, he regained equality in the West, left open the situation in the East, and ensured against any revival of an anti-German coalition of the wartime victors by gaining a veto over any Western acquiescence in it plus terms for reunification and a peace treaty that Moscow would never accept. Yet the analogy to Stresemann is only partial, for he did so by intimate association with the West, not, as Bismarck advised, by keeping the wire open to St. Petersburg.

The convention's key provisions were four. First, the Federal Republic recovered its sovereignty but the three Western powers retained troop stationing rights and reserved jurisdiction over Berlin and Germany as a whole, including reunification and a final peace settlement, which, they agreed, would provide for a united Germany a liberal democratic constitution like that of the Federal Republic and integrated into the European Community—that is, the absorption of East by West Germany. Second, until that occurred the three Western powers endorsed Adenauer's claim that the Federal Republic was the sole legitimate representative of all Germans, that is, that they would not recognize East Berlin and would support Bonn's Hallstein Doctrine to prevent other states from doing so. Third, final determination of Germany's borders would await a peace treaty with a reunited Germany, that is, the three Western powers would not recognize the Oder-Neisse line. They thereby implicitly endorsed Bonn's declaratory policy in favor of its revision. Fourth, the three Western powers would maintain their troops in Berlin and regard any attack on it as one on them. This made it more difficult, if not impossible, for the Western powers to use the Federal Republic's dependence on them to defend West Berlin in order to demand a political price with respect to West German foreign policy or to make concessions to the Soviet Union with respect to it.

These provisions were unacceptable to Moscow, Warsaw, and East Berlin. Adenauer gained a veto power over Western policy on Germany, committed the West to German reunification, blocked Soviet proposals for negotiation, and thus maintained his positions on West German security, equality, *raison d'état,* and, at least rhetorically—and that was enough for his purposes— held open for the future the issues of reunification and the recovery of the 1937 German boundaries.

West German Eastern Policy After Stalin

Two Soviet developments after 1953—Khrushchev's policy of détente with the West and Soviet development of effective thermonuclear deterrent capability—helped to change West German foreign policy, especially toward the East. Adenauer's postwar foreign policy was primarily to recover from defeat, maximally (if only rhetorically) to work toward reunification through a policy of strength, that is, to become so strong that Moscow would feel compelled to give up East Germany. His maximal goal could not be attained by his policies, for the Federal Republic was too weak, the Soviet Union was too strong, and the United States would not use force to support it. Moscow's attainment in 1959 of thermonuclear missile delivery capability over Western Europe and the United States made certain that a "policy of strength" could not force the Soviet Union to decrease its control in East Germany to West Germany's advantage.

Rising Soviet power increased Soviet confidence and nationalism. Stalin bequeathed to his heirs the key prerequisites for Soviet security: the breaking of the U.S. atomic monopoly and the consolidation of the Soviet empire. He also left them a series of unsolved problems, to which their solution was *reculer pour mieux sauter.* Moderation of Soviet policy after Stalin was probably inevitable, if only because of the succession struggle. Khrushchev combined modernization through partial liberalization at home and limited East-West détente and partial devolu-

tion of empire (notably with Peking) abroad. He hoped that détente would help contain his most pressing problems—atomiza-
tion of society through mass terror and low agricultural and industrial production at home and the Korean War, nationalistic
dissatisfaction in China and in Eastern Europe, and the arms
race abroad—and also that he could use détente to exploit the
power vacuum and revolutionary potential left by Western de-
colonization in the third world and to launch a political offensive in Western Europe. In addition, he thought, détente would
guard against the danger of nuclear war and make it easier for
Moscow to move toward strategic parity with the United States.
Moreover, he believed, by satisfying minimal Eastern European
desires for more national autonomy and a higher standard of
living, détente would stabilize the long-term Soviet position,
especially in East Germany, the key to their postwar gains.
Simultaneously, by weakening the Western perception of Soviet hostility, détente would loosen the Western alliance, permit
Soviet cultivation of France, limit West German rearmament
and prevent its atomic rearmament, and he hoped, contribute
toward the maximum Soviet objectives in Western Europe: the
military withdrawal of the United States from the Continent
and the isolation and neutralization of West Germany.

Since 1953, Western and especially West German foreign policy in Europe has reacted to this Soviet détente strategy. By
1954-1955 the United States was becoming vulnerable to Soviet strategic thermonuclear capability and was therefore less inclined to take risks for anything short of its own vital interests,
which did not include German reunification. The more U.S.
vulnerability increased, the higher priority it gave to arms control.[24] In 1953, Eisenhower cut the military budget and therefore could not increase U.S. conventional military capability in
Europe. (He did step up missile development, but this did not
counterbalance increased U.S. nuclear vulnerability.)

France was more vulnerable to and more concerned about
rising West German power and more favorable to Soviet détente
overtures. Washington's lack of support for Paris in Algeria and
in the 1956 Suez crisis, declining French fears of the Soviet

Union, French determination to remain superior to Bonn, and the refusal of French nationalists to accept less than great-power status, turned France away from NATO and European political and military unity toward an independent nuclear capability. As Stanley Hoffmann perceptively put it: "France could not balance German power alone, it could never be sure it could control the joint institutions of the Six, and it did not want to consolidate American preponderance as the price for keeping West German fully integrated into Western Europe."[25]

Soviet détente policy threatened Adenauer's security relationship with the United States, rapprochement with France, and consolidation of West Germany. It also increased his fear of isolation, because he believed that improved Soviet-U.S. relations were based on an exaggerated U.S. evaluation of Soviet moderation and that would shift Washington's primary concern to arms control and the third world, where Bonn was neither necessary for the United States nor over which it had any great influence. He also felt that détente menaced Bonn's desire to convert its growing economic, financial, and technological power into greater political and military influence in order to improve West Germany's position in Europe and the world.

Post-Stalin West German foreign policy thus aimed minimally to prevent its own position from suffering from East-West détente, by losing its equality with its allies or by having foreclosed, though Western acceptance of the Eastern European status quo, progress toward reunification, and maximally to take advantage of Soviet weakness, in particular in Eastern Europe or East Germany.[26] Adenauer was determined to prevent his allies from negotiation with Moscow over his head or contrary to Bonn's interests, to maintain alliance unity and increase alliance strength, and to negotiate with Moscow on the German question only if the above two aims were achieved. By the mid-1950s he, like de Gaulle, was increasingly convinced that the West could profit from the Chinese threat to the Soviets.

It is possible to distinguish five periods of post-1953 West German policy, with particular reference to the East. (1) Adenauer's "holding" policy until 1961, (2) the more flexible East-

ern policy carried on thereafter by the new foreign minister
Gerhard Schröder, which gave way in late 1966 to (3) the Eastern policy of the CDU-SPD coalition, (4) the 1970–1974 new
Ostpolitik of the SPD-FDP coalition, and (5) the post-1974
Schmidt-Genscher Ostpolitik. Movement in Bonn was gradual
and these five divisions are therefore in part artificial, but they
are in my view the most useful for analysis.

Adenauer's Holding Policy
Adenauer's minimal post-1953 foreign policy aim was to preserve
the Federal Republic's previous gains and to prevent a "return
to Potsdam." He profoundly mistrusted Soviet détente policy.
He then continued to give priority to the attainment of Western
European unity and particularly to Franco-German reconciliation before, as he saw it, the inevitable revival of German nationalism could prevent it. He therefore did his best to block
East-West détente, primarily by trying to make progress toward
German reunification a precondition for it. That he saw no
prospect of reunification or that West German integration into
the European Economic Community would lower Soviet and
Eastern European fears of a revival of German nationalism was
not the point. Adenauer had sold his policy of European integration as the only road to reunification, and the surrender of
the goal of reunification would thus cut the ground out from
his foreign policy. He was helped by mounting West German
prosperity and domestic tranquility, Soviet relapses into repression, Foster Dulles's strong support, and his own superior political skill. He therefore neither needed nor wished to improve
Bonn's relations with the Soviet Union and Eastern Europe.

Adenauer was also initially helped by the momentum of the
reactive Western cold war policies. He continued to press for a
European Defense Community. He and Dulles were profoundly
suspicious of Soviet détente initiatives. Indeed, this was the
period of Adenauer's strongest "Atlanticism" (his closest alliance with Washington).

1953: The Last Chance to Unfreeze the German Question?
After Stalin died, Malenkov, Khrushchev, and Beria, competing

for supreme power, initiated East-West détente and partial, controlled liberalization in the Soviet Union and Eastern Europe and in Soviet relations with China. Adenauer was very skeptical of both and of the Western view that they offered opportunities for the West.[27]

Their most notable immediate détente move was to endorse an armistice in the Korean War. Some reports indicate that they were initially willing to accept, and may indeed have favored, some kind of compromise on the German question. Winston Churchill was sufficiently convinced of this to propose four-power negotiations on the subject and to talk to Adenauer of four-power guarantees of a reunified Germany à la Locarno, with some German sacrifices with respect to its eastern borders. Eisenhower and Dulles were skeptical. The French government, weak, divided, and fearing German reunification only less than Soviet domination of Western Europe, followed the American lead. Ulbricht and the Polish and Czechoslovak leaders feared liberalization at home and Soviet concessions to West Germany. Adenauer thus used division in Moscow, Western priority for Western European unity, and West Germany's alliance with the West to block whatever readiness for compromise the new Soviet leadership might display. How much Soviet readiness there may have been is still unclear. One report, by a then high-level East German official, indicates that Moscow may have intended major liberalization in East Germany in preparation for an all-German confederation or even reunification.[28]

The West, including Bonn, knew little of and gave even less credence to these developments. For Adenauer, concessions to the post-Stalin Soviet leadership were another, more dangerous version of what he had seen as Stalin's 1952 trap. The EDC Treaty was not yet ratified by most Western European states. In France, where fear of German rearmament was strengthened by hopes of détente, which might make the EDC no longer so necessary for French security, and by the desire to get Moscow's help to end the increasingly hopeless war in Indochina, EDC Treaty ratification was increasingly in danger. The delay in its ratification postponed the Federal Republic's recovery of its full sovereignty. Adenauer was convinced that the Soviets were determined to prevent it. Therefore, in order to block any East-West compromise and also in response to SPD gains in state elections, he cynically again endorsed the revision of the Oder-Neisse line and the "right to the homeland" (*Heimatrecht*) of the twelve million German expellees.

Churchill fell ill and could no longer push for a summit conference. Then Adenauer's policy was saved by the June 17, 1953, East German rising. Its initial causes were economic and internally East German. Ulbricht's attempts to sabotage the Soviet-imposed concessions (the "New Course") were only partially successful, particularly because his associates Zaisser and Herrnstadt, probably speculating on Beria's victory in the post-Stalin succession struggle in Moscow, were trying to replace him. (Beria wanted to make more concessions, in East Germany and elsewhere, than Khrushchev and Malenkov did; but the fact that the new Soviet high commissioner, Semenov, who brought the New Course directives with him to East Berlin, kept his post after Beria's fall showed that the whole Soviet leadership had agreed to some liberalization in East Germany.) Public evidence of political division and uncertainty in the governing Socialist Unity Party (*Sozialistische Einheitspartei*—SED) and half-hearted, hesitant, economic liberalization created a classic pre-revolutionary situation. Moscow and East Berlin failed to control decompression in East Germany. The result on June 16, 1953, was a spontaneous, flash mass workers' rising in East Berlin, without preparation or leadership, which spread on June 17 throughout East Germany. The rising's initial economic demands turned within hours into a democratic, nationalist one: reunification by free elections. Ulbricht and the SED were swept aside. The divided Moscow leadership, rallying to prevent the reversal of Russia's defeat of Germany in 1945, crushed the rising.

Moscow returned to a status quo German policy: reconsolidation of its hold over East Germany. Convinced of the danger of destablizing East Germany and increasingly confident of its military power (the first Soviet thermonuclear explosion occurred on August 12, 1953), Moscow turned to exploit French war-weariness in Indochina. The West, and especially West Germany, where public opinion became more anti-Soviet by the East German rising, neither wanted nor could afford any conciliatory gestures to Moscow and East Berlin. Adenauer seemed to have won again.[29]

Defeat in Victory: Adenauer's Holding Policy Begins to Fall

In late 1953, Adenauer seemed to have foiled the Soviet attempt to block West German sovereignty and remilitarization. His great foreign ally, Dulles, dominated American foreign policy. He had blocked Churchill's effort to resume four-power negotiations. The final attempts in 1953 and 1954 of the Soviets (and of the SPD) to force four-power negotiations before the attainment of West German sovereignty had failed, and Moscow had turned to full support for Ulbricht. West German economic prosperity was in full swing. Adenauer's internal political position seemed firm. He had successfully rallied all major domestic interest groups, even in part the largely SPD trade unions, behind his foreign policy.

But appearances were deceptive. Adenauer's policy toward the East was apparently offensive, in its demand for reunification through absorption of the DDR into the Federal Republic, but actually defensive in its priority for preventing a "return to Potsdam." Its success therefore required a united Western perception of the overriding security threat of a totally hostile and militarily manacing Soviet Union. Its necessary precondition was an equally hostile Soviet policy toward the West, and particularly toward the Federal Republic. When Stalin's successors changed this policy to one of diplomatic engagement in the context of East-West détente, and as Soviet strength grew, Adenauer's policy was therefore doomed.

Public opinion in Britain, France, and even the United States would not reject out of hand the new Soviet détente policy. Any French government was bound to prefer it, and de Gaulle believed it helped him to maneuver between East and West. Britain, weary of war and empire, also preferred détente. Churchill and Eden thought it helped them to maintain British prestige and their domestic popularity. Eisenhower, a man of peace, preferred East-West détente to confrontation; and although Dulles restrained the president's impulse to negotiate with the Soviets, he would not entirely overcome it. In the Federal Republic, nationalists and Social Democrats renewed their demands for testing Soviet détente policy.

Moreover, a new and increasingly important factor—growing Soviet thermonuclear power—had begun to influence East-West relations. Adenauer's policy was based on unquestioned American thermonuclear superiority and invulnerability. As these declined, Washington and even more London and Paris gave increased priority to arms control in order to avoid an East-West strategic confrontation by accident or miscalculation over the issue of German reunification, which seemed to them increasingly unlikely even if (to Bonn and in part to Washington) desirable.

Khrushchev combined use of his nuclear power for political payoffs with use of arms control negotiations to solidify and guarantee the status quo, particularly in Germany, and thereby to remove German reunification from the international agenda and to gain Western recognition for the East German state and Soviet hegemony over it and the rest of Eastern Europe. Soviet policy thus aimed at consolidation of the status quo in the Soviet sphere and minimal adjustment to pluralistic tendencies in it, combined with a flexible forward strategy outside of it—diplomatic forward engagement rather than Stalin's frozen confrontation. Adenauer feared engagement, for he believed that its destabilizing effects in the West, particularly with respect to West Germany, Western European unification, and NATO, would far outweigh whatever few gains it might bring with respect to East Germany and the rest of Eastern Europe. Moreover, he was convinced that détente would lower West German influence within Western Europe and particularly with the United States, for he correctly sensed that the other Western powers would then increasingly deal with the Soviets over his head and contrary to what he saw as West German interests. Most of all he feared this with the United States after his great ally, Foster Dulles, died in

1959. Adenauer thus believed that détente endangered all his achievements for the Federal Republic, security, prosperity, sovereignty, and equal partnership in a united Europe and, worse, might subject it again to Soviet-U.S. condominium. Moreover, most of the CDU/CSU opposed détente with Moscow for ideological and electoral reasons.

Even so, Adenauer was prepared to negotiate with Moscow in order to check what he saw as Western concessions to the Soviet Union to Bonn's disadvantage. He carefully kept secret what he regarded, with the cold realism that his more ideological associates such as Heinrich von Brentano lacked, as the minimum adjustments he had to make to East-West détente—secret negotiations with Moscow that were intended, with his characteristic icy *conséquence,* to compensate for and limit what he saw as naive American readiness to make useless and counterproductive concessions to Moscow. Even so, he was determined to maintain his previous holding policy as long as he could. His remaining years as chancellor, therefore, were a long, slow, determined, but finally unsuccessful attempt to block the course of history: from cold war to limitation of the East-West conflict relationship.

Adenauer's first priority was to maintain Bonn's equality and influence by preventing a "return to Potsdam." He therefore tried to maintain the linkage *(Junktim)* between reunification and East-West détente by making progress on the former a precondition for the latter and by defining such progress according to the 1954 Paris agreements: a reunited, democratic Germany as a part of a unified Western Europe. When this position began to erode, his priority became not progress toward reunification but an effort to keep what independence and security he had. He tried to decouple the German status quo from détente by advocating worldwide rather than regional European disarmament, which the Soviets had proposed in order to relegate West Germany to a discriminatory status. He also began to negotiate with Moscow to restrain the similar negotiations of his allies.

The Soviet crushing of the June 17, 1953, rising contributed to the impression the Soviets sought to create in the West: that they would keep control over East Germany at any cost, that the United States would silently tolerate it, and that German reunification was therefore not in the cards and the United States would eventually decouple East-West détente from it. Thus Adenauer's holding policy won only a temporary victory. The Soviet crushing of the 1953 rising struck the first blow, as the 1961 Berlin Wall did the final one, to the explicit, public basis of Adenauer's foreign policy: that only integration of the Federal Republic into a strong, united Western Europe allied with the United States could and would bring reunification.

The January 1954 Berlin foreign ministers' conference demonstrated the turn in Soviet policy toward détente in Europe on the basis of the status quo. It saw the first Soviet proposal on European security. The Soviets indicated willingness to help bring peace in Indochina, which, they hoped, would help to prevent French ratification of the EDC Treaty. It also saw the first sign of Moscow's willingness to compromise outstanding East-West issues in Europe: its move toward agreeing to an independent, neutralized Austria free of all foreign troops. (The West had made an Austrian settlement a precondition for an East-West summit conference.) Molotov's reiteration there of some of Stalin's 1952 German proposals (for example, all-German negotiations by equal East and West German parliamentary delegations) also included, however, continued four-power control over a reunited Germany, that is, Adenauer's feared "return to Potsdam." For the first time Molotov coupled this with an "all-European security system" (excluding the United States) to replace both military alliances, NATO and the Warsaw Pact, that is, the withdrawal of U.S. troops from Europe. The Western counterproposal, the "Eden plan," although it insisted on the freedom of alliances for an all-German government, did accept a four-power electoral supervisory system, a dangerous step backward, in Adenauer's view, from previous Western proposals. The conference seemed to have ended without result, but subsequent events showed that it led to the Indochina settlement and the Austrian state treaty—key building blocks in East-West détente.

The rejection of the European Defense Community in 1954 by the French National Assembly was the result of nationalist desire to keep an independent French army and to prevent an independent West German one, weariness with the Indochinese War, preference for East-West détente over West German rearmament, and traditional refusal to place Western European goals above French national interests. It was a major blow to Adenauer's goal of Western European unification. It also threatened the recovery of full West German sovereignty, within such unity, through rearmament. Finally, it showed that events in the third world could unfavorably influence West German interests.

The defeat was largely and rapidly overcome by Eden's October 1954 Western European union compromise, which brought West German sovereignty and entry into NATO substantially under the terms of the 1952 Bonn convention: a treaty commitment by the United States, Great Britain, and France to Bonn's right to sole representation of the German people (*Alleinvertretungsrecht*), that is, to refuse to recognize East Germany and the Oder-Neisse line and to support German reunification through free all-German elections. The Federal Republic in turn reaffirmed its renunciation of force and atomic, biological, and chemical (ABC) weapons and its total military integration into NATO and pledged never to use force "to achieve the reunification of Germany or the modification of the present boundaries of the Federal Republic."[30] The treaty's February 1955 ratification by the Bundestag, over strong SPD opposition, sealed Adenauer's victory. He thus had achieved his minimum foreign policy objectives in the West. Moreover, the defeat to Western European unity was in part only temporary; economic unification soon went ahead again. Nevertheless, it did mark the interruption of the movement toward Western European political unity and thus foreshadowed its subtraction from Adenauer's foreign policy as a credible goal and as a credible instrument for achieving German reunification. Therefore it marked a defeat for his foreign policy that foreshadowed its eventual obsolescense.[31]

The increasing threat to Adenauer's foreign policy became clearer at the 1955 Geneva Summit Conference. Adenauer was concerned before it by what he saw as insufficiently hard-line positions by his allies. He feared that the neutralization of Austria as a result of the 1955 Austrian State Treaty would be used by the Soviets to work toward the neutralization of Germany.[32] In his view the British and the French would accept détente on the basis of the German status quo. Eisenhower gave priority to arms control proposals, and even Foster Dulles seemed to think that major changes in Eastern Europe would have to precede German reunification.

The Geneva conference met because the West accepted a Soviet proposal for it after Moscow agreed to a neutral Austria. Although the West before and at Geneva, under Adenauer's pressure, continued to support German reunification, the Soviets stressed their 1954 Berlin Conference European security proposal and proposed to Bonn the establishment of diplomatic relations. The Geneva summit communiqué papered over East-West disagreement by coupling reunification with European security—that is, with détente. It also included Eden's proposal for limitation and inspection of military forces, with partial military disengagement, in a zone between East and West, which from Adenauer's viewpoint would mean military discrimination against West Germany and limitations on its sovereignty. On his way back to Moscow Khrushchev made clear in East Berlin that Soviet German policy was based on indefinite partition, a communist East Germany, and the best West Germany that Moscow could get, one, as Stanley Hoffman has put it, which appears potentially dangerous but is in fact contained. The Geneva conference showed that neither East nor West intended war. It highlighted "atmospheric" détente and arms control proposals. Adenauer thus saw his fears for the conference confirmed. Moscow in his view won a complete victory. It gained a pause in Western pressure (which is what he saw as the Soviet motive for détente), international recognition, and a Western move toward arms control agreements without progress on German reunification as a precondition for them.[33]

Soviet-West German Diplomatic Relations

Although European security was still coupled with German reunification, which gave him a veto over it, Adenauer knew that the balance was moving against him. His decision to take up the Soviet offer to establish diplomatic relations, although made only after carefully reassuring his allies that he would not return to a Rapallo policy, was in part reinsurance against Western concession to Moscow. In September 1955 in Moscow he established diplomatic relations with the Soviet Union. (Because he feared that this would be interpreted as recognition the status quo, he thereafter issued the first version of the Hallstein Doctrine: a break by Bonn, because of its claim for sole representation, in diplomatic relations with any state that recognized East Germany, except with the USSR, because it was one of the four occupying powers.) After very hard negotiations Adenauer got the release of the remaining German prisoners of war in the Soviet Union, which West German public opinion demanded. (He also successfully, if unilaterally reserved Bonn's position on reunification.)[34]

Adenauer concluded that it was possible to negotiate with the Soviet Union, but only by patience, endurance, and mutual concessions; that the principal Soviet aim, world domination, remained unchanged; but that the Soviet leadership felt that it needed a period of détente to improve living standards at home and weaken Western unity. He was convinced that the time had not yet come for agreement on reunification. But he probably thought that at least some progress in that direction could eventually be made, if only because of Soviet concern about the Chinese.

Why Khrushchev confirmed and intensified Adenauer's view in this last respect remains difficult to understand. In a private conversation between the two, as the chancellor later wrote in his memoirs,

Khrushchev again spoke about Red China. He declared that Red China was the great problem. "Just think, Red China already has a population of over six hundred million. Its yearly increase is twelve million. They all live from a handful of rice. What," and he clapped his hands together, "what will come of all this?"

I thought, "Dear friend, one day you will be very satisfied if you no longer have to keep any troops in the West."

Khrushchev said suddenly, "We can solve this problem. But it is very difficult. Therefore I ask you, help us. Help us to deal with Red China," and after a pause he added, "and with the Americans."

During my Moscow stay Khrushchev three times repeated this request to help him. I did not reply. It would have been a breach of faith toward Europe and America, and to help the Russians at this stage and without firm ties with the rest of the free world would have been to put one's head in the lion's jaws . . . .

Adenauer was convinced that Khrushchev was tempting him toward a new Rapallo. He believed thereafter that Germany's great opportunity would come when Sino-Soviet relations worsened, as Khrushchev apparently feared that they would.[35] (Adenauer later became more convinced that a Sino-Soviet split was likely, in part influenced by a book by Wilhelm Starlinger.)[36]

To analyze why Khrushchev might have discussed China with Adenauer in this respect is impossible because of the lack of evidence. There are only two pieces of published evidence, the 1954 unsuccessful demand by Mao to Khrushchev to return Outer Mongolia to China and the Chinese objection that same year to the Soviet-Yugoslav rapprochement, which could indicate that Sino-Soviet relations were as bad in late 1955 as Khrushchev's statements to Adenauer would indicate.[37]

Recent research has shown that they were worse in 1956 and 1957 than has generally been believed.[38] The Soviet leadership was probably already anxious to prevent West Germany, and probably the United States as well, from exploiting probable future Sino-Soviet differences; and this motive probably played some role, although how important a one is impossible to say, in Moscow's desire in 1955 for détente with Washington and Bonn.

The trip probably also confirmed Adenauer's view that he

needed to wait for the Soviets to make major concessions on German reunification. His success in the negotiations probably made him think that they could be of use in the future to test the Soviets on the German question and to bring quiet pressure on his Western allies not to make concessions to Moscow with which he did not agree. In both respects he was unrealistic, for Moscow did not have to make any major concessions, the West would pursue détente on the basis of recognition of the status quo, Bonn's inactivity would face it with status quo minus, and West German public opinion was found therefore to become increasingly disillusioned about Adenauer's policy of reunification through strength and would eventually demand a more active West German Ostpolitik. That Adenauer did not realize this and act accordingly was the beginning of the ultimate defeat of his Ostpolitik.[39]

The Moscow negotiations also produced differences within the Bonn leadership. Economics Minister Ludwig Erhard had proposed before the negotiations that Bonn should work for partial, gradual liberalization in East Germany. The new CDU foreign minister, Heinrich von Brentano, was extremely skeptical about the negotiations, feared their effect on Western unity (and indeed Washington was apparently somewhat concerned about them), and unsuccessfully tried to persuade Adenauer to break them off rather than to establish diplomatic relations in return for no progress on reunification but only for a Soviet verbal promise (all that Adenauer had been able to get—although it turned out to be valid) to release the Germans imprisoned in the USSR. Hallstein and Kiesinger were also unfavorably impressed by the course of the negotiations. Adenauer, however, was convinced that politically he had to get the imprisoned Germans released and that when at the last moment, after he had implicitly threatened to break them off, the Soviets agreed, he had to agree as well.[40]

Diplomatic relations with Moscow were Adenauer's first, minimal adjustment to détente, for he had shown his allies that he also could deal directly with Khrushchev. But he took no particular advantage of it, perhaps in part because of the very hostile impression the Soviet leaders had made on him in Moscow. Since Moscow's policies remained hostile to Bonn's officially proclaimed aims, little new ensued.[41] Bonn did not reciprocate Warsaw's announced willingness in March and July 1955 to normalize relations. However, for the first time for any Soviet bloc state until the mid-1960s, Bonn did grant Poland a $9.5 million credit.[42]

West German Trade with the East

Although historically German trade with Russia and Eastern Europe had been very great and Germany had been their main source of advanced technology, Adenauer and the CDU/CSU felt that Soviet and Eastern European hostility to the Federal Republic and the necessity for Bonn of solidarity with U.S. policy on the trade embargo vis-à-vis the East should override West German trade traditions and economic interests. As a result West German trade with the Soviet Union and Eastern Europe remained low until the mid-1960s, despite Soviet desire to increase it.[43]

Adenauer, however, unrealistically believed that the Soviets would make political concessions for increased trade, and therefore Bonn refused for several years to conclude a Soviet-West German trade treaty.

Only with East Germany was West German trade substantial, for several reasons. Trade between the two areas had always been large. West German business considered it only proper that it should continue to be so. While East Germany in theory wanted this trade considered "international" (between two states), before the de facto partition in 1949 it had been "inner-German" (*Interzonenhandel*) and West Germany, given its political goal of reunification, maintained that it should continue to be so. East Germany accepted this in practice and therefore the trade was not subject to customs duties. Moreover, when the European Economic Community was established, Bonn insisted on a proviso that "inner-German trade" would continue free of tariffs, which almost made the DDR a secret member of the EEC. Bonn believed that trade with East Germany preserved

West German ties with, and helped economically, the East German population.

As time went on, Bonn also gradually managed to get East Berlin to accept de facto that the absence of DDR harassment of transit to West Berlin was a condition for the trade's continuation. Finally, the DDR wanted to increase interzonal trade, for West Germany was its main and cheapest source of advanced technology. However, Adenauer rejected major increase in inner-German trade, and therefore it increased only slowly after 1955.[44]

Meanwhile, after the summit conference Moscow continued to urge the West to give priority to disarmament and to sign an East-West nonaggression pact that would prevent a NATO nuclear presence in West Germany and would tacitly accept the status quo, including East Germany, and to agree to Ulbricht's confederation proposal, for the same reason. The Soviets formally gave the DDR sovereignty but reserved their four-power responsibilities.[45]

The October 1955 foreign ministers' conference got nowhere, in part because Adenauer pressured the Western powers to define Eden's initially probably deliberately vague zone of troop limitation as one between a reunited Germany and the East, which the Soviets could not possibly accept. Molotov demanded that the zone be between West and East Germany (that it cement the partition) and rejected reunification through "mechanical elections" (free ones) in favor of East-West German discussions about it. The East-West deadlock on Germany was thus total, and Western and West German public opinion began to accept the permanent partition of Germany.

Bonn thereafter concentrated on preventing the international recognition of East Germany, for which it paid for years a high price in economic aid to third world countries. Adenauer met FDP demands for using withdrawal from NATO as a bargaining card for negotiations with the Soviets by arranging a split in the party, whose opponents of his foreign policy left the coalition. For Moscow the Geneva conference was followed by Shepilov's trip to Cairo (the public beginning of Khrushchev's forward strategy in the third world) and the first Soviet-Yugoslav rapprochement, both of which hurt Bonn's and helped East Berlin's interests.

French and British positions in the UN Disarmament Subcommittee, reflecting East-West détente, first gave priority to disarmament over German reunification.[46] Gromyko on March 27, 1956, proposed a one hundred fifty to two hundred thousand troop ceiling on all but the four powers' forces (the proposed Bundeswehr five hundred thousand ceiling would have become impossible) and a Central European arms control and inspection zone composed of the two German states and some others, that is, he discriminated against Bonn and ratified German partition. Both proposals were understandably ominous to Adenauer. Neither came to anything, but the former was another sign that Adenauer's link of détente with reunification was beginning to erode. The first major trouble for Moscow in Eastern Europe and therefore, at least in theory, an opportunity for Bonn came in 1956. These events involved one state, Hungary, that had traditionally been pro-German and anti-Russian, and another, Poland, that although anti-German had always had major trade ties with Germany and was also traditionally anti-Russian. Throughout Eastern Europe the great popular demand for improvement of living standards and greater national autonomy seemed to imply better economic and political relations with West Germany. Although there was little elite or mass East German disaffection, there was disunity within the East German leadership; and the unsuccessful anti-Ulbricht faction, led by Schirdewan and Wollweber, presumably because they calculated that Moscow was considering it, reportedly advocated Ulbricht's removal, liberalization in East Germany, and improvement of relations with West Germany.[47]

Adenauer's policy was unfavorably affected by these developments. The Soviet crushing of the Hungarian Revolution enabled Ulbricht to eliminate his (at least potentially less anti–West German) opposition. Western inaction during the Hungarian Revolution, due to unwillingness to risk nuclear war with respect to Eastern Europe and to its preoccupation with the Suez crisis, made Bonn think that the mutual Soviet-U.S. interest to avoid confrontation and war could lead them to settle crises and, by analogy, that Moscow would never give up its control over East Germany, that thus German reunification was less likely than ever, and that it was by implication even against the interest of America's Western European allies.[48] The United States refused to support Britain and France in their Suez invasion, which worsened their relations with Washington, pushed them toward nuclear capability, and confronted Adenauer with a weakened Western alliance and the fear that the United States might one day refuse to support Bonn as well.

Adenauer and von Brentano drew opposite policy conclusions. Von Brentano and his deputy, van Scherpenberg, felt that Bonn must concentrate on the Eastern European states, notably on Poland, and should envisage a step-by-step approach to reunification, including with the DDR. Adenauer, who did not consult von Brentano on this but only such other advisors as State Secretary Hans Globke, the CDU leader, Krone, the eccentric German ambassador in Moscow, Hans Kroll, and his press chief Felix von Eckhardt, believed that only negotiations with the Soviet Union made sense, the Eastern European states were relatively unimportant, any step-by-step approach to reunification was illusory, and any Western concessions to the Soviets in this respect must be prevented, if necessary by postponing the reunification issue. Von Brentano was unrealistic insofar as he was strongly influenced by his ideological anti-Sovietism and overestimated the role of Poland. Adenauer was also unrealistic, as he later realized, because he underestimated Soviet power and overestimated Soviet willingness to make any concessions on reunification.[49]

Yet parts of both positions foreshadowed future policies. Von Brentano's desire to deal with the Eastern Europeans foreshadowed his successor Gerhard Schröder's Ostpolitik, which also made little progress, for the same reason, and in one respect—the step-by-step approach—the later Brandt-Scheel Ostpolitik. The latter was also foreshadowed by Adenauer's priority for negotiations with Moscow, which Brandt shared while rejecting Adenauer's opposition to step-by-step approaches.

Another reason was West German slowness to exploit the short-lived partial flexibility to Gomułka's post-1956 German policy. Von Brentano and the Foreign Office wanted to improve relations with Poland without recognition of the Oder-Neisse line. Adenauer blocked this because he felt that Moscow was much more important than Warsaw, that because of the expellees it was domestically too risky to move toward recognition of the Oder-Neisse line, and that little would be gained by it. Adenauer was not anti-Polish—he was too Catholic, anti-Prussian, and anti-German nationalist for that. But he saw more clearly than von Brentano, who blindly hated and feared the Soviets, and than Schröder, who thought, incorrectly, that one could successfully pressure Moscow via Eastern Europe, that Bonn could only make progress in the East by negotiating first with Moscow.

Adenauer was willing to exchange trade missions with Warsaw but not to agree to full diplomatic relations, lest such a breach of the Hallstein Doctrine help the DDR in the third world; and he offered Poland no substantial credits. By the time he was ready, in part due to American urging, to make significant concessions to the Poles, retrogression had gone too far in Warsaw. Gomułka returned to orthodoxy at home and support of military disengagement in and denuclearization of both German states and of Soviet policy against Bonn.[50] Thus 1956–1957 briefly awakened West German hopes of progress with the East and therefore strengthened West German opposition to Adenauer's foreign policy, seen as having neglected significant new opportunities.

This did not have immediate effect, however, for three reasons. First, the Soviet crushing of the Hungarian Revolution worsened Soviet-U.S. relations, revived West German fears of Soviet expansionism, cut the ground out from under proposals for negotiations with Moscow, and reconfirmed Adenauer's anti-Soviet attitude. And although after long negotiations Bonn and Moscow did finally sign a trade agreement, it did not seriously improve their relations.[51] Second, Tito's 1957 recognition of East Germany, as a result of Soviet and East German offers of economic aid and in the vain hope of maintaining his rapprochement with Khrushchev and having ties with East as well as West Germany, and Adenauer's consequent breaking of relations with Belgrade, which precluded his establishing relations with Warsaw, were blows to any improved relations between Bonn and Eastern Europe.[52]

Third, because of rising Soviet missile strength, and in order to compensate for Soviet ground forces and tactical atomic weapons without having to increase U.S. conventional forces, Eisenhower decided not only to equip the U.S. forces in East Germany with tactical nuclear weapons but also to supply them, with the warheads remaining under exclusive American custody, to the newly organized West German Army. While he did this primarily for military and budgetary reasons and to counteract the Soviet Sputnik's demonstration of Moscow's missile capability, it also increased Soviet (and Polish) concern about Bonn obtaining its own nuclear weapons and therefore the Soviet desire to pursue détente with the United States to prevent this. Despite frenetic SPD opposition, Adenauer accepted the U.S. proposal, thus giving priority to West German security and self-imposed atomic abstinence as an inducement toward Moscow-Bonn détente. (His fears of the Radford Plan, which would have reduced sharply U.S. troop strength in West Germany, had proven groundless.) Increasing U.S. (and British and French) emphasis on nuclear rather than conventional weapons threatened, in Bonn's view, to downgrade the relative military and political independence of the nonnuclear Bundeswehr and even to cast it as atomic cannon fodder.[53]

Adenauer's main motive in agreeing to the United States giving tactical nuclear weapons to the Bundeswehr was to ensure West German participation in nuclear as well as political decisions by the United States. He believed this increasingly necessary because of rising Soviet nuclear capability, resultant downgrading of the U.S. nuclear deterrent, resultant Soviet-U.S.

bilateralism at Bonn's expense, and rising West German power and self-confidence. These factors reinforced the standard West German motive in military negotiations with the United States: to influence U.S. policy without endangering the U.S. security guarantee to the Federal Republic. For neither he nor the CDU/ CSU, nor even the SPD, ever questioned Bonn's security dependence on Washington—and thus, later, never exchanged U.S. for French guarantees.

This fact made Bonn's military policies remain reactive to U.S. initiatives. Franz Josef Strauss, minister of defense from 1956 to 1962, who pushed development of a Bundeswehr with U.S. tactical nuclear weapons and later became the leader of the "German Gaullists," never questioned the security ties with the United States. But Soviet intercontinental ballistic missile (ICBM) development was proceeding rapidly, and the United States, although still far superior, was becoming more vulnerable to it. Adenauer therefore became less confident of U.S. reliability. The consequent greater U.S. priority for nuclear arms stability through arms control over German reunification reinforced the same tendency in the SPD, which saw arms stability and détente as a precondition for progress toward reunification.[54]

The Rapacki Plan
Within this context Polish Foreign Minister Adam Rapacki announced in October 1957 his plan for an atom-free zone in Western Europe. Its significance remains disputed. Was it a Soviet-inspired proposal to prevent the United States from arming its forces in Germany and through the (U.S.-controlled) "one-key system" the Bundeswehr with tactical nuclear weapons? Or was it primarily or at least significantly a genuinely Polish initiative toward the kind of military disengagement and all-European security system that would not only strengthen détente but bring some gradual, controlled increase in freedom of maneuver for Polish foreign policy, including vis-à-vis the Soviet Union?

To answer these questions one must assess post-1956 Polish foreign policy. (From 1945 to 1956 it had almost completely reflected Stalin's wishes.) Historically Poland has had three foreign policies: alliance with Germany or Russia, alliance with the enemies of both (first France, then Great Britain and the United States), and complete independence. After 1945 Poland's alliance with if not subordination to Russia seemed necessary. No serious Poles, including the lay Catholic leaders, questioned its necessity, above all to defend the Oder-Neisse line. The question was, therefore, how much freedom of maneuver Poland could obtain to follow its own interests and to influence Moscow to its benefit.

After 1956 there developed—or should one say surfaced?—a Polish school of thought, primarily in the foreign ministry, that maintained that Polish interests could best be served by East-West and particularly by Warsaw-Bonn détente, through nuclear disengagement in Central Europe. Its main intellectual inspiration was Prof. Manfred Lachs, supported by Deputy Foreign Minister Józef Winiewicz. Like almost all Poles since 1939, this school believed that Polish interests required that Germany not become united and strong enough, particularly by nuclear weapons, to menace the Oder-Neisse line and to move toward renewed predominance in Central Europe; that therefore Germany must remain divided; and that to ensure this, East Germany's security against absorption by the Federal Republic must be guaranteed.

Thus Moscow, Warsaw, and East Berlin saw Eisenhower's decision to introduce tactical nuclear weapons into West Germany and to give the Bundeswehr U.S.-controlled access to them as a menace to their vital interests. Conversely, for Washington and Bonn denuclearization of Central Europe worsened their military security. In fact, Western technological advantage was changing the military situation in Central Europe.

By 1957 at the latest, although few in the West then realized this, the Soviets had another motive: to stabilize their position in Europe before they would have to face the Chinese. The difficult Sino-Soviet negotiations preceding the November 1957 multiparty meeting probably made this clear to Moscow. But as Adam Ulam has put it, "by pursuing a double aim of outwitting the United States and appeasing China, the USSR was bound to succeed in neither."[55]

The Poles, like the East Germans, had another motive: the fear that the Soviets would compromise with West Germany over their heads and against their interests. The rising economic and technological power of Bonn, Moscow's increasing preoccupation with the Chinese, Khrushchev's ill-fated 1965 attempt, via his son-in-law, Adzhubei, to sound out Adenauer's successor, Erhard, on some kind of bilateral deal, and what Gomuka and Ulbricht reportedly saw in early 1968 as Soviet reluctance to intervene in Prague against a Czechoslovak-West German rapprochement made Warsaw fear a Soviet rapprochement with Bonn. However, Warsaw needed less to fear it than East Berlin did, for Poland was much more stable than East Germany and therefore less menaced by any rapprochement with Bonn; and it needed West German technology and credits much more than East Germany did. But Gomuĺka became increasingly dogmatic, repressive, and anti-German; and Khrushchev's 1958 opening of the second Berlin crisis and the resultant more anti–West pollicy in Warsaw destroyed until after the 1968 Czechoslovak invasion any chance of a significant Bonn-Warsaw rapprochement.

Before that, however, the Rapacki Plan, although only an interlude, was significant for Polish-West German relations. Although it was never put into effect, one of its goals, Bonn-Warsaw détente, did occur in 1970; and another, reduction of conventional forces in Central Europe, added to it later by Rapacki, began to be negotiated in Vienna in 1973.

In its 1958 third version, modified to make it more appealing to the West, the Rapacki Plan proposed controlled freezing and then withdrawal of all nuclear weapons from Poland, Czechoslovakia, and the two German states plus reduction of conventional forces in the same area. Bonn and Washington reacted negatively.

Adenauer saw the plan as a Soviet-inspired attempt to reverse the Bundestag authorization for "one-key" access to tactical nuclear weapons; even worse, to impose on the Federal Republic a discriminatory military and political status; and to isolate it from its Western allies, while offering nothing with respect to reunification. (In 1953–1955, his military advisor, General Heusinger, had worked out a disengagement plan that involved the demilitarization of the DDR only—obviously as a prelude to reunification. By his 1955 visit to Moscow, Adenauer had probably realized that this was totally unacceptable to the Soviets.)

Adenauer therefore proposed general global disarmament and rejected European or other regional arms control measures. Washington, although publicly less hostile to it because of its post-1956 improved relations with Warsaw, rejected it because it would weaken NATO's military posture. Rapacki tried to show the plan did not oppose German reunification but was a necessary precondition for it, but the West knew that Warsaw was firmly committed to the indefinite division of Germany.

The Soviets had little or no reason to oppose the Rapacki Plan. Indeed, which understandably added to Western suspicions of it, Gromyko had proposed such a denuclearized zone in March 1956. Moscow wanted to give Gomułka at least the appearance, and to a minor extent the reality, of some freedom of foreign policy maneuver to please increased Polish sensitivity and to profit from pro-Polish sentiments in the West. Even so, however, Rapacki only with some difficulty persuaded the Soviets to agree to his revisions of it to try to appease Western objections, particularly to avoid conflict with the Hallstein Doctrine and to add a reduction in troop levels. In any case, the second Berlin crisis cut the ground out from under the plan.[56]

The Sino-Soviet Split

The year 1957 was a contradictory one for Soviet foreign policy: success on the surface but underneath the first serious tensions with the Chinese. Khrushchev used the Soviet Sputnik to launch a political offensive to improve the Soviet position in general and to start the second Berlin crisis. Both were directed primarily against the United States but secondarily against China. Khrushchev also seemed to be reconsolidating the Soviet hold over Eastern Europe.

But in fact, although still hidden from the West, the Rumanian[57] and Albanian[58] deviations were already taking shape. Far more dangerous for Khrushchev, at the November 1957 Moscow multiparty meeting, as we now know, the first significant Sino-Soviet differences arose.[59] Although a largely verbal compromise was reached there, Sino-Soviet relations worsened sharply in early 1958 and collapsed in June–September 1959.[60]

Before Soviet-Yugoslav relations worsened, in spring 1958, · Tito had the previous year established diplomatic relations with the DDR, whereupon Bonn had broken off diplomatic relations with Belgrade, as the Hallstein Doctrine required. (By then Bonn had "interpreted" it to require rupture only with countries that recognized East Berlin, not with those, for example, the Soviet Union and Poland, that already had [the so-called *Geburtsfehler* theory].)[61]

Finally, Khrushchev, confronted with the rising Chinese threat to his East and the increasing Soviet technological gap with the West and Japan, must already have begun to consider intensifying détente in Europe and reaching a compromise with Bonn.

The Beginnings of Adenauer's Ostpolitik

In any case, Adenauer, convinced of this, in 1958 took his first important secret step toward Moscow. He felt that the Western alliance was sufficiently reconsolidated after the 1956 Suez and Hungarian crises to make this safe and that the Soviets were more willing to negotiate. Moreover, the Soviets had in January 1958 proposed a summit conference, primarily to prevent U.S. tactical nuclear weapons in Central Europe. Moscow specifically excluded four-power negotiations on the German question, which should, it maintained, instead be discussed between the two German states. Von Brentano and the Foreign Office, responding to Western desires for "new initiatives," again proposed step-by-step measures involving representation of West and East Germany in all-German negotiating bodies. Adenauer flatly rejected this. Instead he reversed his position on priority for reunification before arms control agreements. He proposed that priority be given to "general and complete disarmament," because he correctly expected no progress on the latter and he felt that he had to retreat to his minimum position on the reunification issue: to freeze it lest his Western allies make concessions on it to Moscow.

In March, 1958, before the beginning of the second Berlin crisis, Adenauer secretly proposed to Smirnov, the Soviet ambassador, and to Mikoyan, who visited Bonn, that East Germany should be neutralized and given the status of Austria. He specifically stated that this was based on his priority for easing conditions of life in East Germany over reunification. He seems to have believed that the Soviets could and eventually would accept this. Khrushchev rejected the proposal, since he was determined to maintain Soviet control over the DDR and had no reason to abandon it.

Even so, Adenauer only reluctantly gave way to pressure from West German business, from the SPD, and from the Soviet Union to increase trade with the Soviet Union much more than it was increasing in any case. In summer 1957, negotiations for a trade treaty were opened; and in April 1958, the treaty, which provided for a major increase in trade, was signed. In return Moscow orally agreed to allow repatriation of a significant number of ethnic Germans, which it publicly did in an agreement with East Germany.[62]

The onset of the second Berlin crisis probably made Adenauer even more flexible. By the end of 1958, his state secretary, Hans Globke—the second most influential man in Adenauer's government, much more so than Foreign Minister von Brentano—was secretly drafting the so-called "Globke Plan." Its first version was finished in January 1959 and a revised second edition on November 17, 1960.

The Globke plan went further toward the Soviet position than Adenauer's "Austrian solution." Reunification would occur if, ten years thereafter, majorities in both German states in UN-controlled free elections voted for it. If a majority in one did not, the two states would remain separate indefinitely and Berliners would vote to decide if they would belong to West Germany, East Germany, or be a free city guaranteed by the

UN. During the ten year transitional period all of Berlin would become a free city, with a United Nations guarantee and High Commissioner, and would itself decide if it would join a united Germany. Any reunified Germany would decide for membership in either NATO or the Warsaw Pact; but that part of it, East or West, that as a result left a military pact would thereafter be demilitarized. The reunited Germany would recognize its present boundaries (implicitly, the Oder-Neisse line) and join arms control and security arrangements.

However, the Globke Plan also provided that in the interim before the reunification referendum, East Germany would be fully liberalized, travel between East and West Germany would be free, and East Berlin would be joined to West Berlin in a free city. Moreover, the reunited Germany would not be allowed to choose neutrality—because for Adenauer this meant eventual Soviet predominance. It was overwhelmingly probable that the East Germans would choose reunification and that in the meantime their flight to West Germany would not decline, since they could not be sure that the Soviets would ever allow the referendum. Moreover, in a liberalized East Germany the SED would in all probability be voted out of office. Thus even in the interim, and certainly after the referendum, the status quo in East Germany would decisively be changed in favor of Bonn and the West and Moscow would lose one of its principal gains of World War II, the partition of Germany and Soviet control over its eastern part. It is not surprising, therefore, that Khrushchev initially rejected this plan just as he had Adenauer's "Austrian solution." Even so, he did agree in May 1963 to negotiations about it and his own proposals; but Adenauer was about to resign, so the negotiations never occured. These plans showed that Adenauer would make far more concessions in secret than in public; although always within his overall purpose of giving priority to Bonn's ties with the West, that he gave priority to improving the conditions of life in the DDR over reunification and to dealing with the Soviet Union, not East European states; that contrary to his public image, Adenauer would adjust to East-West détente rather than totally to oppose it and negotiate himself with the

Soviets while loyally informing his allies of his moves; and that he would postpone reunification, which was never for him a major priority except in rhetoric.[63] Adenauer's Ostpolitik—the "Austrian solution" and the "Globke Plan"—was the forerunner of the Ostpolitik of the 1970s.

The Second Berlin Crisis

For several reasons, which like Stalin in the first Berlin crisis he probably saw as defensive ones, Khrushchev launched the second Berlin crisis[64] on November 10, 1958, by proposing to the three Western powers and Bonn that West Berlin become a neutral, demilitarized, "free" city and East Germany control Western access rights to it.[65] In the first East-West negotiations during the crisis, the 1959 Geneva foreign ministers' meeting, Bonn disliked the British proposal for a zone of arms limitation and the U.S. proposal for an all-German federation, although the West had not expected the Soviets to accept either. (When von Brentano made some concessions, Adenauer overruled him.) Because the Soviets rejected it, the final Western proposals took some of his objections into account. Even so, the West agreed to have East and West German "observers," for Adenauer a dangerous step toward the recognition of the DDR.

The West also agreed to continue arms control negotiations, thereby finally decoupling them from progress on German reunification—for Adenauer another retreat toward a "status quo minus" for Bonn. Moreover, after the conference Khrushchev met Eisenhower at Camp David, Maryland. They agreed to continue Soviet-U.S. negotiations over Berlin, of which, Adenauer feared, Bonn would not be informed and in which its interests would not be taken fully into account by Washington.

These developments led to malaise in Bonn, well characterized in a then secret letter to von Brentano from von Scherpenberg: " . . . I have the impression that more and more any foreign policy initiative and freedom of action escapes us, or more accurately, is taken away from us, and that we are sinking back into a situation in which we are only the object of the policies of others. . . . "[66] Von Scherpenberg proposed that Bonn should counterbalance this by an initiative vis-à-vis the Eastern European status quo and by working for a meeting between Khrushchev and Adenauer, that is, to compensate for lack of Western support by improving relations with the Soviet Union and Eastern Europe. Adenauer, always sure that only Moscow mattered and always conscious of expellee hostility, rejected any moves toward the Eastern European states and pursued secret contacts, via Ambassador Kroll, with Khrushchev. Meanwhile, Khrushchev had tried twice, in 1959 and early 1960, to interest Brandt, then governing mayor of West Berlin, in negotiations; but Brandt had reluctantly refused.

Adenauer was particularly appalled by Eisenhower's comment at Camp David that there was an "abnormal situation" (a favorite Soviet phrase) in West Berlin and by his statement, as Adenauer later reported it, at the December 1959 meeting of the Western four chiefs of government in Paris, that the formally agreed legal rights of the Western powers in Berlin were "not so important that public opinion outside Germany would see their violation as sufficient ground for military action. . . ."[67] Although de Gaulle and Macmillan supported him, and Eisenhower, Adenauer later wrote, withdrew his statement, Adenauer's distrust of Washington was intensified.

Thus serious misconceptions had developed between Adenauer and Washington. Adenauer thought the United States was making dangerous unilateral concessions. Washington saw its moves as tactical, largely "public relations" gestures that Moscow would reject.

The watershed in Adenauer's relations with Washington was Foster Dulles's resignation in April 1959 and his death the following month. Although Adenauer had been alarmed briefly by Dulles's "agent theory" (that the DDR could act as agents for the Soviet Union with respect to Western access to West Berlin), which Dulles had thought would indirectly commit Moscow to responsibility for all Berlin traffic, West German as well as Western military, and correctly saw it as unacceptable to Moscow, the two had basically agreed. Adenauer had far more influence on Dulles than did any other statesman. Moreover, although both were more flexible than was thought at the time, they deeply distrusted détente and the Soviets. Eisenhower, on the other hand, was less ideologically anti-Soviet and Dulles's successor, Herter, did not have the same personal relationship with Adenauer. Moreover, the 1958 elections had given control of the U.S. Senate to the Democrats, whose leaders there were not close to Adenauer and gave less priority to West German interests. The interlude of Adenauer's first intending to succeed Heuss as federal president and then abandoning this plan had weakened Adenauer's authority in domestic German politics.[68]

After Khrushchev broke up the May 1960 Paris summit, he postponed a peace treaty with East Berlin until after the U.S. presidential elections and secretly and unsuccessfully tried to persuade Adenauer to agree to a German peace treaty including West German recognition of East Germany and the Oder-Neisse lines—showing how far apart Soviet and West German positions still were.

In September 1960, reacting to East German harassment of transit traffic to West Berlin, Bonn for the first and only time seriously tried to use interzonal trade to put political pressure on East Berlin: It abrogated the interzonal trade agreement. The DDR demanded political negotiations between the two German states, whereupon Bonn renewed the trade agreement, although it reaffirmed the connection between access to West Berlin and trade. Thereafter the DDR tried to become more independent of trade with the Federal Republic, and interzonal trade declined. However, this resulted in serious economic difficulties for the DDR for which Moscow would not compensate by sufficient credits. Thereupon in 1962 East Berlin asked Bonn for major credits to expand interzonal trade but withdrew the request when Bonn posed political conditions. Interzonal trade thereafter rose only very slowly until the late 1960s.

Negotiations for the renewal of the Soviet-West German trade treaty began in October 1960 under the shadow of the Berlin crisis. Bonn tried to insist on explicit inclusion of the "Berlin clause" (that the treaty cover West Berlin as well). Moscow refused and Bonn retreated: West Berlin was only implicitly included.[69]

West German-Soviet trade increased during the Berlin crisis, largely because Bonn did not want to make the crisis worse by limiting it and realized that decreasing it would probably not modify Soviet or East German policy. The only serious problem that occurred, at the end of the crisis, involved a West German contract to export large steel pipe, for oil pipelines, to the Soviet Union. The United States, concerned about the increasing development of Soviet oil production and annoyed by the Franco-German treaty, which had just been signed, successfully pressured Bonn to cancel the contract. Adenauer, despite strong pressure to the contrary from the SPD, the FDP, and West German business, felt that he had no alternative but to give in. The Soviets were surprised and offended by the decision.[70]

Kennedy was at first firmer than Eisenhower on West Berlin and Adenauer was not initially hostile to him—indeed, he reprimanded his Washington ambassador and close associate, Wilhelm Grewe, for being more skeptical. But in Adenauer's view Kennedy soon became even more "flexible" than his predecessor vis-à-vis the Soviet Union and even less concerned with West German interests, particularly when after the unsuccessful June 1961 Vienna meeting Khrushchev renewed his pressure on West Berlin. Kennedy's chief advisors were not men like McCloy and Clay, for Adenauer longtime and trusted "friends of Germany," but too often "leftist intellectuals" whom he instinctively mistrusted.

Kennedy and most of his advisors gave less priority to Bonn and indeed to Western Europe than Eisenhower had and more to the third world. Indeed, as the West Germans realized, while the State Department retained its traditional priority for relations with Bonn, such other advisors of Kennedy as Averell Harriman gave priority to a global dialogue with Moscow centering on arms control negotiations. Moreover, economic competition between the United States and the European Common Market unfavorably affected relations between Bonn and Washington.

Kennedy also had pressing internal problems, notably in civil rights. In short, Adenauer was no longer the most influential foreign statesman in Washington.[71]

True, after the Vienna impasse with Khrushchev, Kennedy rapidly strengthened the U.S. defense posture, called up military reserves, and urged the Western Europeans to do the same. He expressed willingness to risk nuclear war to defend his "three essentials" in West Berlin: Western and West German access, Western troop presence, and economic ties with West Germany. Khrushchev increased Soviet military strength.

But thereafter Kennedy proposed to the Soviet Union an international access authority, an East-West nonaggression pact, and a Soviet-U.S. nonproliferation treaty. He told Khrushchev's son-in-law, Adzhubei, that he opposed West German nuclear weapons because Moscow's security interests would be endangered by them, and he spoke less of reunification than Eisenhower and Dulles had.[72] Moreover, his proposals were not tied to German reunification. Adenauer viewed them as major unilateral U.S. concessions to Soviet and East German interests, which gave priority to détente over Bonn's vital interests. Adenauer feared a "return to Potsdam": joint Soviet-U.S. control over West Germany. He became convinced that Kennedy would make other dangerous concessions to the Soviets, that only the three essentials but not reunification were a precondition to East-West disarmament negotiations, in sum, that Kennedy would not allow Bonn decisive influence over his dealings with Moscow.

But in private Adenauer was anything but enthusiastic about Kennedy's expressed determination to go to nuclear war if necessary to protect U.S. presence in West Berlin. Indeed, an internal Bonn Foreign Office paper indicates that he may well have been prepared to accept the Soviet demand that West Berlin be a "free city" (with Western garrisons) and that access to it, including that of the Western allies, be controlled by the DDR.[73]

In sum, Kennedy gave priority to flexible response and limited cooperation with the Soviet Union rather than to massive retaliation and priority for cooperation with Washington's Western European allies to change the status quo. For Adenauer, both sacrificed vital West German interests; the former threatened Bonn's security and the latter downgraded Bonn's political role and aims.[74] Thus U.S.-West German mutual misperceptions intensified further.

Adenauer also believed, in considerable part incorrectly, that to end Khrushchev's pressure on West Berlin Kennedy was considering measures anathema to Bonn such as recognition of the Oder-Neisse line, denuclearization of West Germany, East German control of Western access to Berlin, UN control or at least presence in West Berlin, and military disengagement in Central Europe. Kennedy's and MacNamara's strategy of "flexible response" seemed to Adenauer to sacrifice effective deterrence in Europe for better protection of U.S. cities. Finally, the U.S.-proposed Multilateral Nuclear Force (MLF), intended by its inventory to satisfy and to contain West German desire for atomic armament and finally, albeit reluctantly, supported by Bonn, became for Kennedy a growing embarrassment. Adenauer believed that Kennedy was ready to sacrifice multilateral Western European (including West German) access to nuclear weapons for arms control agreements with Moscow.[75]

By summer 1961, East Germany faced economic collapse. A forced agricultural collectivization campaign and fear that access to West Berlin would soon end so increased the refugee flow from the DDR into West Berlin that Khrushchev finally agreed with Ulbricht that it had to be stopped. He therefore began to harass allied air traffic to Berlin, whereupon Washington again considered, to Adenauer's grave concern, moving toward recognition of the DDR in return for Soviet guarantees of Western rights in West Berlin.

Simultaneously, Khrushchev renewed his offers of negotiation to Adenauer, including meeting him in Bonn.[76] The West German ambassador in Moscow, Hans Kroll, enthusiastically supported Khrushchev's proposal and on his own responsibility hinted that Bonn might negotiate about recognition of the DDR.[77] Adenauer neither approved nor disavowed this step, which soon became public. Khrushchev replied that Bonn should not allow Western opposition to prevent West German-Soviet negotiations. But Adenauer was still unwilling to make substantial concessions, which, he feared, risked stimulating, not hindering, Soviet-U.S. negotiations. The Soviets thereupon broke off their feelers and Adenauer removed Kroll from Moscow.

Adenauer also refused because Schröder feared that Bonn could only maintain its position with full U.S. support. His position was shared by the FDP, the now pro-United States SPD, and particularly by Brandt, whose relations with Kennedy were much better than Adenauer's and who like Kennedy supported détente.

There was no effective U.S. reaction to the August 13, 1961, East German construction of the Berlin Wall, as there had been none to the 1953 East German rising or the 1956 Hungarian Revolution. (There hardly could have been except for a credible threat of nuclear war.) Indeed, many in Washington felt, as Adenauer knew, that the wall stabilized a crisis area, East Germany. Adenauer and von Brentano neither reacted strongly nor expected Washington to do so. They did not try to use interzonal trade as a weapon against it because the allies would not agree to a trade embargo and the Bonn government was divided on the issue. However, the lack of U.S. reaction was a major shock to West German trust in the United States.[78]

The wall and the lack, as most West Germans saw it, of response to it by Kennedy and Adenauer were largely responsible for the CDU losses in the September 17, 1961, Bundestag elections. The CDU had long been in power and inevitably its public support had eroded. The FDP had become a more credible nonsocialist alternative. The SPD's abandonment of Marxism and neutralism, plus the popularity of its new chancellor candidate, Brandt, further worsened the CDU/CSU position. The CDU/CSU lost its absolute majority in the Bundestag. Adenauer therefore once again had to form a coalition with the FDP.

The main foreign policy results were the replacement as foreign minister of von Brentano, who strongly opposed FDP foreign policy, by Gerhard Schröder and the weakening of Adenauer's position, for he had to pledge to resign before the end of his four-year term. Schröder's policy was less pro-French, more pro-American, and more proactivist Ostpolitik than von Brentano's and more concerned with Eastern Europe (as von Brentano, hesitatingly, had also been) than Adenauer, who always gave priority to the Soviet Union.[79] However, this did not mark the beginning of the new Ostpolitik. The new coalition's foreign policy was little changed. Moreover, Adenauer's secret negotiations with the Soviets foreshadowed the Brandt-Scheel Ostpolitik of the 1970s more than what Schröder soon did vis-à-vis Eastern Europe.

Bonn-Washington relations thereafter were further strained by new U.S. proposals to include West and East Germany in the Berlin international access authority and to have it supervise the West Berlin airfields and the four-power Berlin air safety center, establish West-East German commissions on the basis of parity for technical and economic questions, limit the Western garrisons in West Berlin to nine thousand men, guarantee Central European "demarcation lines," and move toward a nonproliferation agreement. When Washington submitted these proposals to Bonn for immediate comment, they were leaked there to the press, whereupon Kennedy forced the recall of West German Ambassador Grewe, a vocal opponent of détente and of Kennedy's policies. However, Schröder managed to bring Adenauer back to a more pro-U.S. course and the Soviets rejected the international access authority proposal.

On June 6, 1962, Adenauer secretly proposed to Soviet Ambassador Smirnov a new version of the Globke Plan, a ten-year moratorium (*Burgfrieden*) on the German question, simultaneous liberalization in the DDR, and free all-German elections after ten years in order to improve conditions in the DDR and keep the German question out of the Berlin negotiations, lest Bonn's position be worsened. He had two other motives: to demonstrate, particularly to Washington, that he too could develop "new initiatives" and to out-trump Brandt in this respect. Adenauer did not inform Washington and Paris of this until the next year. On July 8, Smirnov rejected the proposal and continued to insist on a peace treaty between the two German states but suggested direct negotiations between Moscow and Bonn. Adenauer did not publish his offer until a year later, but in a Bundestag speech on October 9, 1962, he made clear his priority for improvement of conditions in the DDR:" . . . I again declare that the Federal Government is ready to discuss many things if our brothers in the Zone are able to arrange their lives as they wish. Human considerations play here for us an even greater role than national ones. . . . " Adenauer continued contacts with Moscow, even after he finally recalled Kroll, but his position was steadily weakening, and he felt compelled to resign in 1963. He was replaced by Ludwig Erhard. Thereafter, just before he fell, Khrushchev seems to have intended serious negotiations and, indeed, sent his son-in-law, Adzhubei, to Bonn to prepare them. But he was overthrown in October 1964, and a meeting between him and Erhard never occurred. Even if it had, it seems unlikely that much would have been accomplished, for the CDU continued to reject the two Soviet minimum demands: recognition of the Oder-Neisse line and of the DDR.[80] Thereafter military tension increased, only to be followed by a further Soviet postponement of their Berlin ultimatum until after the U.S. congressional elections—or so it first seemed.

Although Khrushchev had attained his minimum objective, the stabilization of the DDR and the destruction of the basis of Adenauer's reunification policy, he was still determined to try for his maximum goal: change in the status of West Berlin. This was one of the reasons he emplaced Soviet missiles in Cuba. Had he succeeded, he would have significantly, although not decisively, shifted the strategic balance in favor of the Soviet Union and begun to compensate for Kennedy's rapid missile buildup. Then, Khrushchev was convinced, Kennedy would have to make major concessions in Berlin. Khrushchev's gamble failed because Kennedy used U.S. strategic and local conventional superiority to force him to withdraw the missiles. The Soviets then let the Berlin crisis evaporate.[81]

Khrushchev began the crisis to restabilize East Germany by

stopping the massive East German refugee flow to the West; encourage Western disunity; change the Soviet-U.S. balance of power in his favor before his cirsis with China became so that he would be forced farther and faster toward détente in Europe than he wanted; defend himself against the esoteric Chinese attacks that he was insufficiently hard on the Americans; prevent West German access to U.S. atomic weapons (Adenauer rejected this on November 24, 1958, and Khrushchev began the crisis on November 27); slow down or if possible reverse Western European economic integration and Bonn's rising role in it; and force West Germany to participate in negotiations on a German peace treaty that would include East Germany, which Bonn would thereby recognize. Khrushchev's launching of the crisis was vitally necessary for Ulbricht because the swelling refugee flight from East Germany threatened to wreck the East German economy. Khrushchev clearly shared this motive, but he probably gave less priority than Ulbricht to Bonn and the West recognizing East Germany and more to his own minimal defensive aim—restabilizing East Germany. However, Khrushchev's proposed change in the status of West Berlin would probably have destabilized West Germany.

For Bonn and Washington, Khrushchev's move was thus expansionist. Moreover, Khrushchev's November 10, 1959, proposal for two neutralized, largely demilitarized, and completely deatomized German states, both of which would give most-favored-nation tariff treatment for all countries (that is, Bonn would have to leave the EEC), showed how he wanted to use the crisis to get recognition of the DDR by Bonn and the Western allies and to block Western European unification.

Professor Robert Slusser has in my view conclusively demonstrated that there were at the time serious differences of view within the Soviet leadership *inter alia,* on policy toward Berlin, and that Frol Kozlov, then Khrushchev's deputy, took a harder line than Khrushchev himself on Berlin and also on two other issues, Yugoslavia and China.[82] These differences may have accounted in part for Khrushchev's shifting tactics during the crisis.

Khrushchev succeeded temporarily in worsening Bonn-Washington relations. In part this was inevitable, for in a period of global Soviet-U.S. détente and regional European crisis, Washington would give priority to global issues such as arms control rather than unhesitatingly support Bonn's policies. As we have seen, Adenauer had feared just this in the ill-fated preparations for a four-power summit meeting before the Berlin crisis began. As his "Austrian solution," the Globke Plan, and moratorium proposal showed, he decided, because in his view Soviet pressure was so great and U.S. resistance so weak, that he could no longer hope to maintain the "status quo plus" in Berlin or Germany and that he must therefore prevent a "status quo minus," that is, discrimination against the Federal Republic, which would mean "back to Potsdam." For he was convinced that this would totally diminish Bonn's sovereignty and equality and also destabilize the West German polity to Moscow's advantage.

Within the Bonn government the crisis also caused differences of emphasis that foreshadowed future debates on Ostpolitik. Adenauer and his intimate associates, Globke and Krone, convinced that they could no longer trust U.S. policy as they had under Dulles and that Kennedy preferred the status quo, to Bonn's disadvantage, and would no longer push for reunification, attempted to combine American military protection with a political alliance with Gaullist France that would bring pressure on the United States.

Adenauer and his then defense minister, CSU leader Franz Josef Strauss, were also unhappy about growing U.S. unwillingness to agree to a NATO nuclear force (in which Bonn would participate) and later with Kennedy's emphasis on flexible response (as they saw it, not risking nuclear attack on the United States by avoiding use of nuclear weapons at the outbreak of hostilities) and on centrally U.S.-controlled nuclear forces (giving Bonn only a conventional military role.) Nor had they been entirely happy with Eisenhower's tactical nuclear weapons policy, because the Bundeswehr's tactical nuclear weapons were in exclusive U.S. custody. Finally, the worsening of the U.S. balance of payments had made Washington ask Bonn to offset U.S.

deutschmark expenditures for its troops in West Germany by purchases in the United States or by other financial arrangements, which the West Germans resented the more because they saw no alternative but to accede in order to keep the U.S. troops. Less "Gaullist" CDU leaders such as von Brentano and especially Schröder gave priority to alliance with the United States, not with de Gaulle.[83]

The Berlin crisis also brought major changes in SPD foreign policy. The 1959 new SPD *Deutschlandplan* proposed a reunited neutralized Germany, plus a neutral Poland and Czechoslovakia, joined in an internationally-guaranteed regional security system, to be established after a several-stage plan for rapprochement and ultimate reunification. The latter included a first stage of joint organs subject to veto by neither, plus free travel between the two and increased economic ties, to be followed by the withdrawal of all foreign troops, free elections, an all-German government, and, finally, withdrawal of all occupation troops from Berlin. Although Khrushchev made clear in Moscow to two SPD leaders, Carlo Schmid and Fritz Erler, that he would not permit German reunification under any conditions but was determined to get Bonn to recognize the DDR, the SPD published and advocated the plan. But as the crisis intensified, Brandt and Wehner became convinced that it had been utterly unrealistic. The 1959 SPD Godesberg Program abandoned doctrinaire Marxism. In June 1960, Wehner publicly abandoned the SPD's *Deutschlandplan* and its premise, that Bonn could get reunification by negotiations with Moscow, and declared that the SPD agreed with the CDU/CSU on a bipartisan foreign policy: that military defense in NATO was the basis for German foreign policy and that it would not be sacrificed for reunification, which could come only through self-determination via free elections. Wehner did not, however, endorse Adenauer's pro-Gaullist or even his pro-American foreign policy. Indeed, Adenauer's exclusively pro-Western and especially pro-U.S. policy had been greatly weakened by détente and the Berlin Wall and Wehner saw that Bonn needed a revised policy. In October 1960, the SPD designated Brandt as its candidate for chancellor. Brandt also began to advocate more flexibility toward dealing with East Berlin, the more so after the shock to him of the Berlin Wall and U.S. inaction with respect to it.[84]

Adenauer's Rapprochement with de Gaulle

For the three Western powers the most significant development in the crisis was the rapprochement between Bonn and Paris, caused primarily by worsened relations between Bonn and Washington.

The British favored the most concessions to the Soviets. Adenauer therefore practically broke off relations with them. Eisenhower and Kennedy, in the view of Adenauer and all of his associates, were hesitant, convinced that they should not run the risk of war or break off East-West negotiations, particularly on arms control, on issues that would not be supported by U.S. public opinion and no longer willing, as Foster Dulles had been, to give Adenauer full and unhesitating support. This inevitably antagonized the chancellor and his closest associates. In 1945, Adenauer had given priority, as he had in 1919, to reconciliation with France. He had never been pro-British; he had initially mistrusted what he saw as the Americans' naivete and lack of staying power; and he now came to do so again. But his primary motive was tactical: to get de Gaulle to veto American concessions and thus to push Washington back toward his own position.

General de Gaulle had come to power in 1958 determined to get France out of the Algerian War in order to rebuild French prosperity at home and recover independence and power abroad. He intended to do this by rapidly developing the independent French *force de frappe,* blocking European political unity by having France lead a European confederation balancing between the United States and the USSR, extricating France from American *hégémonie* through withdrawal of all French forces from the integrated NATO command, weaning West Germany away from the United States while assuring its nonnuclear status and therefore military inferiority to France, and keeping Great Britain out of the European Common Market—all in order to assure French hegemony in Western Europe and on that basis to negotiate with Khrushchev.[85] (His ultimate objective later became a reunified Germany under East-West control.) If he failed to detach Bonn from Washington, he would, Adenauer feared, revert to the French tradition of alliance with Moscow, or at least of balance between Moscow and Bonn. Thus Adenauer faced what he saw as *the* great danger to Bonn: isolation from *all* its allies by their agreement together or separately with Moscow, over his head and against Bonn's interests.

De Gaulle brilliantly and successfully cultivated Adenauer, but so did Adenauer cultivate de Gaulle. Indeed, during the second Berlin crisis de Gaulle supported Adenauer's policy more than he influenced it. They both shared a long-range sense of history, pessimism about it, and—for Adenauer only after 1959—a distrust of *"les Anglo-Saxons"*: De Gaulle feared return to Yalta, Adenauer, return to Potsdam. Yet they differed sharply with respect to European unity, for Adenauer wanted to submerge West Germany in a Western European state, while de Gaulle wanted a loosely confederated Western Europe under French *hégémonie*. Moreover, Adenauer deeply distrusted German nationalism and feared that French nationalism would revert to anti-Germanism and a deal with Moscow.

Given what Adenauer saw as Kennedy's and Macmillan's excessive willingness to compromise with the Soviets on Berlin, the chancellor found de Gaulle's flat rejection of compromise and insistence on full maintenance of all Western rights welcome, indeed essential.

The motives of their intransigence, however, were different. De Gaulle believed, with Adenauer, that Franco-German reconciliation was important to French and German security. But he saw it as part of a new European system, from which the United States and Britain would be largely excluded, politically although not militarily. (In 1959, Eisenhower, in large part because of Bonn, had rejected his proposal for an Anglo-U.S.-French global "directory.") In it France would lead Western Europe and balance between East and West, thus maintain independence and freedom of maneuver, and then negotiate with Moscow an all-European settlement "from the Atlantic to the

Urals." De Gaulle therefore opposed any new agreement between Moscow and the West on Berlin, which in his view would only stabilize the European status quo, which he was determined to change to France's advantage, and because he saw no tactical reason to negotiate with Moscow under Soviet pressure, make concessions thereby, and thus worsen Western, including French, security.

This required that West Germany be closely allied with France, choose Paris over Washington, but be permanently inferior to France, especially in two respects: that West Germany have no access to nuclear weapons, thus guaranteeing French military superiority over it, and that not West Germany but France take the lead in negotiating with the Soviet Union—in short, that Bonn have no active Ostpolitik.

Adenauer was hardly deceived by de Gaulle. He knew that de Gaulle was a French nationalist. He always feared the isolation and encirclement of West Germany by a Franco-Russian entente. He wanted above all else to maintain the unity of the West and the Federal Republic's nondiscriminatory position in it. He genuinely believed in Franco-German reconciliation and was determined to prevent Franco-German conflict. He knew that the Federal Republic was constantly increasing its economic lead over France. He therefore maneuvered with de Gaulle as de Gaulle did with him. And he knew that Bonn needed the U.S. security guarantee far more than Paris did and that, indeed, de Gaulle could leave the joint NATO command because Bonn remained in it. Adenauer, therefore, had to try to balance between Washington and Paris.

Soviet Miscalculations

Soviet tactical policy in the second Berlin crisis was characterized by a series of ultimata and time limits, postponed when the West rejected them and designed to erode the Western position without provoking military confrontation or ending the negotiations. Khrushchev overestimated how much he could get out of the West. He turned down one after another Western compromise proposal that would have given him at least the "status quo partially minus" in West Berlin: the U.S.-proposed international access authority, limitations on Western troop presence and propaganda activity, and East and West German representation in joint bodies to supervise access. He miscalculated strategically by believing that he could face Kennedy down in the 1962 Cuban missile crisis and thereby gain all his demands with respect to West Berlin.

Results of the Crisis
The Berlin Wall was *the* decisive watershed in postwar West German foreign policy, for it forced West Germans to accept the reality of long-term partition of Germany. It severed East and West Berlin, thus cutting the major travel link between West and East Germany, and made West Germans realize that neither U.S. nor West German foreign policy had prevented it. It destroyed the basic premise of Adenauer's foreign policy of strength through the Western alliance, that it would bring reunification. It further tarnished the West German image of the United States as the protector of Bonn's interests. (This was especially the case with Willy Brandt, then mayor of West Berlin, and his close associate, Egon Bahr.) It thus stabilized East Germany, unsettled West Germany, and worsened Bonn-Washington relations— three major objectives of Soviet policy in Europe. The wall was the primary impetus for the increasing West German popular conviction that a new West German policy must be sought to ease the hardships of, and restore ties with, the millions of East Germans.

The crisis convinced the more conservative, Catholic, Western European-oriented elements in the CDU, plus Strauss and the CSU, that U.S. and West German interests had so diverged, and French and West German interests converged, that, while preserving the U.S. security guarantee, Bonn should have a primary political relationship with Paris.[86]

The crisis stabilized East Germany and the Soviet hold over it. The wall gradually, grudgingly, but surely made East Germans reconcile themselves to stay in East Germany, cooperate with the SED for its industrialization and modernization, and thus build state consciousness. As West Germans realized this, they all the more wanted a more active Ostpolitik to prevent East German national consciousness developing as well.

Thus by cementing the status quo, intensifying East-West détente, consolidating the DDR, and maintaining West Berlin, the second Berlin crisis furthered an independent West German foreign policy less automatically supportive of the United States. This was especially true of Adenauer and Strauss, whose mistrust of the United States remained strong thereafter, and of Brandt and Bahr, who had always shared some of Schumacher's firece desire for West German independence and who were shocked by U.S. inaction at the time of the construction of the Berlin Wall.

Even so, after the crisis ended, and in large part because it ended, Bonn-Washington relations initially improved. The remaining issues between the two were more containable. Kennedy realized that there had been no point in trying to force Adenauer to accept proposals that Moscow rejected anyway. The "Europeanists" in the State Department gained ground. De Gaulle's veto of Britain's entry into the European Common Market and the U.S.-U.K. Nassau agreement on nuclear weapons so worsened French-American relations that arguments that Washington must counteract "German Gaullism," that is, a Franco-German entente, found U. S. converts. Their proposal for a multinational nuclear force (MLF) pleased Bonn, which saw it primarily as a political instrument to prevent further Soviet-U.S. bilateralism and move toward equality with Britain and France vis-à-vis the United States. American MLF policy was contradictory, for its U.S. proponents wanted to use it to satisfy future West German demands for access to nuclear weapons and also to prevent them from really getting it. But Moscow saw the MLF as the opening step in conversion of West German economic and technological power to nuclear power, whereby Bonn would either rapidly become the principal influence on U.S. policy in Western Europe or, worse, increasingly independent of it and thus militarily more menacing.[87]

Schröder and von Hassell, the new defense minister, got along with Washington far better than von Brentano and Strauss (who had fallen over the *Spiegel* affair). Adenauer's foreign policy valedictory, the Franco-German treaty, had been attenuated, in part because of U.S. pressure, by the Bundestag's adding a pro-NATO preamble when it ratified it.[88] But the differences between Kennedy and the West German conservatives remained unbridged. Kennedy concluded that he must now intensify political détente with Moscow in order to avoid other crises in the future. This was bound to be seen in Bonn as a threat to West Germany's special relationship with the United States. Thus Bonn-Washington tension was bound to revive.

Although Kennedy's 1963 trip to West Berlin had made the news primarily for his statement, *"Ich bin ein Berliner,"* he declared later that day: "The peaceful reunification of Berlin and Germany will, therefore, not be either quick or easy . . . in the meantime, justice requires us to do what we can do in this transition period to improve the lot and maintain the hopes of those on the other side. . . . "[89] And earlier that month, in his major American University address on June 10, he had announced the beginning of negotiations with Moscow on a test-ban treaty and made clear that avoidance of nuclear war was the key world problem and, by omitting any mention of it, that German reunification was not.[90]

Later that year Adenauer was very seriously disturbed (although Schröder apparently was less so) by the test-ban negotiations and the signing of the test-ban treaty. He believed that in them any link with German reunification had clearly been abandoned, thus upgrading the DDR, which signed the treaty; they were carried on without meaningful consultation with the Federal Republic; and they threatened to make Washington favor the Soviet proposal for NATO-Warsaw Pact nonaggression pacts, which would upgrade the DDR even more. Schröder favored ratification of the treaty; von Brentano, Krone, and Strauss opposed it. Adenauer, unenthusiastic, realized that Bonn had no alternative but to ratify it; for further Soviet-U.S. negotiations over Berlin and general East-West relations were planned and de Gaulle had just announced that he was removing the French naval units in the Atlantic from NATO control. Bonn's refusal to sign would thus isolate it further and weaken NATO. Bonn signed the treaty in August 1963 and the Bundestag ratified it the next year.

The affair caused Adenauer's latent distrust of the United States to well up again. This was one reason he carried on secret negotiations with the Soviets, largely via ex-Ambassador Kroll. For a brief time he believed that the bad 1963 Soviet grain harvest could be used, by means either of a Western grain sale boycott or of mass economic aid, to make progress on the German question; but a meeting with Khrushchev was prevented by Adenauer's declining political power and then his resignation.[91]

Adenauer's rule was thus drawing to its close and with it Bonn's rigidity on Ostpolitik and his inclination to move away from Washington toward France. Yet rising West German economic power and disillusionment with Washington would make Bonn pursue a more national policy.

The Global Preconditions

July 1963 saw two interrelated major events occur in Moscow: the signature of the Soviet-U.S.-U.K. partial test-ban treaty and the collapse of Sino-Soviet party negotiations. Both contributed to the post-1971 Sino-U.S. rapprochement, the intensification of Soviet-U.S. détente, and the German settlement. But initially Soviet policy remained hostile to West Germany. East Germany, shielded by the Berlin Wall, began to consolidate. Franco-American relations became more strained, in part because de Gaulle, confident after the Cuban crisis that the Soviet Union was no longer so dangerous, pushed détente with the Soviet Union and Eastern Europe. Johnson initially improved West German–U.S. relations, but later his popularity declined in Bonn because of his renewed priority for arms control over German reunification.

In Eastern Europe reconsolidation of Soviet power began to give way again in the early 1960s to renewed fissures, caused by reviving Eastern European nationalisms, desire for more rapid economic development, cultural liberalization, and the decline in Soviet authority resulting from the Sino-Soviet split.

Rumania's move away from Soviet control had begun in the late 1950s with the realignment of its foreign trade pattern toward Western Europe, because of superior Western technology and credit terms plus Rumanian resentment over economic pressure by East Germany, Czechoslovakia, and the USSR for integration into the Council for Mutual Economic Aid (CMEA), which would slow down Rumanian industrialization. The second Soviet-Yugoslav rapprochement began after 1960, in part because Sino-Soviet relations worsened, but opposition to its going too far grew in the more developed western republics of Croatia and Slovenia, intensified by their desire for more access to Western technology and credits. Rumania and Yugoslavia, and even more traditionally pro-German Hungary and Bulgaria, felt that these could best be obtained from West Germany, the more so because they need not fear a German foreign trade monopoly: Bonn's share was too small and Moscow's too large. Moreover, Italy accounted for almost as much trade with the Balkan states as West Germany. Finally, in 1962, a major economic crisis and the first signs of liberalization developed in Czechoslovakia.[1]

Thus Bonn's relations with its Western allies, notably the United States, were less satisfactory and those with Moscow were hostile. It saw some prospect for improving relations with some Eastern European states. Adenauer therefore felt out Moscow secretly on the prospects for a temporary compromise on the German question. They also influenced Schröder, with Adenauer's rather unenthusiastic approval, to adopt a more flexible policy toward the Eastern European states.

These developments also had more general causes:

1. Frustration over the severing by the Berlin Wall of human contacts with East Germany, resultant consolidation of the East regime, consequent decline in prospects for reunification, and fear of gradual disappearance in East Germany of the sense of belonging to one German nation made West German public opinion move toward a more flexible policy toward the East to counteract these tendencies.[2]

2. Frustration over stagnation in European political unification had set in with de Gaulle's nationalist policies and was strengthened by his veto over U.K. entry into the EEC and his blocking of all attempts toward European political union. Many West Germans were therefore thrown back to a national goal, improving conditions of life in East Germany. This was especially true for many of the politically active West German youth, who felt no personal guilt for the Nazi regime and therefore did not share their elders' inhibitions about supporting German nationalism, and most of all for its leftist segment, which was internationalist and therefore did not give first priority to reunification but was primarily concerned with liberalization in East Germany and in Eastern Europe in general.

3. Discontent with the disunity of Bonn's allies and their lack of support for West Germany's national goals, plus rising Franco-American tension and the increasing tendency of Paris and Washington to negotiate separately and bilaterally with Moscow threatened to weaken the Atlantic alliance and to maneuver

Bonn back into a discriminatory status.[3] NATO, "Atlanticism," and Kennedy's "Atlantic partnership" thus became less attractive.

West German discontent centered on the United States, which many West Germans thought was moving toward agreements with the Soviet Union contrary to Bonn's vital interests. West German-American differences during the second Berlin crisis were reinforced by Bonn's concern about U.S. lack of consultation during the U.S.-USSR partial test-ban treaty negotiations, particularly as to whether the modus of its signature would upgrade East Germany, plus the U.S. move away from support of the MLF toward Soviet-U.S. arms control agreements. In 1967 and thereafter these fears were further intensified by U.S.-USSR nonproliferation negotiations.[4]

West Germans thus increasingly saw the United States giving less priority to reunification and more to détente and Vietnam. They feared U.S. neoisolationism and were less attracted to the United States as a model because of failure to win in Vietnam and U.S. domestic disturbances. Finally, they resented rising American financial demands on Bonn, because of the worsening of U.S. balance of payments, to offset foreign currency expenditures for U.S. troops. De Gaulle's policies were less resented than Washington's because of support in CDU and CSU Catholic circles for his advocacy of an independent Europe, even if under French leadership, as an equal ally of the United States.[5]

4. Disillusionment with the United States among educated, leftist West German youth, and to a lesser degree among the whole West German population, strengthened this trend. In part this was inevitable, for postwar political passivity was bound to give way to a more normal degree of political engagement, including the revival of the historic German radical tradition, so long submerged by nazism and the cold war. East-West détente and U.S. involvement in Vietnam and in domestic political crises, plus less fear of Soviet aggression, also helped revive the native German radical left and lowered U.S. popular attractiveness.

Much of this also reflected the 1960 global New Left youth politics. But in the Federal Republic it also reflected something deeper, more traditionally German: a revival of the traditional German rejection of the West's materialism, consumer society, and Weberian "ice age" of "rational bureaucracy" in favor of tradition, prebourgeois (and postbourgeois) *Gemeinschaft* (community) values, this time radical, egalitarian, and anarcho-Marxist, but sharing with the Nazi students of the 1930s the priority for emotion, violence, and revolution over reason, democracy, and the rule of law. This was true only of the small radical West German student Left, yet in the mid-1970s only in West Germany were student radicals still influential in several universities.

5. The changing perception of the DDR in the Federal Republic intensified the rising alienation among West Germans from its Western allies, and above all from the United States. Once the flow of technologically qualified personnel to West Germany had stopped, Ulbricht had felt able to rationalize his economy and end drastic police terror. While East German economic reforms were not as extensive as Hungarian ones, when coupled with traditional German efficiency and East Germans' resigned realization that they no longer had any other place to go, they did result in rapid economic growth, rising standards of living, and, as Ulbricht often, to Soviet disapproval, stressed, to by far the most productive "developed socialist society."

By the late 1960s most West Germans became increasingly disinterested in the DDR as compared to the problems of the Federal Republic and their lives in it, since they saw less and less possibility of reunification and favorable economic and social development in West Germany itself. Their concern about the Soviet threat to West Germany declined as détente intensified and their perception of Poland became more positive; and as the years went on they became more favorable to the developing West German Ostpolitik. This process centered in the young, the more prosperous, and the better educated. (There is some evidence that a somewhat similar process has been going on in the DDR.) Thus the changes in West German Ostpolitik reflected as well as stimulated similar changes in West German public opinion. (Yet one should be wary of assuming that these tendencies will necessarily continue. The stability of the West German, and, indeed, East German, politics are primarily the result of economic and social progress. Were these to change, the stability would be seriously threatened. And the classic nationalisms of such partitioned nations as Poland and Ireland, and more recently of Korea and Vietnam, should warn us that while most West Germans probably now no longer view their state as only provisional, all-German nationalism can rise again.)

Conversely, the West German radical Left viewed favorably the DDR's consolidation and its advantage over West Germany in mass education and social mobility, in contrast with what they saw as deliberate West German backwardness in these areas in order to favor the upper half of the population. Again, behind these perceptions were deep historic traditions: Prussian, precapitalist priority for *Kultur, Gemeinschaft,* self-sacrifice, discipline, and *Ordnung* over affluent, hedonistic, "degenerate, pornographic, drug ridden" Western *Zivilisation.*

6. West German national self-confidence was rising, due, in addition to (2) and (3) above, to the ebbing of postwar antinationalist sentiments and to the rise of West German power. This led to a desire for a more national foreign policy and, in part of the Left, to higher priority for Ostpolitik.

7. Optimism that Eastern European developments offered new opportunities for West Germany was favored by arguments by analogy that the same trends were at least potentially present in East Germany and that therefore a less hostile West German policy toward it would encourage elements in the East German leadership to favor détente with West Germany and more liberalization and autonomy from the Soviet Union. These tendencies were strengthened by rising West German public awareness of the post-1962 liberalization in Czechoslovakia and by rapidly increasing West German tourism and cultural exchange with Eastern Europe.

8. Bonn felt it necessary to avoid isolation in the West about détente with the East. During the second Berlin crisis this danger had not been so great, because de Gaulle obdurately opposed negotiations with the Soviets under threat. But his shift

to détente, in part in order to keep ahead of Washington and Bonn in this respect, and the intensification of it by the United States, threatened Bonn with isolation, which Adenauer moved after 1962 to avoid, the more so to prevent Paris from balancing between Moscow and Bonn.

9. West German business wanted to increase trade with Eastern Europe.[6] Bonn hoped that greater political influence would result from economic penetration.

10. In late 1959 the SPD, under Herbert Wehner's leadership, as a result of the Berlin crisis abandoned its neutralist, disengagement policies for support of NATO and rapprochement between East and West Germany in order to move gradually toward reunification and to gain respectability among the bourgeoisie in order to participate in a CDU-SPD "Grand Coalition" and thus eventually become the majority party. Some CDU leaders also began to feel that the failure of Adenauer's "policy of strength" required a coalition in order to contain the danger of frustrated German nationalism. There was thus no longer any major obstacle to a CDU-SPD foreign policy rapprochement.[7]

The West German Political Realignment and Ostpolitik
The factors outlined above, plus the post-1959 decline of Adenauer's authority and the rivalries for his succession, led to a complex realignment of West German politics, which primarily concerned internal politics and relations with the West but also involved differences about and had great effect upon Bonn's policy toward the East. It appeared by 1960 and coalesced during the revival of détente after the 1962 end of the Berlin crisis.

It resulted in three main West German foreign policy groups: the "flexible Atlanticists," the "inflexible conservatives," and the "flexible leftists."[8] The differences between the first two in part reflected the historic division along Protestant-Catholic and northern versus western-southern German lines on policy toward Eastern and Western Europe. That between the first and the third reflected a less sharp difference in the SPD. These catagories were not mutually exclusive. Brandt, for example, was between the flexible Atlanticists and the flexible leftists. Erler, although primarily a flexible Atlanticist, also had elements of a flexible leftist. The distinction between the first and third groups was one of relative priority for Atlantic ties and between the first and second, for Western European ties in contrast to those with Moscow and East Berlin.

Most flexible Atlanticists were sophisticated German nationalists. Typified by Protestant Gerhard Schröder, they included most of German industry, the right and center of the FDP, and most of the Foreign Office, the trade unions, and the SPD leadership, notably Fritz Erler and Hulmut Schmidt. They did not think France strong or reliable enough to guarantee West German security against the Soviet Union, and they saw de Gaulle as an outmoded French nationalist, not even an advocate of a French-led united Western Europe.

Like most Protestants and northern Germans, they were pro-British and pro-American, not pro-French. Although they shared much of the general Western European disillusionment with American policy, they saw no alternative, given Soviet strength and West German weakness, but to maintain the American alliance and to influence American policy on negotiations with Moscow and on nuclear policy in favor of West German interests. Although firmly for Western European unity and British participation in it, they felt that major progress was unlikely and that therefore West German policy should emphasize West German influence on and participation in U.S. policy-making. They therefore supported the MLF. That project, however, even before Erhard's demise, had fallen prey to Washington's shift toward priorities for arms control arrangements with the Soviet Union and for the Vietnam War, to strong opposition by de Gaulle and the "German Gaullists," and, with the advent of the Grand Coalition, to SPD priority for Ostpolitik versus nuclear sharing, and thereby for maximum West German freedom of maneuver.[9] The flexible Atlanticists and Gaullists also split on the nonproliferation treaty. Schröder and the SPD favored it to avoid isolation, while Adenauer, no longer chancellor, and

Strauss opposed it, because it would allegedly upgrade the DDR and prevent a Western European "nuclear option"—a European nuclear force.[10]

While the old *Russland* versus *Randstaatenpolitik* controversy (priority for relations with the Soviet Union or with the Eastern European states) still existed within the flexible Atlanticists, Schröder had concluded that Adenauer's "policy of strength" needed to be adjusted to East-West détente and U.S. support of it, Gaullist policies, and new opportunities in Eastern Europe. Erler and other SPD leaders, conversely, had been led by the second Berlin crisis, the Berlin Wall, and their aim of forming a Grand Coalition to move toward an Atlanticist policy while retaining their previous commitment to contacts with the East but to hostility toward East Germany. Schröder's and Erler's Ostpolitik was West German, not Western European. They were for Western European unity and NATO. But they drew the consequences from the American priority for East-West détente and from de Gaulle's nationalistic policies toward the East: a nationalist West German Ostpolitik.[11]

Since they foresaw little progress with Moscow or East Berlin and knew that the CDU/CSU would resist rapprochement with East Germany, they began with the other Eastern European states. There, they believed, liberalization was likely and would favor Bonn, because Eastern European economies would require Western technology and credits, which Bonn could best supply, for a political payoff. West German business leaders supported but did not decisively influence this view. They hoped that as West German influence grew in Eastern Europe Moscow would negotiate with Bonn, and West Germany could thus work toward improvement of conditions in the DDR and contribute toward eventual German unification. They therefore opposed rapprochement with and advocated the isolation of East Germany. In order to avoid the problem of the Hallstein Doctrine, they initially urged only increased economic and cultural contacts with the Eastern European states, institutionalized through establishment of West German trade missions in the Eastern European capitals. (As early as 1957, Wilhelm Grewe, one of Adenauer's close associates, had begun to sketch out such a policy toward those Eastern European states such as Hungary and Rumania with whom West Germany had no border problems; and von Brentano had favored it as well.) Thereby, they hoped, Bonn would break the East German monopoly on representation in the Eastern European capitals, and, by the so-called "Berlin clause" (giving Bonn the right to represent West Berlin as well), work against the Soviet-East German "three German states" theory (that West Berlin, as a "free city," would be a third German state). Anxious not to give West or East any reason to underrate Bonn's commitment to German reunification, they stressed that Bonn's *Alleinvertretungsrecht* should not be surrendered. East Germany should not be recognized, and efforts to negotiate with Moscow should continue. These views, prevalent in the Bonn Foreign Office for some time, were developed in a Bundestag subcommittee in 1960 and 1961 and embodied in a unanimous Bundestag resolution of June 14, 1961, which, although inevitably very generally worded, marked the beginning of the new German Ostpolitik. It declared:

The Federal Government is called upon to pursue with its allies an eastern policy aiming at the restoration of a free and all-German state that maintains friendly and prosperous relations with the Soviet Union and the East European countries. To this end, the Federal Government should grasp every opporunity to bring about a normalization of relations between the Federal Republic and the East European countries without abandoning vital German interests.[12]

The second group, the inflexible conservatives, was made up primarily of Catholics from the Rhineland and Bavaria. Pro-French, not anti-American but opposed to Washington's priority for negotiations with Moscow, ideologically strongly anti-communist, and favoring absolute priority to Western European unity, they continued Adenauer's "policy of strength." After he relinquished the chancellorship, Adenauer joined them, although, as we have seen, he had secretly been more in touch with Moscow than they would probably have preferred. Ironically, he was using German nationalism against Moscow and Washington and for a Western Europe allied with but equal to the United States, based on his cherished Franco-German alliance and cutting the ground out from its extremist version.[13]

The inflexible conservatives included Adenauer's supporters, Heinrich Krone and Heinrich von Brentano and CSU head Franz Josef Strauss. They did not object to *Randstaatenpolitik* but considered *Russlandpolitik* futile, and they gave the former much lower priority than Western European unification. They believed that an independent West German Ostpolitik would interfere with Western European unification and particularly with priority for good relations with France, surrender German legal and moral claims, and antagonize their electoral constituencies, with little prospect of it accomplishing much in Eastern Europe. Their disillusionment with the United States had convinced them that only a united Europe, even if (temporarily) under French leadership, could be an equal partner of the United States and thereby effectively defend Western European interests against Soviet-American bilateralism and the rising economic power of the U.S. multilateral corporations. Like Adenauer, the other inflexible conservatives claimed that only Western European unity and strength could bring, or at least keep open, the possibility of German reunification; but this probably reflected more rhetoric than a real priority with most inflexible conservatives, as it did with Adenauer.

The inflexible conservatives were less, not more, national minded than the flexible Atlanticists, for they were unenthusiastic about the Bismarck Reich and wanted a united Europe, independent of although allied with the United States, with a European nuclear force. They were prepared to accept leadership by de Gaulle as the only way to move toward Western European unity, in which after him Bonn's position would become stronger, and only after which Eastern Europe could be reunited with the West. (Strauss declared in 1967 that he did not expect to see again a German state within anything like the 1937 boundaries.)[14]

The third group, the flexible leftists, centered in the SPD and included many left-wing intellectuals. Its policies and goals were similar to but its motives different from the first two. Its primary aim was, by "small steps" (*kleine Schritte*), to improve conditions of life in East Germany, as an end in itself and as a means for progress toward German reunification. Because it was convinced that German reunification could only come after the reunification of Europe and that liberalization and autonomy in Eastern Europe were increasing, it felt that the West, and particularly the Federal Republic, by aiding it could contribute to the "reunification of Europe"—but, unlike Schröder by compromise with, rather than pressure on, the Soviet Union and the DDR. As one of its major theoreticians, Richard Löwenthal, later put it, "Intra-German solidarity on the one hand and the consciousness of a role in Central Europe on the other began to replace in the thoughts of many citizens of the Federal Republic the blocked alternatives of reunification and integration into Western Europe."[15] Brandt put this policy into effect in West Berlin and brought it, as foreign minister, into the Grand Coalition in 1966.[16]

This group wanted negotiations with Moscow. It believed that only through détente could it reach its aims. (The first group felt that West Germany could not afford to be isolated from détente and the second opposed it.) It believed, or at least hoped, that industrialization would lead to convergence between East and West and contacts with East Germany would gradually liberalize it. It rejected the isolation of East Germany for change there through rapprochement (*"Wandel durch Annäherung"*). It was led by Brandt, the new SPD chairman, and by Wehner.[17] (Its main theoretician was Brandt's press chief Egon Bahr.) It was strong in Brandt's West Berlin SPD, which wanted to ameliorate the partition of the city. It profited from the initial successes in the negotiations between West Berlin and East Germany on easing travel restrictions.

The flexible leftists may be subdivided into cosmopolitans and nationalists. The former, left-wing intellectuals, went beyond the official SPD position to advocate the recognition of the DDR in order to stabilize it and thereby to encourage the potentially less pro-Soviet part of the SED elite to favor more contacts with West Germany. Many, fearing a revival of German nationalism, opposed German reunification, for like Adenauer they believed that the Bismarck Reich had been a disaster for Germany and the world. Others were convinced that the post-1945 international system precluded German reunification, because all of Germany's neighbors, the United States, and the Soviet Union, opposed it. Bonn's clinging to it, they were convinced, was a major obstacle to liberalization in the DDR. (For the German New Left, which concentrated on internal problems and "antiimperialism," that is, domestic and international systemic changes, Ostpolitik was at best irrelevant and at worst dangerous because it was "systemstabilizing.")[18]

The leftist internationalists continued the cosmopolitan, internationalist tradition of the enlightenment and of the Left during the Weimar Republic, and like them they had little political influence. The nationalist flexible leftists, notably Brandt, Wehner, and Bahr, were less cosmopolitan and more nationalist. They, not the cosmopolitan flexible leftists, led West German Ostpolitik after Brandt became chancellor in 1969.

They believed that German policy toward the East required firm alliance with the West and particularly with the United States. Brandt shared some of de Gaulle's and Schumacher's scepticism about Washington and wanted to improve Bonn's relations with Paris. Like Adenauer, he believed that European unity should produce a strong power allied with but also not dependent on the United States. He saw himself as neither a pure "Atlanticist" nor a pure "European." (His ideas in this respect partially revived his wartime émigré views.)[19] He and Bahr had also been greatly disillusioned about the United States by what they had seen as American passivity with respect to the Berlin Wall.[20]

Brandt, an extreme left-wing socialist before World War II, was a conciliatory, integrating leader of the SPD. He still, however, held the optimistic views of old-time socialists about human nature in general and about the prospects of change to the east, including in the DDR, in particular. Without this optimism, and the courage of his convictions, he would hardly have gone as far and as fast as he was to go with Ostpolitik. Wehner and Bahr came from Thuringia. Wehner had been a leading German Communist and had broken with Moscow in 1942. Bahr had been discriminated against under the Nazis. Conscious nationalists, they carried on the Schumacher SPD tradition: priority for German reunification through negotiations or, as a minimum, increased contacts with and improvement of conditions of life in the DDR over Western European unification. (Bahr, in addition, became increasingly convinced that reunification was out of the question.) Bahr, like Brandt, had been decisively and lastingly disillusioned by U.S. inaction when the Berlin Wall was built. (The Atlanticists were much less influenced by it, and the German Gaullists hardly at all.)[21] Neither wanted to abandon the Western alliance or Western European unity, although Bahr may well at least initially have thought of an eventual European security system involving the dissolution of both military blocs. Neither was in any sense procommunist; Schumacher's anticommunism remained alive in them. But while for the cosmopolitan leftist intellectuals neither German reunification nor Western European unity but East-West détente and peace had priority, for Wehner and Bahr German reunification as the ultimate goal and until then improvement of living conditions in and contacts with East Germany had priority over the other two.

In July 1963, Bahr set forth his (and Brandt's) views in the first programmatic statement of what in 1969 became the Brandt-Scheel Ostpolitik. The only realistic goal, he maintained, was *Wandel durch Annäherung* (change through rapprochement): "the narrow path of improvement of the conditions of life in such homeopathic doses that there will not arise the danger of a revolutionary upsurge which would result inevitably, out of Soviet interest, in Soviet intervention. . . . " Second, he maintained, economic improvement in East Germany would lead to political relaxation there. Third, he insisted, "The preconditions for reunification can be established only with the Soviets. They cannot be obtained in East Berlin, not against the Soviets, not without them. . . . The Zone must be transformed with the consent of the Soviets. . . . " Bahr did not speak of even de facto recognition of the DDR but he tried to downgrade the issue.

And he insisted that "Reunification is not a simple event . . . but a process with many steps and many stages."[22]

Brandt's and Bahr's Ostpolitik was thus forward vis-à-vis the DDR, for it was intended to liberalize it, against its own will, through negotiations with Moscow and thereby to make progress toward eventual reunification. (It was thus similar to the initial maximum goals of the Soviet Westpolitik: the destablization of West Germany and its eventual "Finlandization.") In the short run, however, it would stabilize the DDR just as the Soviet Westpolitik would stabilize West Germany. Both policies, SPD and Soviet, unlike Stalin's and Adenauer's rigid cold war confrontation, were policies of conscious political engagement in Europe between the two German states.

After the 1962 resumption of East-West détente, the SPD returned to its support for détente and German reunification and therefore for a more flexible Ostpolitik. While the inflexible conservatives denigrated them, the flexible Atlanticists and the flexible leftists were encouraged by (and overestimated) the prospects for liberalization and national autonomy in Eastern Europe. Finally, the post-1962 West German New Left pressured the SPD to intensify its new Ostpolitik.

Schröder's Ostpolitik
Schröder's Ostpolitik began in 1961–1962, with Adenauer's initial approval and SPD support. He aimed to establish West German trade missions (including the "Berlin clause"—that Bonn would also represent West Berlin) in the Eastern European states, increase trade with Eastern Europe through higher levels of governmentally guaranteed West German industrial credits *(Hermes-Bürgschaften)*, and increased cultural exchange and tourism.

Schröder's Ostpolitik consciously and specifically excluded the DDR, which it hoped to isolate so that Moscow would eventually force East Berlin to make major concessions to Bonn. This could not succeed, for Soviet control over the DDR was for Moscow a guarantee against liberalization and nationalism elsewhere in Eastern Europe and against the reunification of Germany.[23]

Moscow and the Eastern European states were of two minds about Schröder's Ostpolitik. It made it more possible to get West German technology on favorable credit terms at a time when the East-West technological gap was widening steadily. It diluted the Hallstein Doctrine, since Bonn's trade missions would mean symbolic acceptance of Eastern European diplomatic relations with East Berlin and perhaps the beginning of recognition of the DDR by Bonn. But its success would increase West German influence in Eastern Europe, isolate the DDR, and, insofar as the Eastern European states accepted the Berlin clause, the trade missions, or both in lieu of full diplomatic relations, lower their price for normalization of relations with Bonn.

Moscow and even more East Berlin therefore opposed it as long as it aimed to isolate, not recognize, East Germany and because while Schröder's "policy of movement" was not explicitly or consciously confrontational, as was Adenauer's policy, its effect was "objectively" confrontational.

The resultant West German–East German negotiations were long and tedious. The Berlin clause was the main obstacle. The Soviets, having recognized Bonn in 1955 and seeing the advantages as well as the disadvantages, supported the Eastern European states in the negotiations and pushed them to give priority to Poland in them, so that Bonn could not begin with states less hostile to it. (Actually, Bonn started with Poland lest it seem not to give priority to the state that Hitler had treated the worst.) Ulbricht supplemented Soviet pressure on Gomu*l*ka, with whom his relations had become close.[24] Trade mission negotiations were concluded with Poland on March 7, 1963,[25] with Rumania on October 17, 1962,[26] with Hungary on November 10, 1963,[27] and with Bulgaria on March 6, 1964.[28] In Prague, where Novotný was still in power, they dragged on, because Prague demanded that Bonn declare the 1938 Munich agreement invalid *ex tunc* (as of its signature), Moscow pressed Prague against Bonn, and the Sudeten German lobby in Bonn successfully pressuresd Adenauer and Erhard to reject this concession.

One other factor made Bonn's new Ostpolitik more difficult: the beginning of the EEC agricultural policy (CAP), whose preference for intra-EEC agricultural imports made Eastern European agricultural exports to West Germany more difficult, Neverthless, Bonn increased credit guarantees to the Eastern European states when the trade mission agreements were signed, so that the 1962–1963 decline of West German trade with them, due to the CAP, was reversed in 1964. West German trade with East Germany and the Soviet Union also began to increase after the Berlin crisis ended. Cultural exchange and tourism with West Germany also began to expand rapidly, since those Eastern European states with tourism potential (all except Poland), realizing how West German tourism had helped revive the Yugoslav, Greek, and Spanish economies, gave favorable tourist exchange rates to get hard currency.

The Erhard Interlude

The complex intrigues that led to the forced resignation of Adenauer in 1963 can only be sketched here. Schröder had become foreign minister in 1961 primarily as a result of FDP pressure. Strauss was forced to resign as minister of defense because of his role in the *Spiegel* affair.[29] Age and FDP opposition forced Adenauer to resign in October 1963. Minister of Economics Ludwig Erhard, the author of the postwar West German "economic miracle," replaced Adenauer because he was the only sure CDU vote getter and in spite of the well-known fact that he was an indecisive, ineffective administrator and would probably be an indecisive chancellor, as indeed, he turned out to be. Erhard, a Protestant from Franconia, was like Schröder, pro-American and far from Francophile.

Adenauer's disillusionment with Washington and his sympathies for France and de Gaulle made him try, through the Franco-German Friendship Treaty, to tie West Germany closely to France. But opposition by the CDU's north German Protestant wing and by the SPD forced the Bundestag to add a preamble reaffirming NATO solidarity and thus implicitly reject one of de Gaulle's aims in concluding it. When worsening U.S.-French relations made Washington pressure Bonn to choose it over Paris, Erhard, Schröder, and the SPD preferred the former. Adenauer and Strauss, rejecting the necessity of the choice, went into de facto opposition, including against Schröder's Ostpolitik.

Although Erhard basically favored Schröder's Ostpolitik, his indecisiveness slowed it down, particularly when because of pressure against it by the Sudeten Germans, led by Federal Minister of Transport Seebohm, and by Adenauer and Strauss he hesitated to agree to resume diplomatic relations with Rumania, preparations for which were successfully completed in 1964–1966, lest they accuse him of abandoning the Hallstein Doctrine and thus worsening Bonn's international position. Erhard's increasingly obvious weakness made it clear that he would be only an interim chancellor. The struggle for the succession between Schröder and Strauss grew and Schröder would therefore take fewer risks about Ostpolitik.

During the Erhard period prolonged and complex negotiations between West Berlin and East Germany also went on about lessening travel restrictions between East and West Berlin. Pressure from West Berlin public opinion and from the Berlin SPD made Bonn permit them. SPD support for them was increased by its new chairman, Willy Brandt, then mayor of West Berlin, who favored East-West German negotiations to make progress on the German question. West German public opinion also increasingly supported them. Schröder, Erhard, and the Bonn Foreign Office, however, feared that they would lessen East Germany's isolation and upgrade its international status and therefore opposed any concessions to the DDR. (In January 1963, Khrushchev sounded out Brandt on a meeting, but CDU opposition prevented it.)

Ulbricht wanted to use them to improve his international status and to sow discord between the SPD and the CDU. Since he controlled access to East Berlin, he gradually compelled Bonn to allow West Berlin to negotiate with and thus upgrade East

Germany. In return, Berlin travel pass agreements were reached for Christmas 1963 and again, for a longer period, in September 1964, after both sides agreed to disagree about terminology regarding the DDR. But because Ulbricht's minimum aim was to prevent human contacts and raise tension between West and East Germany, when he did not succeed in his maximum aim, Bonn's recognition of East Germany, he broke off the negotiations.[30] However, this policy of "little steps" (*kleine Schritte*) broke the ice, accustomed Bonn to deal with East Berlin, increased SPD support for *Wandel durch Annäherung*, and strengthened the flexible leftists, for, if only briefly, it had increased human contacts between East and West Berliners. Encouraged by them, in August 1964 Brandt urged U.S. Secretary of State Rusk to include the DDR, below the level of recognition, in greatly increased East-West economic relations, especially in joint energy and transport projects.[31] Brandt's moves also led to a long dispute between him and the Erhard government. Erler and Wehner also thought that Brandt was moving too far and too fast toward negotiations with East Berlin.

West German Trade Policy under Erhard

The Erhard period saw some improvement in West German trade relations with Eastern Europe, including the DDR, but its trade position vis-à-vis the Soviet Union worsened in relative terms and its balance of trade with Moscow became increasingly passive. The latter occurred primarily because of West German political reasons. Bonn's position on credits to Moscow, despite West German business pressure, remained relatively inflexible. The pipe embargo episode had made Moscow more hostile to Bonn on trade matters. The other Western European states were giving Moscow better trade and credit terms. Moscow refused to negotiate another trade treaty with Bonn. There was also an economic reason: The Soviet economy was going through a period of lower economic growth and Moscow did not dispose of so much foreign currency. Perhaps the most important reason, however, was Bonn's continuing inflexibility on Ostpolitik.

Trade began to grow with Poland but soon became the largest

with Rumania, with whom there were no territorial problems, which exported oil, and which did not have problems like Poland's with the CAP. Although Bonn did not establish a trade mission in Prague and therefore did not encourage expansion of trade with Czechoslovakia, for structural reasons (the developed Czechoslovak economy), trade with it increased as much as with the other bloc countries. Travel improved, if little, between West and East Berlin, largely because Bonn made economic concessions to the DDR in return.[32]

The "Exchange of Speakers" Episode

The SPD position developed further in early 1966 as a result of its negotiations with the SED on the latter's "exchange of speakers" (*Redneraustausch*) proposal. East Berlin's initiative reflected Soviet and East German policies. Moscow's maximum aims in Western Europe were improvement of relations with France, isolation of West Germany, and rapprochement between Communist and Socialist parties. Ulbricht wanted to appeal to the SPD voters over the heads of their leaders. In February 1966, therefore, the SED, with Soviet approval and probably at Soviet encouragement, published an "open letter" to all SPD members proposing a dialogue between the two parties, presumably in the expectation that the SPD leadership would reject the overture and the SED would thereby profit with the left-wing SPD rank and file.

Wehner, reversing his previous position, accepted the SED proposal and thus seized the initiative. The SPD proposed freedom of speech in both German states and as a minimum a detailed dialogue proposal. The SED then proposed two debates, which the SPD immediately accepted and at which it designated its three top leaders to speak. Thereupon the SED delayed until the SPD Dortmund Party Congress. However, it did publish the exchange of correspondence. West German opinion supported the SPD's acceptance but SED party cadres objected that the proposal was unsettling to the East German population. The SPD Dortmund Party Congress was a victory for the leadership. Its proposals for a "qualified, regulated coexistence (*Nebenein-*

ander) limited in time" with the DDR, below the level of de jure recognition but on the basis of international agreements, full diplomatic recognition of the Eastern European states, and readiness to accept sacrifices in the border question did not fulfill Ulbricht's hopes. They did, however, foreshadow the Grand Coalition's Ostpolitik, the Brandt-Scheel Ostpolitik, and the 1970–1973 treaties. Finally, using the pretexts of the passage by the Bundestag of a law granting exemption from prosecution to SED speakers, plus the refusal of the SPD to condemn the United States in Vietnam and to recognize the existence of two German states, the SED called off the debate.[33]

This episode showed that one assumption of the SPD Ostpolitik was correct: *Wandel durch Annäherung* helped the SPD in West and East Germany. After the episode the SPD and the FDP continued to move toward a more flexible Ostpolitik. The SPD intensified its policy of *Wandel durch Annäherung* and gained more support for it in West German public opinion, thus making its adoption by the CDU in the Grand Coalition more likely. Moreover, after the exchange of speakers project collapsed, the Soviet ambassador to the DDR, Abrassimov, for the first time held a series of meetings with Brandt, in which he indicated Soviet interest in Brandt's "small steps" policy.[34]

The Erhard period also saw West German public opinion swing toward the new Ostpolitik, led by the two churches. In October 1965, the Committee for Public Responsibilities of the Evangelical Church declared that Poles as well as German expellees had suffered wrongs, the twenty years of Polish settlement east of the Oder-Neisse line could not morally be brushed aside in favor of the expellees' "right to their homeland" *(Heimatrecht)* but, rather, two rights were in conflict, and Bonn should begin to prepare West Germans for the inevitable sacrifices that peace and reconciliation would demand. In spite of expellee protests, the Evangelical Church did not disown the memorandum and the controversy about it increased Protestant CDU support for the new Ostpolitik.[35]

In December 1965, the West German Catholic hierarchy published their reply to the letter sent them by the Polish hierarchy at the Second Vatican Council. Although not as conciliatory as the Evangelical memorandum, in part because it was more official, it also supported the new Ostpolitik and thus increased support for it in Catholic CDU/CSU circles.[36] West German elite and mass public opinion, particularly in the SPD and among influential left-wing intellectuals and media public opinion leaders, moved in general in favor of a more flexible Ostpolitik.[37] The CDU and even more the CSU, on the other hand, maintained their old perceptions, rejected any upgrading of the DDR, and continued to insist on maintaining Bonn's claim to speak for all of Germany. However, the SPD became more specific and united in its desire for movement but the CDU became more divided and uncertain.

Elite and mass opinion, although supporting reunification and more willing to sacrifice for it, was less optimistic about its chances and even less about regaining the territories east of the Oder-Neisse line. Except for the organized expellees, it supported a more flexible Ostpolitik, including contacts with the DDR, and even before the invasion of Czechoslovakia a large majority saw the SPD best able to carry it out.[38]

The "Peace Note"
The most important formal expression of Schröder's new Ostpolitik was the "peace note" of March 25, 1966. It was a compromise document, since by early 1966 the Erhard government was already torn by the chancellor's weakness and the Schröder-Strauss feud, more a summing up of Bonn's policy rather than a bold new initiative, and in considerable part a reaction to Western pressure and in the hope of influencing Eastern Europe. But it did move Bonn's policy forward in the direction of Schröder's Ostpolitik. Moreover, it had been shown in draft to the SPD, which basically endorsed it, although it would have gone further. It marked a further development toward improving relations with Eastern Europe, especially with Czechoslovakia, and acceptance of détente and some arms control measures not conditional on progress toward reunification. It included the first formal Bonn declaration that the Munich agreement had been torn

up by Hitler and was therefore no longer valid and that Bonn made no territorial claims on Czechoslovakia. It expressed the desire to improve relations with Warsaw. Its statement that Germany would have to make sacrifices in the peace treaty was counterbalanced, however, by the repetition of Bonn's traditional refusal to recognize the Oder-Neisse line. In a passage added in cabinet discussion, under expellee pressure, to the Foreign Office draft, it reiterated the validity of the 1937 boundaries; and it quoted from the most violent anti-West German statements made by Moscow. With respect to arms control, it proposed that other nations should agree, as Bonn had in 1954, not to produce nuclear weapons and that atomic powers should refuse to proliferate; but it left open the question of Bonn's participation in Western European or Atlantic nuclear forces. It also proposed mutual exchanges of observers at military maneuvers, scaling down of atomic weapons in Europe, stricter International Atomic Energy Authority (IAEA) control of nuclear materials, and—the most important point for the future—exchange of nonuse of force declarations with the Communist powers. (Previous proposals in Bonn for this had always been blocked by the argument that they would mean de facto recognition of the Eastern European states.) The note did not mention East Germany at all, reflecting Bonn's continuing policy of isolating it. The responses to it by Moscow, Warsaw, and Prague were hostile, centering on Bonn's refusal to recognize the Oder-Neisse line and the DDR, but less so by Belgrade and Budapest; and there were no responses by Bucharest or Sofia.[39]

The Soviet Response

Soviet response to Schröder's Ostpolitik is difficult to analyze because Khrushchev's German policy in the last two years of his rule showed considerable ambivalence. Initially—and incorrectly—Khrushchev probably thought Erhard more pragmatic than Adenauer; but in fact Erhard's indecisiveness made him less so, as Khrushchev soon realized.[40] Ulbricht saw from the first that Schröder wanted to isolate the DDR. Khrushchev preferred bilateral negotiations with Washington, directed primarily against the MLF, at Bonn's expense, and negotiations with Paris to disrupt the Franco-West German entente; but he at least toyed with improving Moscow-Bonn relations in order to check the growth of West German power, prevent its access to nuclear weapons, lower West German and American conventional military power, and improve Soviet-West German commercial relations. (Khrushchev hardly intended to decrease Soviet influence in East Germany but rather to consolidate Germany's partition.) On December 31, 1963, Khrushchev proposed to Erhard negotiations for nonuse of force in border conflicts. When Erhard rejected them, Moscow signed a new treaty of alliance and friendship with the DDR that, although it reserved Soviet four-power obligations, specifically referred to West Berlin as a "separate political unit." Moscow also blocked a Bonn-Prague agreement on trade missions.[41]

Toward the end of his rule and against some opposition in Moscow, Khrushchev planned a personal initiative toward rapprochement with Bonn: a meeting there with Chancellor Erhard. His major aims were probably to increase Soviet-West German trade and to stop the MLF. Then signs of opposition to Khrushchev's move began to appear. A March 7, 1964, TASS declared against the MLF was much sharper than previous ones. The economic counselor of the West German embassy in Moscow was expelled, with no reason given, ten days thereafter. In late July Khrushchev's son-in-law, Adzhubei, visited the Federal Republic, stressed the Chinese danger to both countries, and made clear Khrushchev's desire to visit Bonn, as was announced by the federal government on September 3. On September 6, a mustard gas attack on a West German technician at Zagorsk (perhaps organized by Khrushchev's opponents) caused Erhard to delay the visit. *Pravda* then attacked West Germany and in early October Brezhnev and Suslov, who presumably organized the conspiracy against Khrushchev, praised the DDR. Khrushchev's fall shortly thereafter ended this curious episode.[42] The immediately following first Chinese atomic explosion probably intensified

Brezhnev's inclination to harden the line against Bonn, although not against the other Western powers, whom he wanted to split from the Federal Republic.

The Brezhnev-Kosygin leadership was more repressive at home and more cautious abroad. Its hostility to the U.S. military engagement in Vietnam and to the Ostpolitik of Schröder and the Grand Coalition and its concern with liberalization in Czechoslovakia, rising Chinese hostility during the Cultural Revolution, and Ulbricht's and Gomułka's hard-line pressure on it, intensified its hard line toward Bonn.[43]

The "Policy of Movement": A Balance Sheet
Schröder's Ostpolitik, although it made some progress in Eastern Europe and decreased Bonn's isolation from the West, did not and could not reach its main objectives, for three reasons. It overestimated potential Eastern European freedom of maneuver. By excluding the Soviet Union and the DDR, it prevented their Eastern European allies from moving toward Bonn. Third, by refusing to recognize the Oder-Neisse line, it prevented any real progress with Poland. Yet it is hard to see how Schröder could have gone much farther without SPD participation in the coalition. Even so, he did break the ice with Eastern Europe and modified the CDU/CSU position, thereby making easier the Grand Coalition's task.

The Grand Coalition (CDU-SPD)

Chancelor Erhard was forced to resign in late 1966 for primarily domestic reasons: economic recession and decline in CDU votes in state elections, both blamed on his indecisiveness. Some, but relatively minor, foreign policy issues were also involved: Bonn's difficulties with Washington about American demands for more German troop cost compensation, plus Washington's priority to arms control agreements with the Soviet Union, especially a nonproliferation treaty, and over German participation, even if multilateral (MLF), in nuclear weapons.[1] The CDU also resented President Johnson's October 7, 1966 speech, an important declaratory change in U.S. policy, which stated that reunification could only be the end result of, not the precondition for, East-West détente.[2] But this change, then still opposed by some in the State Department, was overshadowed by Johnson's increased involvement in the Vietnam War. Johnson's assumption, in my view never correct, that he needed and could get Soviet help to end the Vietnam War, made him give more priority to détente with Moscow and less to Western Europe. (The SPD, by then, favored U.S. arms control initiatives and priority for East-West détente.)[3] The CDU/CSU inflexible conservatives also feared that Franco-German tension would result from the worsening of relations between Washington and Paris after de Gaulle's 1966 withdrawal from the NATO integrated command and from his attempted French-led "European" détente. They blamed this danger on Erhard's allegedly anti-French (because pro–United States) policies. Thus the fear that Washington and Paris were less reliable allies mobilized Erhard's supporters and opponents against him.[4]

After a CDU attempt at coalition with the FDP failed, the Grand Coalition (CDU-SPD) was formed.[5] The Baden-Würtemberg minister-president, Kurt Georg Kiesinger, a polished Catholic Suabian orator, became chancellor. Strauss, who had reconsolidated his power in the CSU, became minister of finance; Schröder, minister of defense; Brandt, who had been initially opposed to a Grand Coalition, foreign minister; and Wehner, minister for all-German affairs (that is, for dealings with

East Germany). The Grand Coalition reflected in part a widespread feeling in both major parties that the Federal Republic was confronted with problems so serious and opportunities so great that all political forces must concentrate to solve them. It also marked the victory of Wehner's policy of SPD participation in the government.

Ostpolitik and Western Allies[6]

In theory the Grand Coalition's Ostpolitik aligned Bonn's Eastern policy more closely with those of its Western allies. However, the alignment was not yet complete and with respect to France perhaps less so than before. The Western powers' priority for East-West détente was inevitably greater than Bonn's, for the United States, Great Britain, and France were saturated status quo powers, while the Federal Republic was not. For West Germany, therefore, détente was either not necessarily good in itself or as for much of the CDU/CSU, good and bad; but it could only be good insofar as it offered an opportunity—indeed, as its proponents declared, the only opportunity—to change the status quo in Central Europe to Bonn's benefit, if not territorially, then by liberalizing, and having more contacts with, East Germany.

Britain had always been for East-West détente. The United States was increasingly so. The French attitude was different, more complex, and more difficult for Bonn to deal with. Relations between de Gaulle and Bonn had improved somewhat after Kiesinger became chancellor, for this had been part of the CDU price for entering the Grand Coalition. Formally de Gaulle maintained the French adamancy toward any concessions to Moscow that he had demonstrated during the second Berlin crisis. But in reality, as Bonn realized, his policy became one of armed neutrality in order to assure French predominance in Europe before West Germany became strong enough to prevent it, guaranteed by the continued division of Germany, the balance between Bonn and Moscow, further Eastern European autonomy from the USSR, and eventual U.S. withdrawal from Europe. Only thereafter was de Gaulle prepared to permit the gradual reunification of a nonnuclear Germany, no longer occupied but supervised by the four occupation powers and therefore inferior to France.[7] This any Bonn government had to reject, for it would deprive West Germany of U.S. nuclear and troop protection, its equal status with its Western European allies, and its goal of Western European unity. Conversely, after Bonn abandoned its demand that reunification or progress toward it be a prerequisite for détente, its exposed military situation made it, like the United States, support arms control with the East. But de Gaulle was interested only in confirming permanent West German military inferiority to France, which the *force de frappe* and West Germany's nonnuclear status guaranteed. Therefore he rejected all arms control proposals and maintained solidarity with the other Western powers only on issues involving West Berlin, where Bonn still needed him to block Washington's making concessions to the Soviets.[8]

Ostpolitik: Concepts and Contents

The Grand Coalition's foreign policy was a compromise. The CDU/CSU and SPD agreed on a more independent foreign policy, less dependent on Washington, less hostile to Paris, and more active toward the East.[9] The inflexible conservatives got higher priority for relations with de Gaulle; but since by then he was also pushing détente with the East, they could oppose it less. Johnson's October 1966 advocacy of peaceful engagement, supported by the CDU flexible Atlanticists and the SPD, also favored West German rapprochement toward Eastern Europe. The SPD, much more united on its Ostpolitik than the CDU/CSU, therefore successfully insisted on *Wandel durch Annäherung* with East Germany, in return for agreeing to improve relations with Paris.[10]

The two basic new concepts of the Grand Coalition's Ostpolitik were that reunification could come only after and as a result of détente. As Kiesinger put it,

A reunified Germany has a critical size. It is too big to play no role in the balance of power and too small to hold in balance the powers around it. It is therefore very difficult to see how a reunited Germany could join one side or another, given the continuation of the present European political structure. Therefore one can only envisage the growing together of the separated parts of Germany as being an organic part of the overcoming of the East-West conflict in Europe.[11]

Progress should come generally in East-West détente and move toward a European security system, in which West Germany's neighbors (particularly the Eastern European states) would accept a gradual rapprochement between the two German states, and specifically in improvement of conditions of life in the DDR through high-level contacts with the DDR government.

Brandt's and the SPD's views went farther. His European security system proposal included mutual renunciation of use of force, renewed West German renunciation of national atomic armament, balanced force reductions and other confidence-building arms control measures, Soviet and U.S. participation in it, and the continuation of NATO and the Warsaw Pact. However, he also saw as possible, and according to one controversial report Bahr in theory preferred, their replacement by an all European security system. Either would eventually lead to a European peace structure (*Friedensordnung*) in which the partition of Europe and Germany would be overcome.[12]

Brandt's views foreshadowed in considerable part the events of the early 1970s. They were a compromise between the SPD's pre-1959 advocacy of a European collective security system and Adenauer's Western orientation. They tried to reconcile a more independent and forward West German policy with maintenance of the primary alliance with the United States, good relations with France, and détente with the Soviet Union and Eastern Europe.

The Grand Coalition therefore abandoned any attempt to isolate East Germany for "regulated coexistence" (*geregeltes Nebeneinander*): contacts and cooperation with the DDR at all levels below diplomatic recognition (Bonn still maintained its claim to *Alleinvertretungsrecht*,[13] including willingness, contrary to Erhard, to include the DDR in renunciation of use of force agreements, and a positive attitude toward East-West détente in principle), and abandonment of the previous insistence on progress on German reunification as a precondition for détente. The Grand Coalition also abandoned any conscious effort to play Eastern European states against the Soviet Union and made clear to Moscow that it would not try to profit from the Sino-Soviet conflict. (Even so, it underestimated the DDR's influence in Moscow and its resumption of diplomatic relations with Rumania was seen as hostile by the Soviet Union.)[14] Otherwise the Grand Coalition intensified Schröder's Eastern policy: strong support for East-West détente, including arms control measures before, and as the best means toward, reunification: emphasis on humanization of conditions in East Germany, with reunification only the eventual goal; modification of the Hallstein Doctrine to permit full diplomatic relations with the Eastern European states;[15] declaring the Munich agreement "no longer valid;" and stress on Bonn's desire for good relations with the Soviet Union and insistence that the new Ostpolitik was not intended to split Moscow from Eastern Europe or to isolate East Germany. (In fact, however, it tried to put pressure on Moscow via Eastern Europe more than to negotiate with it.) By summer 1968, Bonn also advocated a European security system, based upon the continuation of NATO and the Warsaw Pact and including mutual troop and nuclear stockpile reductions and exchanges of observation missions and nonuse of force declarations.[16] But the Grand Coalition really had not one but two Eastern policies, CDU/CSU and SPD. Unable, therefore, to advocate either confrontation or compromise, it ended up intensifying, not decisively changing, Schröder's policies.

The Grand Coalition's intensified drive for diplomatic relations with Eastern Europe was coupled with an attempt greatly to increase West German trade with and credits to Eastern Europe, with two aims. The less important was to improve the Federal Republic's export trade and thus help overcome an economic recession. The adoption, at SPD insistence, of the new SPD Economics Minister Schiller's neo-Keynesian countercyclical economic policy made additional credits available for German export trade, including to Eastern Europe. (The combination of countercyclical economic policies with export of manufactured goods and credits to Eastern Europe may have been reminiscent, at least to the Soviets, of Dr. Schacht's similar policies in the 1930s; but the analogy did not hold, because post-1945 German economic penetration was so diluted by Italian trade with Eastern Europe that anything like the German monopoly position of the 1930s is impossible. In any case, Soviet political military power remained predominant in the area.) The primary aim was to increase West German political influence in Eastern Europe, further its greater freedom of maneuver vis-à-vis Moscow and East Berlin, and eventually convince the Soviets to moderate East German policies.

The Grand Coalition's Ostpolitik thus gave tactical priority for détente over reunification in order to use détente to work toward liberalization and eventual reunification of East Germany with the Federal Republic. (As a minimum, the CDU wanted East Germany to be transformed into something like Austria, while the SPD would have been satisfied with something like Yugoslavia.) It hoped to persuade Eastern European governments and Soviet and East German counterelites, in an active contest with Ulbricht, to liberalize and increase contacts with East Germany, by means of a carefully regulated combination of inducements and pressures leading to controlled, limited movement, enough to make progress but not enough to bring effective Soviet action against it.[17]

The SPD went farther than the CDU toward recognition of the Oder-Neisse line,[18] modification of the Hallstein Doctrine, arms control proposals, and movement toward de facto recognition of East Germany.[19] The CDU/CSU inflexible conservatives were hostile to these and Schröder and Kiesinger favored them less and less. The basic difference on the German question remained the same as before the Grand Coalition. The SPD gave priority to improvement of relations with East Germany as well as with the Soviet Union and believed that considerable progress could be made in this respect.[20] (Brandt and Bahr were much influenced by their experiences in Berlin, particularly by the wall and the negotiations with the DDR for easing travel.) The CDU flexible Atlanticists were pessimistic about progress with

Moscow or East Berlin, although committed to letting Brandt and Wehner try and giving priority to improvement of relations with Eastern Europe. The result was that the Grand Coalition postponed the crucial issues, in particular recognition of the status quo, in favor of concentrating on improving the atmosphere and progress on peripheral problems.[21] It is not surprising, therefore, that it was not very successful.

Ostpolitik: Tactics

Kiesinger made clear that the Grand Coalition would press Ulbricht on specific points for more contacts and stated that Bonn was prepared to negotiate with East Berlin, at all levels up to that of heads of government, with respect to increased inter-German trade, larger west German credits to East Germany, joint economic ventures, freer and more extensive travel, cultural exchange, exchange of newspapers, and so forth, but not to negotiate on de jure recognition of the DDR. Under pressure from the SPD Kiesinger replied to a May 11, 1967, letter from DDR Premier Stoph—the first time Bonn had ever done so—but East Berlin rejected the reply because it did not accept all the DDR's demands.[22] Later Bonn specifically proposed to include the area of East Germany in exchanges of declarations renouncing the use of force. Bonn's terminology with respect to the DDR became less negative and the Hallstein Doctrine was modified to mean "freezing," not breaking off, relations with third states that recognized the DDR.[23]

The SPD and the CDU continued to quarrel over how far Bonn should go toward recognition of East Germany. Brandt and especially Wehner went verbally much farther than Kiesinger and the CDU/CSU in this respect.[24] In October 1967 Kiesinger attacked the "recognition party" (*Anerkennungspartei*), that is, leftist tendencies toward recognition of East Germany.[25] The West German left wing continued its advocacy of an intensified Ostpolitik, and many of them pushed for the de facto and even de jure recognition of East Berlin.[26]

Significant for the extent to which de facto recognition of the DDR was increasingly accepted as a probable if unpleasant necessity in order to bring détente with East Germany was the publication at the end of 1967 by Wilhelm Wolfgang Schütz, head of the interparty, government-financed *Kuratorium Unteilbares Deutschland*, of a *Deutschland Memorandum* that systematized what the SPD had been moving toward. He declared that Bonn did not, because it could not, represent East Germans, that the two German states composed a "community" and that therefore one could not be considered as foreign territory by the other, that the question of diplomatic recognition thus did not arise, but that Bonn should intensify economic and cultural and even establish consular relations with East Berlin in order to improve the conditions of life of the East Germans and to bring East Germany into the "responsibilities of the world of states." This memorandum unleashed an extensive public discussion; but Schütz, who maintained his arguments, kept his office.[27] In March 1968, the Evangelical Committee for Public Responsibility[28] and a Catholic discussion group, the Bensberger Kreis,[29] renewed their support for reconciliation with Eastern Europe and, with respect thereto, improvement of relations with East Germany.

In 1967–1968, before the Soviet invasion of Czechoslovakia, a group of West German parliamentarians and academics drafted a reappraisal of West German policy toward the East that foreshadowed many of the elements in the subsequent Brandt-Scheel Ostpolitik. It declared that the previous policy of hope for reunification without any clear basis was counterproductive and misled the citizens of the Federal Republic. It called for a modus vivendi between Bonn and East Berlin and a plebiscite about reunification after twenty years. But it came close to endorsing the status quo, for it declared that there could be no solution of the German question that changed the balance of forces significantly between East and West, that did not guarantee the integrity of Poland and Czechoslovakia, that would again make Germany more powerful than its neighbors, and that did not involve West German cooperation with the DDR.[30]

The Nonproliferation Treaty

During the whole period of the Grand Coalition the question of

Bonn's accession to the nonproliferation treaty was a major issue within the coalition and within the CDU/CSU. The German Gaullists in the CDU and all of the CSU opposed it, or at least demanded its revision before accession, while the flexible Atlanticists in the CDU and the SPD and all the flexible leftists favored it. Officially the Grand Coalition favored ratification in principle, but it was incapable of ratifying it in practice.

All parties were concerned lest the treaty forbid West German progress in peaceful utilization of atomic energy. All wanted to prevent it from forbidding Bonn's participation in NATO nuclear planning. All wanted to avoid any damage by the treaty to EURATOM (the EEC joint atomic agency). All wanted to avoid threats by nuclear powers against nonnuclear powers. All wanted it to lead to further progress toward disarmament. In addition, the CDU/CSU demanded that the "European option" (of a Western European nuclear force) be kept open, so that the treaty would not permanently confine Western Europe to the secondary position it then had. During long negotiations all these concerns were largely, if not entirely, satisfied by U.S. clarifications and unilateral declarations.

Behind these concerns lay serious differences between the CDU/CSU and SPD. The former gave priority to preventing the treaty from further accentuating the U.S. tendency toward bilateralism with the Soviet Union and wanted to use "clarifications" to it in order to push Washington back toward closer relationships with its alliance partners. The latter viewed the treaty positively, as a necessary precondition for détente with the Soviet Union and its Eastern European allies, along with renunciation of use of force and troop reduction in Central Europe. This basic difference, which foreshadowed the later struggle over the German treaties, when added to the Soviet invasion of Czechoslovakia and the increasing tensions within the Grand Coalition, forced the postponement of Bonn signing the treaty, which only took place after the Brandt-Scheel government came to power in 1969.[31] However, Brandt's negotiating strategy of trying to cooperate with Washington rather than defying it and

of close cooperation with the other nonnuclear powers successfully avoided most of the strains in Bonn-Washington relations
that the test-ban treaty had produced.

West German Trade Policy

The Grand Coalition wanted even more than the Erhard government to use expansion of West German trade to further its
Ostpolitik. However, Soviet and Eastern European opposition
prevented it from having much success. It actively tried to get a
new Soviet-West German trade treaty, the negotiations for
which had broken down, as we have seen, over the "Berlin
clause" at the end of the Erhard government. But it continued
to insist on the Berlin clause being included and it was not willing to grant the Soviets long-term credits. Moscow, on the other
hand, became more negative because of its opposition to the
resumption of diplomatic relations between Bonn and Bucharest, the continuing rise in West German-Rumanian trade, and
the anti-Ostpolitik pressure of Ulbricht and Gomulka. The Soviets were aware that Bonn was trying to use trade as a means of
expanding its influence in Eastern Europe without recognizing,
as Moscow demanded, the Oder-Neisse line and the DDR and
were thus the more determined not to conclude a trade treaty
with Bonn. Even so, Soviet desire for trade with West Germany
was so great that while publicly refusing to increase it, privately
Moscow encouraged its rise.

With respect to the DDR, the Grand Coalition actively pursued a policy of expanding trade. This was particularly favored
by the SPD, which viewed it as a means for, and a symbol of,
the abandonment of Schröder's policy of the isolation of East
Germany. The Grand Coalition for the first time offered the
DDR long-term credits for interzonal trade. However, while this
increased West German exports to East Germany, it also resulted in massive East German trade deficits with the Federal
Republic, so that in 1967 interzonal trade actually declined. In
December 1968, however, after the Soviet invasion of Czechoslovakia, a new interzonal trade agreement was signed providing
for its expansion and for further West German incentives for it.

The Grand Coalition also intensified Schröder's policy of

actively pushing the expansion of trade with Eastern Europe. This was particularly true with Rumania and Czechoslovakia. By mid-1967, West German credits to Rumania had reached DM 2.2 billion. A mid-1967 agreement with Prague provided for the opening there of a West German trade mission. Thereafter, particularly when the 1968 Prague spring began, Bonn indicated its readiness to aid in the reorientation of Czechoslovak foreign trade to the West. (As I set forth below, however, I regard as unfounded the Soviet statements that their intervention was primarily or even seriously motivated by fear of Prague reorienting itself toward Bonn.)[32]

Soviet Reaction to Ostpolitik

Soviet counterstrategy against the Grand Coalition's Ostpolitik was an intensified version of its strategy against Schröder's Ostpolitik and of its whole post-1955 policy toward Bonn.[33] Bonn, Moscow declared, must recognize the Oder-Neisse line; recognize East Germany de jure and thereby abandon its *Alleinvertretungsanspruch*, its claim for self-determination for the East Germans, and its use of economic pressure to prevent other states from recognizing East Germany; recognize that West Berlin is de jure a separate political entity with respect to which Bonn has no rights whatsoever; recognize the 1938 Munich agreement as having been invalid *ab initio*; and formally forswear vis-à-vis Moscow any kind of access to nuclear weapons by signing the nonproliferation treaty without reservations. In short, Moscow demanded, Bonn should formally recognize the status quo and contribute toward stabilizing and upgrading East Germany.[34]

Initially Moscow's attitude toward the Grand Coalition's Ostpolitik was not as totally hostile as Ulbricht's and Gomułka's, because the Soviets hoped that they might gain from it an upgrading of East Germany, move Bonn toward Paris and thus weaken its alliance with Washington. Totally opposing it, Moscow felt, would create difficulties for the Soviets with France, drive West Germany away from France and closer to the United States, and make a common position with the Eastern European states toward it more difficult. But Bonn's rapid if somewhat reluctant establishment of relations with Bucharest, which wanted to confront Moscow and its allies with a *fait accompli* before they could coordinate their opposition to its policies, plus East German and Polish pressure in Moscow against Czechoslovak and Hungarian desires to resume relations with Bonn even before it recognized the DDR, contributed to a rapid stiffening of Soviet policy lest there be an Eastern European push to Bonn. (The same was true of its resumption of relations with Belgrade—without Bonn's immediate payment of reparations. In this respect Bonn's successes with Bucharest and Belgrade were somewhat pyrrhic, for they made successes elsewhere more difficult.) In a January 13, 1967, speech at Gorki, Brezhnev shifted to a harder line toward Bonn, although he still did not go as far as Ulbricht did. A Soviet note of January 19, 1967, echoed the stronger line. By March 1967, at a series of meetings with Eastern European leaders, Moscow had made clear that they could not follow Rumania's example but must delay and demand that Bonn accept the above five preconditions for diplomatic recognition, set forth publicly in detail first in the July 1966 Bucharest Warsaw Pact Political Committee meeting[35] and maintained thereafter, notably at the February 1967 Warsaw conference and the April 1967 Karlový Varý Conference, at which, however, Moscow finally almost adopted Ulbricht's hard line. (Brezhnev did not demand that Bonn recognize the DDR de jure and kept the door slightly open to Bonn.)[36]

Moscow maintained that the Grand Coalition's Ostpolitik reflected only a change in West German tactics but that Bonn's goal, the revision of the post-1945 status quo in Europe in its favor, remained unchanged. The Soviets therefore tried to make the new Ostpolitik confirm rather than threaten the status quo, especially with respect to East Germany. From its own perspective Moscow had a point. Although the Grand Coalition's Ostpolitik was intended to contribute not only toward adjusting Bonn's foreign policy to East-West détente and improving of relations with Moscow and the Eastern European states, its long-range purpose was to utilize West German economic, technological, and financial power, along with the interest of some Eastern European states and of the majority of the Eastern European populations, to push for greater national independence, economic development, and internal liberalization. The SPD thus wanted to change the status quo in East Germany contrary to the wishes of East Berlin—and the CDU/CSU wanted to change it contrary to Moscow's as well. So long as Moscow, Warsaw, and East Berlin were determined to prevent this, the Grand Coalition's new Ostpolitik, no matter what its proponents intended, was thus directed against Moscow's, Warsaw's, and East Berlin's perceived interests and could therefore only be viewed by them as hostile and as an attempt to ally with their opponents in Bucharest, Belgrade, and Prague against them.[37]

Bonn therefore could not, at least in the short run, simultaneously improve its relations with Moscow and its Eastern European allies and also with those Eastern European states whom Moscow saw as its opponents. Because Bonn would not do the former, since it considered the Soviet price too high, as its attempts to feel out Moscow and East Berlin made clear, it could only do the latter.[38]

It was thus not surprising that Soviet reaction toward the Grand Coalition's Ostpolitik became more hostile. Moscow could no longer either hope to isolate Bonn from the West, a prospect the new Ostpolitik prevented, or to move Bonn away from NATO. Bucharest's reestablishment of diplomatic relations with Bonn, plus the expressed interest to do the same by Budapest, Sofia, Belgrade, and Prague, showed the destabilizing effect of the new Ostpolitik on Warsaw Pact and international communist cohesion. Soviet strategy therefore reverted to its minimum objective: to lessen the impact of the new Ostpolitik on East Germany and Eastern Europe. This more hostile Soviet attitude was also furthered by a general hardening of Soviet foreign policy toward the West, reflecting the rapid Soviet strategic arms buildup vis-à-vis the United States and the growth of Soviet worldwide intervention capability, of Soviet naval power in the Mediterranean, and of Soviet political and military presence in the Middle East. Moreover, the rush forward of liberalization in Czechoslovakia, where the June 1967 Writers Congress marked the first public organization forum in which dissent was publicly expressed, intensified Soviet hostility to Ostpolitik. Indeed, the parallel (although unrelated) course of Bonn's new Ostpolitik and of Czechoslovak liberalization was probably a major factor in the Soviet decision to move against both.

The Soviets therefore retreated from their maximum objective, isolating Bonn or changing its policies and lowering U.S. influence in Western Europe, to their minimal one, reestablishing their control over and conformity within Eastern Europe. This was reflected in the Warsaw Pact's July 1966 Bucharest European security proposals, Moscow's increasing hostility, and that of Ulbricht and Gomuľka, to the Grand Coalition's Ostpolitik, and their attempts to contain liberalization in Czechoslovakia.[39] Rising Soviet hostility to the new Ostpolitik was reflected in rising Soviet, East German, and Polish propaganda attacks on it. It was specifically and accurately registered in the prolonged and (until July 1968, when the Soviet and thereupon the West Germans published their exchanges of notes) secret diplomatic exchanges between Bonn and Moscow on mutual renunciation of the use of force.[40]

Schröder's 1966 "peace note" had first proposed mutual renunciation of use of force declarations, but it had been ambiguous as to whether Bonn would exchange such a declaration with East Berlin and was therefore seen in Moscow and East Berlin as continuing Bonn's anti-DDR policy. Kiesinger's December 1966 government declaration, Bonn's February 7, 1967, draft (without any preconditions), and his correspondence between May and September 1967 with East German Premier Stoph specifically but still somewhat ambiguously also proposed this with respect to East Germany, that is, without, because of CDU/CSU opposition, indicating any willingness for direct negotiations with East Berlin. (Not surprisingly, this exchange got nowhere.) The first (then unpublished) Soviet reply to Bonn's "peace note," on October 12, 1967, insisted that before an exchange of such declarations with Moscow Bonn must exchange them with East Berlin in the same form as with the other Eastern European countries. A further (then unpublished) Soviet note of

November 21, 1967, commenting on the February 7, 1967, draft declaration, escalated Soviet demands by insisting that Bonn prohibit nazism, militarism, and agitation for territorial revisionism and by declaring that the rights of the Soviet Union according to the Potsdam Agreement and Articles 53 and 107 of the United Nations Charter remained valid and included the right to intervene in the Federal Republic to ensure the prohibition of these activities. A further (also unpublished) Soviet note of December 8, 1967, to the three Western powers charged that the Federal Republic was secretly rearming and planned to acquire nuclear weapons.[41] The further Soviet hardening probably reflected East German and Polish pressure, spiraling liberalization in Prague, and the imminent resumption by Bonn of diplomatic relations with Belgrade.[42]

Probably not coincidentally, the January 1968 replacement of Novotný by Dubček in Prague was immediately followed by a Soviet *aide-mémoire* to Bonn, a demarche by Soviet Ambassador to East Berlin Abrassimov to West Berlin Mayor Schütz, and a Soviet note to the three Western powers demanding a reduction in Bonn's presence in West Berlin. In March and April, the Soviets allowed the DDR to resume harassment of West German travel to West Berlin, only to have Abrassimov then invite Brandt to meet him in East Berlin.[43] The invitation was probably designed to deter Bonn from pressing Ostpolitik.

Meanwhile, two days before the resumption of Bonn-Belgrade relations, a new Soviet memorandum to Bonn on January 29 had included a new demand, that Bonn renounce its "illegal claims" on West Berlin, and had reiterated that Bonn must exchange renunciation of use of force declarations binding in international law with the DDR as well as with other Eastern European states, and thus recognize the DDR de jure. Brandt got the CDU to agree, provided that it not involve de jure recognition—to just what Brezhnev, Ulbricht, and Gomuka were determined to get.[44]

The (unpublished) conciliatory West German reply of April 9, 1968, proposed the exchange of renunciation of force declarations as a point of departure for reduction of atomic weapons and exchange of maneuver observers. Yet it fell short of de jure recognition of the DDR, for although it proposed to negotiate these declarations with every member state of the Warsaw Pact (including the DDR), it also proposed talks "with the other part of Germany about binding renunciation of force as a step towards detente and rapprochement between the two parts of Germany, which do not regard each other as foreign countries.[45] It reiterated the Oder-Neisse formulation of the December 13, 1966, Grand Coalition government declaration, that is, it still rejected de jure recognition of the DDR. The reply was amplified by Brandt's statement on June 24, 1968, to the Reykjavik NATO Ministerial Council meeting that East Germany could not be regarded as a sovereign state and four-power responsibility for Berlin and for self-determination for all of Germany remained in effect. He reiterated his proposal for mutual renunciation of use of force with East Berlin and added to it a renunciation of "any attempt to alter by force the social structure in the other part of Germany.[46]"

The Reykjavik meeting also agreed to propose mutual balanced force reduction (MBFR) negotiations to the Soviets. This proposal was an integral part of Brandt's Ostpolitik. He felt that it would contribute to détente in general and in Central Europe in particular, to allaying Soviet fears of the rising power of the Bundeswehr, and to helping forestall unilateral American troop reductions on the Central European front.[47]

But Moscow's line continued to harden, as the April 1968 Communist Party of the Soviet Union (CPSU) Central Committee plenum demonstrated, along with the flood of liberalization in Prague, where that same month the revisionist "action program" was published. The final Soviet document in the exchange of July 5, 1968, was the most extreme of all. It accused Bonn of being anti-DDR, refusing to recognize the Oder-Neisse line, endorsing the Munich agreement by refusing to declare it invalid *ab initio*, trying to annex West Berlin, and defending and furthering neonazism; and it reiterated the Soviet right to intervene in West Germany.[48] The Soviet publication of its notes on July

11 made clear that the new Ostpolitik had worsened relations with Moscow.[49]

Yet Soviet hardening was not total, as differences between Soviet and East German formulations had shown. In addition at an April 1968 Moscow "scientific conference" of specialists on Germany from the USSR, Poland, Czechoslovakia, Hungary, and the DDR, although most speeches were strongly anti-West German, one, by the leading Soviet German specialist D. E. Melnikov, was more differentiated. He stressed that although both Atlanticists like Schröder and Europeans like Strauss were strongly anti-Soviet, the SPD had become more moderate and thus implied that it might become more so. At the end, N. N. Inonezemtsev, a leading Soviet expert on international affairs, although he took a hard line, echoed Melnikov's qualification as well. Moreover, Abrassimov told Brandt in June 1968 that the Soviet Union wanted the Berlin situation to remain quiet.[50] Moscow and East Berlin thus retreated from détente on the German question as Bonn moved toward it.

SPD Ostpolitik

Brandt's ideas about Berlin went farther in private than in public. They influenced the Grand Coalition's Ostpolitik and even more the SPD's. Basically defensive, as Western and West German policy toward exposed West Berlin had to be, they were directed against the Soviet and East German moves to cut back, and if possible to terminate, such symbols of Bonn's rejection of the partition of Germany and Berlin and of relations with the DDR as the meetings in West Berlin of the Bundestag and its committees and the election there of the federal president. Already in 1965 the DDR had claimed the right to screen West German Bundestag members traveling to West Berlin for Bundestag meetings, a claim they had circumvented by flying into the city. In March, the DDR prohibited West German "neo-Nazis," and in April all West German ministers, from traveling to West Berlin. In June, East Berlin instituted visas for visitors from West Germany and West Berlin to East Germany and raised the compulsory daily currency exchange quotas for them.

Moscow and East Berlin were thus working toward a "status

quo minus" within East Berlin, in part probably as a reply to the Grand Coalition's Ostpolitik. The Federal Republic, the United States, Great Britain, and France at the June 1968 Reykjavik meeting therefore reaffirmed the three Western powers' determination to maintain access to West Berlin.

However, Brandt did not succeed at Reykjavik in his maximum aims, ones quite similar to the 1972 Berlin agreements: to establish joint West German-East German committees on a fifty-fifty basis, by authority of the four powers, to regulate Berlin traffic and to have the three Western powers formally approve Bonn's presence in the city. Instead, the final communiqué said only that Berlin "cannot be excluded from general political détente in Europe."[51]

The SPD and the PCI

Brandt and the SPD developed a more flexible position on other Ostpolitik issues and met strong CDU/CSU criticism as a result. One of their most novel moves was their dialogue with the Italian Communist party (PCI). This was initiated by the PCI in late 1967 as a result of the Grand Coalition's Ostpolitik and the April 1967 Karlový Várý European Communist conference on European security and because SPD-PCI contacts would help the PCI in Italy. The SPD hoped to use the PCI for an indirect dialogue with Moscow and East Berlin. The main SPD negotiators were Brandt's associate, Leo Bauer (an ex-Communist who had been imprisoned in East Germany in Stalin's anti-Semitic purges and released from Vorkuta after Adenauer's 1955 visit to Moscow), Egon Franke, a leading right-wing SPD official, and Egon Bahr. This was followed in February 1968 by a long SED-PCI discussion in Rome, with Longo, then head of the PCI, who had been in prison with Bauer, and Paul Verner of the SED leading the two delegations. All three parties viewed favorably a PCI proposal to solve the problem of the ban against the KPD in West Germany by founding a new Communist party there (which appeared in 1968 as the *Deutsche Kommunistische Partei—DKP*). The SPD also indicated that it was prepared to agree to recognition or respecting of the Oder-Neisse line and signing of the nonproliferation treaty. The discussions gave the SPD another channel to communicate with the Soviet and Eastern European party leaderships and to help moderate the SED position.[52]

At the March 1968 Nürnberg SPD Party Congress, Brandt declared that Bonn must "respect and recognize the existing boundaries in Europe, including the Western boundary of Poland" (the Oder-Neisse line.) The next month he stated that Bonn was prepared to negotiate about all the Soviet and Eastern European demands but would not accept them as preconditions to negotiations.[53]

The Grand Coalition and Eastern Europe

Those Eastern European states with economic and political reasons for reestablishing relations with Bonn (Rumania, Yugoslavia, Hungary, and Bulgaria) maintained that the Bucharest Declaration demands were necessary for a peace treaty (for "complete normalization") but that in the meantime diplomatic relations could be established.[54] When the Grand Coalition was formed in December 1966, terms for the resumption of diplomatic relations between Bonn and Bucharest had already been agreed on at the working level. The same was basically true with Hungary, and Bulgaria had indicated great interest. Less progress had been made with Yugoslavia, which had established diplomatic relations with East Berlin in 1957, that is, it had not, like the other Eastern European states, had them from the beginning ("*Geburtsfehler*"), to which Bonn was less hostile. Thus the less flexible politicians and diplomats in Bonn maintained, West German recognition of Belgrade would be more likely to unleash an avalanche of recognition of East Berlin by third world states. Moreover, they declared, it would favor Yugoslav claims for reparations.

Rumania

Kiesinger and Brandt had initially to decide with which country in Eastern Europe they should first resume relations. The Grand Coalition and particularly the SPD needed a rapid, public success for its new Ostpolitik. Many argued for Hungary, because recognition of Rumania first would unnecessarily offend the Soviet Union. But Budapest was under increasing Soviet, East German, and Polish pressure to demand more concessions from Bonn while Rumanian policy had already deviated from Moscow's. Rumanian reorientation of its foreign trade toward the West and particularly toward the Federal Republic, obstruction of Soviet wishes within the Warsaw Pact and CMEA, and good party relations with Peking had shown that Bucharest wanted to carry on an autonomous foreign policy, including with Bonn. Bucharest insisted that Bonn should resume relations. Therefore, although Bonn realized that this would worsen its chances elsewhere in Eastern Europe, it resumed diplomatic relations with Bucharest in January 1967 and raised the level of guaranteed credits for exports to it from the Federal Republic.[55]

Bonn-Bucharest relations developed rapidly and favorably. Rumania resisted Soviet, East German, and Polish pressure against Bonn; it joined Yugoslavia in supporting the Czechoslovak move toward greater autonomy from Moscow; and it moved away from the Soviet line on Israel and the nonproliferation treaty. Its trade with West Germany rose rapidly, as did its trade deficit with Bonn, which tried with little success to encourage West German imports from Rumania. West German-Rumanian cultural relations also grew rapidly. However, presumably because it needed their skills, Bucharest refused to allow many ethnic Germans in Transylvania to emigrate to West Germany, as Bonn desired.[56]

Bucharest's establishment of relations with Bonn alarmed East Berlin, Warsaw, and Moscow, who knew that Budapest and Sofia wanted to do the same. Soviet pressure against it was stepped up and none of them, except Yugoslavia, which Moscow could not control, did so.[57] This initial apparent lack of progress of the new Ostpolitik made many West Germans impatient, but liberalization in Czechoslovakia again raised their hopes.[58]

East Germany

Ulbricht pressed Moscow to take a more hostile line against Bonn.[59] East German political consolidation and economic and technological growth and Moscow's loss of influence in Rumania and Czechoslovakia made him more influential in Moscow.[60] Bonn's establishment of diplomatic relations with Rumania and trade missions with some other Eastern European countries threatened him with "selective coexistence" (isolation). Ulbricht therefore concentrated on blocking the Grand Coalition's Ostpolitik. At the February 8–10, 1967 Warsaw Pact Conference, he urged that no pact member establish diplomatic relations with Bonn before the latter recognized the DDR, the Oder-Neisse line, and the status of West Berlin as a "special political unit." Although Rumanian opposition prevented its formal adoption by the conference, its support by the Soviets made the other Eastern European Pact members accept it in practice. The April 24–26 Karlový Váry declaration of European Communist and workers parties (with Rumania absent) then formally endorsed this "Ulbricht doctrine."[61] Ulbricht concluded bilateral agreements with Eastern European states to block Bonn's Ostpolitik.[62] The Kiesinger-Stoph exchanges got nowhere. In a secret SED document distributed before the April 1967 SED Party Congress and, albeit less clearly, in his speech there, Ulbricht stressed that neither the DDR nor the USSR would allow German reunification unless or until West Germany became communist.[63] In the spring of 1968, with Soviet approval, Ulbricht tried to expand his control of West German travel to and from West Berlin. But Moscow, not wanting another Berlin crisis, kept DDR harassment at a low level and restricted to West German travelers.[64]

Ulbricht was also restrained by his desire to maintain DDR trade with West Germany.[65] Western reaction was minimal. The condition Ulbricht demanded for discussing Kiesinger's proposals about improved travel and economic and cultural relations, that Bonn recognize the DDR de jure, made it clear that he was determined to force Bonn to capitulate and to prevent West German influence in East Germany.[66]

Meanwhile, Bonn continued to combat East German influence in the third world. East Berlin's influence rose, along with Moscow's, in the radical Arab states, particularly after Bonn's secret military aid to Israel (at U.S. request) became public. In early 1965, Ulbricht paid a state visit to Cairo. Thereupon, having failed to prevent this by offering to stop arms deliveries to Israel, Bonn recognized Israel, whereupon almost all Arab states broke off relations with Bonn. However, no noncommunist state recognized East Germany, even after Bonn resumed relations with Belgrade and East German influence in Guinea, Ghana, and Indonesia declined after Sekou Touré's move away from Moscow and the overthrow of Nkrumah and Sukarno. Even so, Berlin's influence had increased and Bonn's declined in the Arab states—hardly a success for the Hallstein Doctrine.[67]

Ulbricht continued to try to use the Grand Coalition's refusal to recognize East Germany and West German impatience with slow progress of Ostpolitik to gain support in the Federal Republic. He apparently hoped that the New Left and the small neo-Nazi National Democratic Party (NPD) would worsen Bonn-Moscow and Bonn-Washington relations. But the former, more anarchist than Marxist, opposed East as well as West Germany and the latter's votes declined in 1968 as the West German economy recovered.[68]

Poland

Poland was initially also totally hostile to West German Ostpolitik.[69] Polish-West German relations had been out of phase—when Warsaw was flexible, in 1956–1957, Bonn was not, and vice versa. After late 1958, when Warsaw made recognition by Bonn of the Oder-Neisse line a precondition for diplomatic relations—in 1956 it had not—Polish policy toward Bonn hardened. West German policy toward Warsaw, largely unintentionally, hardened as well. Polish-West German trade rose slowly and Bonn's trade mission in Warsaw, established in 1963, the first one in Eastern Europe, remained politically uninfluential. In 1965, due to the rapprochement between Warsaw and East Berlin and perhaps also to Soviet influence, Poland made de jure recognition of East Germany an additional condition for resumption of relations. Gomułka thus adopted Ulbricht's opposition to any rapprochement with Bonn.

The hardening of the Polish position was also due to the post-1962 liberalization in Czechoslovakia. Gomułka had hoped to compensate for fissures in Eastern Europe and rising West German economic power by close Polish political and economic relations with the two other "northern tier" states, East Germany and Czechoslovakia, and with the Soviet Union. Furthermore, as popular support for his regime declined, he became increasingly more anti-German in order to retain popular support. By 1966, Gomułka felt threatened by Czechoslovak liberalization, national autonomy, and improvement of relations with Bonn. He therefore urged Moscow to prevent Eastern European states from recognizing Bonn unless Bonn recognized East Germany as well as the Oder-Neisse line.

Gomułka's hostility to the Polish aspects of the new Ostpolitik—the attempt by Kiesinger and Brandt to show that they understood Poland's need for settled frontiers, SPD "respect" (de facto recognition) for the Oder-Neisse line, and so forth—was also due to his realization that noncommunist elements in the Polish elite, notably the Polish Catholic hierarchy, were becoming less hostile to West Germany. The exchange of letters in late 1965 between the Polish and West German Catholic bishops showed that Cardinal Wyszyński, the Polish Primate, while adamantly defending the Oder-Neisse line, wanted to improve the climate of German-Polish relations, since he wanted to increase West German support for the new Ostpolitik. Because Gomułka thought anti-Germanism was one of the few issues on which he could get popular support, he violently attacked the cardinal, which backfired in the cardinal's favor. An uneasy church-state truce ensued. When the March 1968 "Bensberger memorandum" of a West German Catholic group showed understanding toward Poland, the Polish hierarchy replied favorably in September, after the invasion of Czechoslovakia.[70] Polish press reaction was not totally hostile.[71]

There may well also have been differences of opinion within the Polish leadership on Bonn's new Ostpolitik. After 1967, it was rent by the struggle between Gomuka and the so-called "Partisans," led by General Mieczysław Moczar, Gomułka's would-be successor. Some reports indicate that before the invasion of Czechoslovakia Moczar may have wanted to improve relations with Bonn in order to increase Poland's area of maneuver vis-à-vis the Soviet Union. Moreover, some younger, less dogmatic Polish Communists found Gomułka's anti-Germanism sterile and counterproductive. Intellectual dissidence and student riots in Poland in spring 1968, plus Moczar's nationalism, must have made Moscow listen more attentively to Gomułka's pressure for a stronger Soviet line against Dubček.

The invasion of Czechoslovakia was a major defeat for the Partisans. Gomułka reconsolidated his position and his anti-German policy. In November 1968, after the Czechoslovak invasion, he added two more preconditions for Polish normalization of relations with Bonn: West German recognition of the invalidity of the Munich agreement *ab initio* and abandonment of all claims to West Berlin.

Hungary

Of all the Eastern European states that Moscow forced to reject the Grand Coalition's Ostpolitik, Hungary was the most reluctant. Hungarian relations with Germany were traditionally good. It wanted more West German trade and tourism. Kádár had liberalized domestic policy and tried to keep on good terms with Prague and Belgrade and to mediate between the Soviet Union and Czechoslovakia. Budapest was ready to establish relations with Bonn when the Grand Coalition came into power; but Bonn began with Bucharest rather than with Budapest, and by early 1967 Ulbricht and Gomułka had persuaded Moscow to block Kádár's plan. However, Hungary still wanted more trade. The invasion of Czechoslovakia and its probably reluctant participation forced Hungary even closer to the Soviet anti-German line.[72]

Bulgaria

Bulgaria also had no anti-German tradition and wanted trade with West Germany, and therefore improved relations with Bonn. But pro-Russian tradition was strong. Anti-Yugoslav (over Macedonia) and rather anti-Rumanian (over the Dobrudja), Bulgaria wanted all the more to keep good relations with its main ally, Moscow. Soviet pressure prevented Sofia in 1967 from resuming relations with Bonn, with whom Bulgarian trade had been rising rapidly. The invasion of Czechoslovakia temporarily blocked improved relations between Bonn and Sofia but trade gradually increased.[73]

The Chinese People's Republic

Post-1945 relations, or their absence, between Bonn and Peking were always primarily determined by the relations of each with its allies and enemies. Bonn was primarily concerned about its relations with Washington, Tokyo, and Moscow and its attitude toward the DDR. Peking was primarily concerned about Moscow, Washington, and East Berlin.

Until 1955, there were no contacts between Bonn and Peking, and Chinese relations with East Berlin were close. In 1955, after Adenauer reestablished diplomatic relations with Moscow, Peking put out feelers for relations with Bonn as well: but Adenauer, although already anticipating a Sino-Soviet split, did not reciprocate, for he foresaw an eventual easing of Soviet hostility toward Bonn. In 1956, the FDP proposed a West German approach to Peking but Adenauer again blocked it. However, in 1957, informal trade relations were established, with Bonn's approval, by the West German private *Ostausschuss der deutschen Wirtschaft* and West German-Chinese trade began to increase.

After the Sino-Soviet split, Peking in 1962 made informal, unsuccessful approaches to Bonn for diplomatic relations. Bonn reciprocated only in 1964; and negotiating sessions, at the working level, were held between the West German and Chinese embassies in Bern. That summer Mao made clear his appeal to West German (and Polish and Rumanian) territorial revisionism against the Soviet Union. The United States and Japan pressured Bonn against diplomatic relations with Peking. During a visit that summer to Washington, Chancellor Erhard declared that diplomatic relations would not be established. China refused to accept the "Berlin clause" (that Bonn would represent West Berlin). Thereupon only a trade agreement was signed, and the Chinese in October 1964 broke off the Bern negotiations. They were displeased by Erhard's giving in to U.S. pressure. It also may be that they saw Khrushchev's fall, that same month, as an opportunity to improve Sino-Soviet relations, although Chou En-lai's subsequent statements made no concessions on Sino-Soviet issues and Sino-Soviet relations did not improve. Peking may still have hoped to split East Berlin from Moscow. Thereafter the Cultural Revolution paralyzed Chinese diplomatic initiatives for some years.[74]

Yugoslavia

One of the main objectives of the Grand Coalition's Ostpolitik and especially of the SPD was to reestablish diplomatic relations with Belgrade. German-Yugoslav economic relations had traditionally been close and Yugoslavia offered great prospects for West German exports. Bonn wanted to block Ulbricht's cultivation of Tito so that Tito's influence in the underdeveloped world would not be used to Bonn's disadvantage. However, resumption of relations with Belgrade would contravene the Hallstein Doctrine more directly than with Rumania, to whom the *Geburtsfehler* theory could be applied. Bonn, and particularly the CDU, also did not want to resume relations only with states, like Rumania and Yugoslavia, on bad terms with Moscow, lest this impede improvement in West German-Soviet relations.[75] Finally, Belgrade initially demanded extensive reparations from Bonn. (However, it soon agreed to postpone these claims.)

By 1966, Belgrade was also increasingly interested in improving its relations with Bonn. The 1966 fall of Ranković had resulted primarily from opposition to him in Croatia and Slovenia, traditionally not anti-German. Economically developed, Catholic, and Western, they favored priority for Western Europe and West Germany. Yugoslavia wanted credits and high-level technology plus greater Western markets for Yugoslav agricultural products. West Germany was the main source of both. Yugoslavia's liberalization of foreign trade and semiconvertability of the dinar required better ties with Western Europe and led to a rising Yugoslav foreign trade deficit, particularly with the Federal Republic. Thus Belgrade needed more West German credits. Yugoslavia wanted associate EEC membership to counter-balance increasing integration within EEC and CMEA, for which it needed Bonn's support. Many Yugoslavs, particularly Croats and Slovenes, also favored priority for Western Europe because they were disillusioned with the disunity and impotence of the third world and Tito's concentration on it. But in 1963–1965 the Sino-Soviet split, Brezhnev's lower priority for "collective mobilization" against the Chinese, and Tito's wish not to become too dependent on the West and to balance among the Yugoslav republics furthered Soviet-Yugoslav rapprochement. Moscow and East Berlin cultivated Belgrade *inter alia* to keep the latter on bad terms with Bonn.

West German inaction on the extensive Yugoslav reparations claims and on improving the status of Yugoslav workers in West Germany, plus the anti-Titoist violence of Croat Ustaši émigrés in the Federal Republic, with, Belgrade maintained, the toleration if not encouragement of Bonn, also worsened Yugoslav attitudes toward the Federal Republic. Therefore, despite Schröder's Ostpolitik, by 1964 Bonn-Belgrade relations were the worst since the first Yugoslav-Soviet rapprochement in 1955.

Then they began to improve. Although Yugoslav *raison d'état* and Tito's *raison du parti* opposed a West Germany so strong that it might again become the economic or even political hegemonic power in Eastern Europe, they wanted the Federal Republic sufficiently strong to resist Russian westward expansion. They also wanted Soviet détente with the West and toleration of gradual liberalization in Eastern Europe, which would increase Yugoslav security vis-à-vis and influence on its neighbors. Yugoslavia therefore opposed Soviet policy in the second Berlin crisis. Belgrade wanted Bonn to recognize Belgrade and accept continued Yugoslav-East German relations. When, after Khrushchev, Soviet policy became less prodétente, more anti-Bonn, more opposed to Rumanian nationalism and to Czechoslovak nationalism and liberalization, and, after 1965, more committed to collective mobilization against the Chinese, Yugoslav policy aligned itself with Bucharest and, after Novotný's 1968 fall, with Prague. Thus by late 1966, Yugoslavia favored improved relations with Bonn. (Yugoslav agreement to raise East Berlin's Belgrade representation from legation to embassy status was probably intended to protect its eastern flank while it did so.)

The Soviet-East German-Polish counterattack against the new Ostpolitik, plus constant SPD pressure, finally made Kiesinger agree to resume relations with Belgrade.

At first the CDU had tried, without much hope of success, to persuade Belgrade to reduce them to their previous legation status. Realizing, however, that he need only wait to have Bonn resume on his terms, Tito refused to agree. After Kiesinger's autumn 1967 trip to India and other Asian countries, he correctly assured the CDU that resumption with Belgrade would not bring recognition of the DDR by third world states.

The December 1967 resumption of Bonn-Belgrade relations increased West German trade and credits to Yugoslavia, improved the status of the Yugoslav workers in West Germany, and furthered West German suppression of anti-Titoist Yugoslav émigré activity and West German sponsorship of Yugoslav associate status in the EEC.[76] (The question of reparations was postponed by mutual agreement.) The Soviet invasion of Czechoslovakia made Yugoslavia fear that it was next, greatly worsened Soviet-Yugoslav relations, and intensified Yugoslav interest in good ties with the West and especially with the Federal Republic.[77]

Czechoslovakia

The 1968 Czechoslovak developments interrupted and then improved relations between Bonn and the East. Liberalization in Czechoslovakia, which had set in slowly after 1962 and reached a crescendo in 1968, arose from the 1962 economic recession, the drastic discrediting of the Novotný regime by its unwilling disclosures of its complicity in Stalinist crimes, the recoalescence and return to influence of the intelligentsia, bringing with it a changed attitude toward the Germans and Russians, and the rise of Slovak nationalism. These events led at the end of 1967 to Novotný's replacement as first secretary by Alexander Dubček, the Slovak first secretary, and in April 1968 to his replacement as President by General Ludvík Svoboda.

Two of these factors are especially important for this study: the economic recession and the changing attitude toward the Germans. By 1967, Czech and Slovak economists and the intelligentsia realized that Czechoslovakia needed massive inputs of high-level Western technology to make its manufactures internationally competitive.[78] Only the Federal Republic could and for political reasons—the new Ostpolitik—would grant such credits. Thus there was a decisive economic reason for Prague to improve its relations with Bonn. Moreover, Czechs had never been as anti-German as Poles or Russians, and their memories of nazism had faded somewhat. East Germany was constantly attempting to restrain Czechoslovak liberalization. Moreover, the Slovaks, never anti-German, had achieved independence under German hegemony and the Slovaks were determined to regain at least their 1945–1948 autonomy.

Bonn had been cultivating Prague since the early 1960s; and although Novotný, under Soviet pressure, decided against resumption of diplomatic relations, a West German trade mission was established in Prague in early 1967. Once Dubček came to power, contacts between Prague and Bonn intensified rapidly and Bonn indicated its willingness to compromise on the Munich agreement and to extend extensive credits to Prague, to modernize Czechoslovak industry. Ulbricht, seconded by Gomuľka, increasingly pressed Moscow to prevent liberalization in Prague from destabilizing and isolating East Germany. Bucharest and Belgrade supported Prague, Ceauşescu for nationalist and anti-Soviet and Tito for nationalist and liberalization motives. Thus the summer of 1968 saw signs of a de facto revival of the interwar Little Entente of Czechoslovakia, Rumania, and Yugoslavia, this time directed against the Soviet Union, East Germany, and Poland and favorable to Bonn. Hungary tried to steer a middle course between Moscow and Prague and improve its relations with Bonn.

Kiesinger and Brandt tried hard in spring and summer 1968 to avoid giving the impression of interfering in or being too enthusiastic about the developments in Prague; indeed, the farther Czechoslovak developments went, the less active the West Germans were. In retrospect, Bonn might have been even more restrained, but this hardly would have prevented the Soviet invasion. For it was clear to Moscow as well as to Bonn that

Czechoslovak developments threatened to destabilize East Germany, Poland, and the Soviet Ukraine[79] and increase Western, particularly West German influence.

Yet Soviet concern about Dubček's improvement of relations with Bonn played only a secondary role in the Soviet decision to invade. Soviet declarations that Czechoslovakia was falling in into the hands of the "Bonn revanchists" were consciously exaggerated. The Soviets invaded Czechoslovakia primarily because of Czechoslovak domestic developments.[80]

The Grand Coalition's Ostpolitik after the Soviet Invasion of Czechoslovakia

The August 20-21, 1968, Soviet invasion of Czechoslovakia resulted in a temporary caesura in Bonn's Ostpolitik.[81] Ironically, however, it was also a precondition for its success. Initially, it reversed West German gains in Czechoslovakia and lessened prospects for improved relations with Hungary and Bulgaria. Gomuľka's and Ulbricht's hard anti-German line triumphed. Moscow rationalized and generalized its invasion: The "socialist commonwealth" (the Soviet Union) must intervene to prevent a "danger to socialism itself."[82] Although Bucharest declared that it would fight any (that is, Russian) invasion, it also became more cautious toward Bonn. Only defiant Yugoslavia still wanted to expand its ties with Bonn.

Thus one of the major premises of the Grand Coalition's Ostpolitik, that Bonn could control its successes and therefore persuade Moscow to allow them to continue, was disproven because of events in Prague and in Moscow over which West Germany had, and could have, no control.

The invasion had proved that although what de Gaulle called *la force des choses* in Eastern Europe—nationalism, liberalization, and economic reform—favored the new Ostpolitik, *la force sovietique* would block or reverse its gains. Moscow remained decisive for Eastern Europe. Bonn's strategic aim, to encourage liberalization in East Germany, seemed blocked.[83] West Germans were shocked at the Soviet invasion and feared that it meant a greater Soviet menace to West Germany and West Berlin. Bonn therefore tightened its ties with the United States.

The minimal U.S. reaction to the Soviet invasion disappointed many in Bonn and increased their frustration without offering any alternative to it. De Gaulle's reaction was even more minimal. The invasion underscored the failure of his détente efforts with Moscow, his hopes for French leadership in Europe, and his weakness and unreliability should Moscow march against West Germany or—a more immediate West German concern— start another Berlin crisis.

The invasion seemed to justify CDU doubts about détente with Moscow and East Berlin. The right-wing SPD shared much of the CDU's disillusionment but the left wing argued that Bonn must finally accept the status quo.[84] The result initially improved the CDU's position.

But neither party had a satisfactory alternative to Ostpolitik, which remained easier than revising the Grand Coalition agreement. It still unmasked Ulbricht as the chief enemy of détente. Its gains in Yugoslavia and Rumania continued. It prevented Bonn from becoming isolated from Washington and Paris when it needed them more than before. It kept the door open for a less hostile Soviet policy. Finally, the invasion made it possible for the Soviets, once they reestablished their control over Prague, to make concessions to Bonn, convinced the SPD and FDP that they must recognize de facto Soviet control over Eastern Europe, and drove Peking toward Washington—and therefore Moscow toward Washington and Bonn.

Thus the opponents of Ostpolitik only temporarily gained ground. Even before the 1969 SPD-FDP coalition, West German elite public opinion began to realize that the invasion ended any hope of successful pressure on the Soviet Union via the other Eastern European states or of a change in Eastern Europe that would make German unification soon possible and that therefore a more flexible Ostpolitik was necessary. For if the Red Army had destroyed liberalization in Czechoslovakia, how much more would it prevent German unification. And how much longer could the Hallstein Doctrine be maintained and would not the attempt to do so only isolate Bonn? Thus the Soviet invasion of Czechoslovakia was a precondition for the German settlement of 1970–1973 in two respects: It changed West German public opinion and made the new Ostpolitik possible and it so reconsolidated Soviet control over Eastern Europe that Moscow believed it could afford to make concessions to Bonn.[85] Thus thinking in Bonn was by early 1969 moving toward intensification of Ostpolitik. Only in October 1969 when the Brandt-Scheel government came to power, did a breakthrough occur. But even before, Ostpolitik was furthered in Bonn, and in Moscow, by the worldwide diplomatic revolution.

The Great Turn: The Globalization of European Politics
In 1969, a diplomatic revolution was beginning in international politics, centering around the Sino-American rapprochement and the intensification of Soviet-American détente, which for the first time since the end of World War II linked European with Asian politics. Since I have analyzed these developments elsewhere at length, I shall treat here only their impact on relations between the Germanies and the East.[86]

The most important factor in this diplomatic revolution was the Sino-American rapprochement.[87] This resulted from the desire of Peking and Washington to contain rising Soviet power. The year 1969 was also one of very high Sino-Soviet tension, highlighted by the Sino-Soviet border incidents and the massive increase in Soviet troop deployment on the Chinese frontiers, which had by the early 1970s reached some four hundred fifty thousand men, with conventional and atomic armament. This made China give overriding priority to containing the Soviet military threat and committed the Soviets indefinitely in East Asia.

The United States was disengaging from Vietnam, thus ending what Peking had seen as a serious American military threat, just when it saw the Soviet military threat rising rapidly. Washington was concerned about rising Soviet strategic and naval power and China, about rising Soviet strategic and land power. Ironically, the Soviet military buildup to China's north was thus responsible for bringing about what Moscow had long feared, a Sino-American détente. The Chinese also tried to counter the Soviets in Eastern and Western Europe. This intensified the Soviet fear that China would be rearmed by West Germany, Japan, or America. Therefore, to avoid threats in Europe and Asia, Moscow moved toward détente on its western flank.

The second major cause of Moscow's intensification of détente in 1969 was its growing technological gap with the Atlantic-Japanese developed world. The Soviets therefore wanted Western and Japanese technology and credits.[88] Obtaining them required a prolonged period of East-West détente in Europe and elsewhere.

The United States, Moscow realized, also had its problems. Washington was scaling down its commitments abroad as a result of public disillusionment with the Vietnam War.[89] Increasing economic rivalry between the United States and Western Europe and Japan led to several devaluations of the dollar and American and EEC trade disputes. U.S. neoisolationism threatened American troop commitment in Europe.

The U.S. image in Western Europe was becoming tarnished by the Vietnam War, U.S. racial problems, drugs, environmental backlash, and so forth. The United States became less a model to be admired than a future to be feared. Western Europe was also more prosperous and self-confident. The Western European image of Soviet hostility was becoming blurred. Western European youth, lacking their parents' cold war experience, reacted against what they saw as their elders' excessive "cold war" anti-Sovietism. Finally, a radical West German Left was arising, anti-American, anti–cold war, and often rather pro-SED, the latest example of the recurrent German revolt against Western bourgeois, affluent, materialistic society, as opposed to ascetic, egalitarian, Prussian, romantic virtues, now seen by some radicals in the "Prussian socialism" of the DDR.

The new Soviet Westpolitik
The Soviet Union intended to use Ostpolitik to prevent Western Europe from becoming politically or, worse, militarily or, worst

of all, thermonuclearly united and, in particular, to prevent the Federal Republic from becoming dominant in Western Europe, obtaining independent access to nuclear weapons, or otherwise greatly increasing its military strength.[90]

Conversely, as the Soviets realized, intensification of East-West détente at a bilateral Soviet-American level might well increase U.S.-Western European tensions, for the Western Europeans would feel that these negotiations were being conducted over their heads and contrary to their interests. (That the East Germans would feel the same about Soviet negotiations with the United States and West Germany was also clear to the Soviets, but they controlled East Germany; the United States did not control West Germany.) Moscow also hoped that a less antagonistic policy toward West Germany would encourage the radical Left within and to the left of the SPD. Finally, Moscow must have realized in spite of its historic distrust of the German Social Democrats, it could more easily reach a favorable agreement with them. By 1969, therefore, Moscow wanted to get advanced West German technology, prevent Bonn from playing with Peking against Moscow, and get German recognition of East Germany and the Soviet sphere of influence in Eastern Europe in order to stabilize East Germany and Poland. The renewed Soviet move toward Bonn was thus an integral part of a defensive Soviet policy of détente with the West, counterbalanced by internal and bloc restabilization and a forward strategy against Peking.[91]

Renewed Soviet-West German Negotiations

Bonn's attempts to negotiate a nonuse of force treaty with Moscow had been interrupted by the invasion of Czechoslovakia. Even without that, they could not have succeeded as long as the CDU was participating in power in Bonn, for it refused to accept Moscow's minimal demand: recognition, at least de facto, of the DDR. Even so, Moscow resumed negotiations with Bonn *before* Brandt or Moscow could have calculated that he would become chancellor, and before Bonn committed itself to de facto recognition of the DDR and the Oder-Neisse line. Had the

CDU won the October 1969 elections, the negotiations would at least have been far more prolonged and quite likely would not have succeeded. Brandt's coming to power probably was a precondition for their success.

The change in Soviet policy was initially very gradual. Although postinvasion Soviet press polemics became even more violently anti-West German, Moscow was careful to reassure Bonn, beginning on the day of the invasion, that the Soviet Union was not threatening West German security. In his October 3 UN speech Gromyko coupled an exposition of the "Brezhnev doctrine" (the ideological justification of Moscow's invasion of Czechoslovakia) with desire for economic cooperation with Bonn and willingness to resume the nonuse of force discussion.[92] On October 8, Gromyko insisted to Brandt that Bonn recognize the postwar borders and the DDR but repeated his willingness to continue negotiations on nonuse of force declarations.[93]

In November 1968, the Soviet German specialist D. E. Melnikov reiterated his favorable April 1968 reference to "German democrats."[94] On the other hand, DDR harassment of access to West Berlin also increased.[95] A prolonged Soviet reassessment of policy toward Bonn was followed by Tsarapkin's return to Bonn at the end of 1968 after a three month absence and his resumption of nonuse of force discussions with the Bonn foreign ministry on January 10, 1969. On February 5, he indicated to Brandt that Moscow was prepared to make concessions on the intervention issue—probably in order to overcome CDU/CSU demands that this be a precondition for Bonn's ratification of the non-proliferation treaty (NPT), in which Moscow was vitally interested.[96]

However, on February 7, a new Berlin "minicrisis" broke out, ostensibly over the forthcoming election of the West German president in West Berlin.[97] East Berlin declared the election "illegal" and banned transit to West Berlin of members of the Bundestag. The three Western powers protested strongly.[98] Moscow supported the DDR's move, but not in very strong terms. After the Western protest, Soviet propaganda became even less strong. On February 23, Tsarapkin told Kiesinger that the Soviet Union would help enable West Berliners to visit their East Berlin relatives in another DDR city. (A February 21 Ulbricht letter had made the transfer of the presidential election out of West Berlin a precondition for passes for West Berliners to East Berlin. Tsarapkin made no such precondition and reportedly told Kiesinger that he had not known of the Ulbricht letter, a claim that hardly seems true.)[99] Thereupon Bonn centered its ire on East Berlin, not Moscow, but made clear that it would only move the election if assured by Moscow that in addition to the passes it would get a general Berlin settlement. (This foreshadowed the eventual 1971 Berlin agreement.)

The new Nixon administration refused to intensify détente with Moscow, notably on SALT, as long as harassment of West Berlin continued and ostentatiously gave full support to Bonn's firm stand, symbolized by Nixon's February 1969 visit to West Berlin. France, weakened after the May 1968 student revolt and fearful after the Czechoslovak invasion, also gave Bonn full support.

Then the March 2, 1969, Sino-Soviet Ussuri border clash convinced Moscow, as it soon began to make clear, that it must lower tension in the West. On that same day the Soviets threatened the security of Western commercial air flights to West Berlin that would the next day be flying in the West German electors for the presidency. But on the following day the flights occurred without incident, as did the presidential election, a fact hardly unrelated to the Ussuri incident. Moscow reacted favorably to the victory of Heinemann (SPD) over Schröder (CDU). On March 11, Tsarapkin called on Kiesinger and then on Brandt to give them the Soviet version of the Ussuri border clash—the first time that Moscow had ever officially raised the Chinese issue in Bonn. That same week Soviet propaganda on West Berlin deescalated sharply and the Berlin minicrisis evaporated.

The minicrisis demonstrated direct interaction between German and Sino-Soviet issues and was the first Soviet move in the West to compensate for the Ussuri crisis by giving priority to détente over full support of Ulbricht. In late March, in another indication of Soviet-East German differences, Suslov and Ulbricht publicly differed, esoterically but significantly, on the KPD's 1933 policy toward the SPD.[100]

The Budapest Declaration

The March 1969 Budapest Declaration of the Warsaw Pact was less extreme vis-à-vis the United States and the Federal Republic than similar ones in 1966–1968. It called for the immediate convocation of a European security conference with emphasis on East-West economic cooperation. While it still demanded West German recognition of the Oder-Neisse line, the East-West German border, the "existence" of the DDR, a "special status" for West Berlin, and the abandonment of Bonn's "sole represen-tation" claim, they were made preconditions for European security but not for negotiations with Bonn. Tsarapkin soon made clear that these demands were not even preconditions for a European security conference but proposals for its agenda. Moreover, Bonn's recognition of the invalidity of the Munich agreement *ex tunc* was not mentioned, and the declaration stated that West Berlin was "a special entity and does not belong to West Germany," not, as the previously Karlový Varý Declara-tion had, that it is "an independent political entity"—an indica-tion that Moscow was moving toward recognition of the West Berlin status quo.[101] Moreover, the declaration emphasized less than previous ones the liquidation of military blocs. Indeed, it seemed to assume their continued existence—not surprisingly, after the Soviet troop deployment in Czechoslovakia. Moscow thus demonstrated its priority for consolidating control over Eastern Europe over increasing its influence in Western Europe.

Although Moscow continued to demand withdrawal of U.S. forces from Europe, its opposition to U.S. and Canadian partici-pation in a European security conference began to lessen. The Soviet-arranged May 1969 Finnish invitation to the conference included both, thus showing that Moscow realized it had be-come counterproductive for it to insist on their exclusion and would compromise with the West to have the conference meet. Conversely, Moscow continued to oppose all Western proposals for troop reductions in Europe. Soviet-West German economic negotiations became more serious in April 1969 when Soviet Foreign Trade Minister Patolichev met West German Economics Minister Schiller. They arrived at a major natural gas agreement, with West Germany providing steel pipes for massive export of natural gas from the Soviet Union to the Federal Republic. Visits to Moscow by FDP and SPD delegations, led by Scheel and Schmidt, led to more favorable Soviet press treatment of these two parties than of the CDU.[102]

The Budapest Declaration had indicated that Moscow no longer demanded that Bonn recognize the DDR as a precondition to Soviet-West German negotiations and therefore that Bonn could expect to get something for such recognition, Bonn's price was Soviet and East German confirmation by treaty of Kennedy's "three essentials" for West Berlin: Western presence, free access, and economic ties with the Federal Republic, which recognition of the DDR would enable it to menace. In short, if Bonn and the West were to recognize the status quo in the DDR, Moscow and the DDR had to recognize it in West Berlin.

This became clear when an April 10 NATO declaration coupled willingness to discuss a European security conference with four-power negotiations to improve the Berlin situation.[103] On May 19, Gomułka, in a speech reportedly without previous consultation with Moscow, which did not publicly endorse it, proposed Polish-West German negotiations on recognition of the Oder-Neisse line and omitted his previous precondition, recognition of the DDR.[104] Gomułka probably made this proposal in order to get more West German technology and credits and to indicate to Moscow that Poland would not be left behind the Soviet Union in normalization of relations with the Federal Republic. His speech, preceded by a softening of the Polish propaganda position on the Federal Republic, reflected higher Polish priority for obtaining West German technology and credits.

On July 4, Bonn proposed to Moscow the resumption of nonuse of force negotiations. Gromyko said on July 10 (and confirmed in a Soviet note of September 12) that Moscow was prepared to resume them, discuss the situation in Berlin and the German question with the three Western powers, and begin

SALT negotiations with Washington.[105] He did not mention Bonn's recognizing the DDR or even, as the Budapest Declaration had done, its "existence." Rather, he stressed recognition of existing European frontiers—thus making clearer the growing gap between the Soviet and East German positions.[106] The three Western powers thereupon proposed negotiations on Berlin, to which Moscow agreed.

On September 22, 1969, Brandt and Gromyko met again in New York. Gromyko said that Moscow would resume nonuse of force negotiations. He made clear the Soviet interest in Bonn's participation in a European security conference and ratification of the NPT. Brandt indicated that improvement in Bonn's relations with the DDR would make Bonn's participation in the conference easier. As Brandt later wrote, "This discussion was in some respects the bridge" to his later Ostpolitik, for in it he made clear that movement by Bonn toward recognition of existing frontiers, NPT ratification, and the security conference and détente between Bonn and East Berlin—that is, there would be linkage *(Junktim)* between the two.[107] Bonn and the Western powers had thus demanded that Soviet-West German negotiations be linked to four-power negotiations on Berlin. Bonn therefore had to coordinate its Ostpolitik even more with the Western powers and particularly with the United States.[108]

As the Bundestag elections approached, Brandt's position became more conciliatory and Kiesinger's less so.[109] In March 1969, a sharp controversy had arisen within the Grand Coalition about Cambodia's recognition of the DDR. Although it resulted in a compromise (Bonn "froze" relations with Pnom Penh instead of breaking them), Brandt concluded that if possible the SPD should rule without the CDU/CSU after the next Bundestag elections. [110] The next month new Bundestag elections resulted in an SPD-FDP coalition government.

The Grand Coalition's Ostpolitik in Retrospect

The Grand Coalition's Ostpolitik was ahead of, behind, and unadjusted to its time: ahead because Soviet moderation toward Bonn was beginning when the Grand Coalition ended; behind because due to CDU/CSU opposition it would not make the minimum concessions—recognition of the Oder-Neisse line and the DDR—that Moscow demanded; and unadjusted because the CDU/CSU and SPD overestimated the potential for controlled liberalization in Eastern Europe, underestimated the speed and uncontrolled nature of liberalization in Czechoslovakia and the determination of the Soviet Union to reverse it, and overestimated the potential influence of the Federal Republic in Eastern Europe.

Compromise was the inevitable result. Yet, if one concluded, as the SPD had but the CDU/CSU had not, that one could only change the status quo in the DDR by rapprochement, not pressure, one could not reject recognition of the Oder-Neisse line and the DDR. Compromise only stimulated Soviet and East German appetites and suspicions. For were the East to agree, Bonn would get what it wanted and the East would not get its main goal: recognition of the status quo. Moreover, as the East's reaction to the establishment of Bonn-Bucharest relations in early 1967 had shown, the Grand Coalition's Ostpolitik was much more tempting to Hungary, Rumania, Bulgaria, and Yugoslavia than to the Soviet Union, Poland, Czechoslovakia, and East Germany. It thus threatened bloc unity and required a hostile Soviet response. Finally, this compromise Ostpolitik was sufficiently behind the actual as opposed to the rhetorical positions of Bonn's Western allies so that it tended to create tension with them.

Yet although the Grand Coalition's Ostpolitik failed to reach its own objectives, it laid the ground for later progress toward them. It prepared the ground for a more realistic West German view of the potentialities of Ostpolitik and thus began to convince Moscow and Eastern Europe that West German public opinion was really changing. It took the first steps toward recognizing the Oder-Neisse line, annulling the Munich agreement, and modifying the Hallstein Docrtine. It began to discredit the Communist propaganda against West German "revisionism." By abandoning Schröder's policy of isolation of the DDR, it moved Ulbricht to isolate himself. It established diplomatic relations with Rumania and Yugoslavia. Finally, the SPD gained experience in dealing with the East, confirmed its view that one must recognize the status quo in order to modify and, it, hoped, eventually overcome it, and became more realistic about what could be accomplished.[111]

The 1969 SPD-FDP Coalition

The 1969 West German Bundestag election was very close.[1] If the Free Democratic and NPD (neo-Nazi) vote had been less than 1 percent, the Grand Coalition almost surely would have continued. Had the FDP not moved to the left, the new coalition could hardly have been formed. Finally, Brandt was then not as charismatic a figure as CDU Chancellor Kiesinger; the SPD was more popular than he.

The election thus was not a major shift. It did, however, reflect slow, continuing SPD rise because of West German modernization, urbanization, and secularization, which strenghed its willingness to change and the belief that change could be effective, provided they did not threaten high risks and did not run contrary to basic societal values.

The SPD gained from the CDU, particularly among white-collar workers. Post-1959 SPD strategy forswore nationalization of industry and neutralization in foreign policy to make the Social Democrats "respectable" to the middle class. The strategy paid off handsomely. The SPD's respectability had grown after Social Democrat Gustav Heinemann became federal president in March 1969. The successful Grand Coalition economic policies were identified with SPD Minister of Economics Karl Schiller. Finally, although the FDP lost considerably, its left wing did better than its right wing; and the FDP was thus more likely to join a coalition with the SPD than with the CDU. (The extreme right and extreme left parties got nowhere.) The SPD gained enough to form a coalition with the FDP and rapidly did so.

Foreign policy was not a major issue in the election. What there was primarily concerned relations with the Soviet Union, Eastern Europe, particularly Poland (the Oder-Neisse line), and East Germany (reunification and diplomatic recognition.) The FDP's essentially German nationalist foreign policy—East-West détente and agreement with the Soviet Union and East Germany to achieve reunification, even if this meant moving out of NATO into a European security system—was not favored by the

voters. The Christian Democrats stressed Western European unification plus relations with Eastern Europe without recognition
of East Germany or the Oder-Neisse line. The SPD stressed Western European unification and détente, including acceptance of
the status quo.

West Germans, in contrast to 1967, were prepared to give
support to détente, recognize the Oder-Neisse line, and improve
relations with East Germany but not to recognize it or to abandon reunification.[2] Public opinion came to see the Federal Republic to be a Western European medium power for an indefinite
period and lost its illusions about German reunification or rapid
Western European political union. The self-image of Brandt and
the SPD, not implicated in the Nazi regime, became that of
most West Germans, for whom a guilt complex was no longer
necessary or justified.

The major foreign policy change from the Grand Coalition
was that the new government gave its new Ostpolitik the same
priority as Western European unification and NATO and both
were consciously coordinated in the concept of a "European
peace order," summarized above. Second, its new Ostpolitik
was based on détente with the Soviet Union, East Germany, and
the other Eastern European states; and its first priority was
agreement with the Soviet Union so that Moscow would pressure East Germany to increase contacts between the two German states. The new coalition proposed to offer Moscow mutual
renunciation of use of force declarations, recognition of the
Oder-Neisse line, de facto recognition of East Germany,[3] and
signing of the nonproliferation treaty in return for the Soviet
Union giving up its claim to the right of intervention in the Federal Republic, its public hostility to West Germany, and acceptance of West German de facto, not de jure recognition of East
Germany, that is, "special relations," after which East German
diplomatic relations with all other states would be accepted.[4]
Reunification, Bonn's ultimate goal, was thus postponed to the
far, far distant future, if ever.[5]

The new coalition's security policy was based on continued

defense ties with the United States and on membership in NATO, coupled with conscious use of these ties to further East-West détente. The new government gave priority to the entry of the United Kingdom into the EEC over closer EEC political unity, in part because, unlike the CDU, it was so concerned with Ostpolitik as not to risk it vis-à-vis rapid, tight EEC political union. Western European political unity remained an integral, but not overriding, part of Bonn's foreign policy.

The differences within the new coalition on foreign policy can be best analyzed as differences between flexible Atlanticists and left nationalists. SPD flexible Atlanticists Helmut Schmidt and Georg Leber gave priority to the Atlantic alliance over Wehner's and Bahr's (left nationalist) priority for Ostpolitik, including over priority for Western European unity. Brandt, conciliatory by nature, tried to mediate between these two opposite views. However, the CDU/CSU accusations that Wehner and Bahr were pro-Soviet or pro-East German were unfounded. On the contrary, their Ostpolitik, whether or not nationalist, was potentially more dangerous to the Soviet Union and East Germany than the CDU/CSU's.

The CDU/CSU had been the governing party since 1949 and was unprepared for opposition. Its narrow defeat split its leadership and lowered its morale. Its initially near-total opposition to the Brandt-Scheel Ostpolitik was allegedly because it diminished priority for Western European reunification and Atlantic security, abandoned West Germany's legal claim to reunification, and endangered West German political stability, all in return for illusory gains in the East. The CDU/CSU somewhat but not decisively limited Brandt's flexibility, but it was also a useful argument vis-à-vis the Soviets.[6]

The new Ostpolitik of Brandt and Scheel, like the new Soviet Westpolitik, was primarily defensive: to maintain "the substance of the nation," the ties and sense of nationhood that existed between West and East Germans, by increasing contacts between West and East Germany. Since the Soviet Union would prevent reunification or major East German liberalization, Bonn could only encourage gradual change in the DDR through rapprochement with it—normalizing relations with it and defusing the Berlin problem.[7]

The new Ostpolitik had three other minimal aims: to join its Western allies in support of East-West détente, to maintain priority for Western European unity, and to compensate for the danger that the United States would be less inclined to take risks for Bonn because of the Soviet nuclear near-parity, U.S. Vietnam war-weariness, and pressure for unilateral U.S. troop withdrawal. These plus the shock of the Czechoslovak invasion made "security through normalization" more important for the SPD-FDP coalition than "change through rapprochement."[8] (Brandt's fear of Washington's reliability was exaggerated but nevertheless real.) These minimal aims would also contribute to the maximal objective: to expand West German influence in the Soviet Union and Eastern Europe and contribute to ultimate German reunification.

Thus by 1969, Moscow and Bonn wanted to recognize and stabilize the status quo in order eventually to change it. For both, the minimal motive was predominant, because both realized that this was in their interest and neither expected that the status quo could soon be changed. Bonn was too weak and too constrained to change it as long as Moscow's military power was so overwhelmingly superior and atomic weapons froze boundaries. To West Germany, and indeed to Western Europe, Moscow's political and economic attraction was low but the new Soviet Westpolitik could hope to prevent Western Europe from becoming more united and strong and to decrease U.S. presence there. Moreover, Moscow probably thought, West German economic and technological influence in Eastern Europe could be prevented from being converted into political power. Bonn hoped to preserve "the substance of the nation," or at least to slow down its erosion, and to demonstrate to East Berlin that Moscow would compromise with Bonn against East Berlin's wishes. Thus Moscow and Bonn's engagement with each other would aid the minimum aims of each, while only the future would tell which would eventually come closer to gaining its maximum aims. Agreement, therefore, was probable.

Multiple East-West Negotiations and the German Question

The resultant East-West negotiations on the German question had eight stages: (1) Soviet-Western negotiations on Europe, and the German question in particular, within the context of Sino-Soviet and Sino-American relations, (2) Soviet-West German negotiations, interacting with (3) Berlin negotiations and (4) other East-West negotiations in Europe—the Conference on Security and Cooperation in Europe (CSCE) and, later, mutual force reduction negotiations (MBFR), (5) Polish-West German negotiations, (6) West German-East German negotiations, (7) Czechoslovak-West German negotiations, and (8) normalization of relations between West Germany and Hungary and Bulgaria. The negotiations may be divided into three periods: (1) 1969–1970, when Soviet-West German negotiations were primary but West German-East German and West German-Polish negotiations were also going on; (2) 1971–1972, when Berlin negotiations were primary but West German-East German negotiations were also taking place; and (3) 1973, when West-East German negotiations became central.

Soviet motives were primarily defensive: to stabilize Eastern Europe and East Germany, to limit the rise of West German power and influence therein, and to get much more West German technology and credits. (Moscow also may have hoped eventually to destabilize and isolate West Germany.) For Moscow, Bonn's recognition of the boundaries to its east, not renunciation of use of force, was the key new element. Brezhnev personally identified himself with East-West détente, import of Western and Japanese technology and credits, improvement of domestic living standards, and renewed intellectual repression. All four were interrelated, since the second required the first, the third required the second and therefore the first, the first in his view required the fourth, and the third and fourth required each other. Moreover, since technology and credit imports required long-term credits from the West, they and East-West détente had to be long-range strategic policies, and so, therefore, did improvement of domestic living standards and renewed intellectual repression. Brezhnev encountered some opposition in Moscow on these four policies and in his rise in power, but by the Twenty-Fourth CPSU Congress in April 1971 he had pushed them through and consolidated his position. (As we shall see below, shortly thereafter Ulbricht fell and the Soviet position in the Berlin negotiations suddenly softened.)[9]

U.S. motives were even more defensive: to secure West Berlin, get an MBFR agreement because of domestic pressure for unilateral U.S. troop reduction in Europe, and prevent destabilization of West Germany or NATO and expansion westward in Europe of Soviet influence.

West Germany's motives were also primarily defensive: to lower the Soviet security threat, particularly since unilateral U.S. troop withdrawals would endanger the stability of West Berlin, liberalize East Germany via Soviet pressure on East Berlin, thereby "maintain the substance of the nation" and thus prevent the development of an East German "national" consciousness (Nationalbewusstsein). Bonn's long-range motives were potentially exapnsionist: to reunify Germany and in the short run liberalize, or, as Moscow and East Berlin saw it, destabilize, East Germany.

East German motives were also primarily defensive: to stabilize and legitimatize the SED regime by obtaining Western, and particularly West German, recognition of the partition of Germany and the legitimacy of the DDR and to end the West German pressure in West Berlin and thereby to move it toward being an "independent political entity" and eventually being abosrbed into the DDR.

Moscow's and East Berlin's policies increasingly diverged. Moscow gave priority to détente with the United States and agreement with Bonn over support of East Berlin's maximum demands, while Ulbricht remained opposed to détente and compromise with Bonn.

The DDR's problems had become much more difficult. The

Soviet invasion of Czechoslovakia had ended Moscow's fear that Ostpolitik would dangerously destabilize Eastern Europe. The Sino-American rapprochement moved Moscow toward détente. The new West German Ostpolitik, which gave Moscow its minimum demands, border recognition and international respectability for the DDR, did not give the DDR its maximum demands, recognition de jure, that is, Bonn's formal abjuring of any claim to German reunification, and a drastic status quo minus in West Berlin. It thus threatened to force the DDR to accept détente with Bonn without attaining either maximum demand and thus to make West German "infiltration" into the DDR easier and its prevention through *Abgrenzung* (demarcation) more difficult.

True, the DDR's inability to use either nationalism or liberalization (because of nationalism) to increase its popular acceptance was increasingly counterbalanced by the resignation of its population to its government, because of the Berlin Wall, the resultant blow to hopes of reunification and of flight, and by the rising East German standard of living. Still, Moscow was moving toward Bonn and Bonn's influence in the West was increasing because of its rising economic power and acceptance of Western détente policy.[10] Ulbricht therefore became more flexible in tactics but remained stubbornly rigid in substance. In short, he reacted to Brandt's abandonment of Bonn's previous policy of isolating the DDR by isolating himself, thus laying the ground for his fall.

Poland and Czechoslovakia wanted to limit West German power. Warsaw also wanted massive inputs of West German technology and credits, for which after the invasion Prague had no hope. Hungary, Rumania, and Bulgaria, much less concerned with West German power, also wanted West German technology and credits. However, Bulgaria was almost totally, and Hungary largely, bound to support Soviet foreign policy toward Bonn and thus could not get all they wanted, while Rumania, which was not, could and did. Yugoslavia also wanted to limit West German power. But it was so dependent on West German tourism and remittances of Yugoslav workers in West Germany; so anxious to increase its trade with the EEC; so desirous of West

German technology, credits, and trade; relatively invulnerable to Soviet pressure on the German issue; and anxious, for its own security, to strengthen détente to Europe that it favored the new Ostpolitik and opposed East German sabotage of it.

France was ambivalent about Soviet-West German détente. It wanted very close relations with Bonn to ensure its security against the Soviet Union and nationalistic, militaristic, and anti-French or pro-Soviet West Germany. For de Gaulle, West German Ostpolitik integrated into détente in Europe could work against these dangers. But he also realized that successful Ostpolitik would soon overshadow his own Eastern policy, make Paris less interesting for Moscow, and increase West German influence. French policy, therefore, was to give Bonn no reason to doubt its support of Ostpolitik but also to pursue its own Eastern policy, nuclear program, and economic and technological development. However, the May 1968 student riots weakened de Gaulle's authority, the August 1968 Czechoslovak invasion revived French fears of Moscow, and after de Gaulle's resignation in 1969, Pompidou conducted a less ambitious, less global, and less anti-U.S. foreign policy. Paris could do little about Ostpolitik except to try to safeguard its own interests, for Moscow soon made clear that it was much more interested in West Germany than in France.

Great Britain supported West German policies and favored détente and Ostpolitik, but its internal economic weakness eroded its foreign policy possibilities. The other Western European states played no particular role.

The United States primarily wanted a new Berlin agreement and mutual force reduction negotiations to ward off Senator Mansfield's drive for unilateral U.S. troop cuts in Europe. It favored Soviet-U.S. détente and therefore Soviet-West German détente as well in order to help limit strategic weapons, contain rising Soviet power, and get Soviet help for a compromise settlement of the Vietnam War. Nixon and Kissinger, like their predecessors, in principle favored priority for the U.S. alliance with Western Europe but negotiated with Moscow more than most

Western European governments liked. Moreover, Kissinger at first had considerable reservations about Brandt's new Ostpolitik and the Soviet proposal for a European security conference because he thought that both would strengthen the Soviet position in Eastern Europe, increase its influence in Western Europe, and destabilize the Federal Republic. Such conservative American figures as Acheson, Clay, and McCloy, long associated with U.S. policy toward Germany, strongly anti-Soviet, and with close ties with the CDU, also opposed the Brandt-Scheel Ostpolitik. Nevertheless, Nixon and Kissinger went along with it and when in 1971 the Soviets began to make concessions to Berlin they abandoned their initial reservations.

The New Ostpolitik and the Soviet-West German Treaty

The new Ostpolitik was not a revolutionary or hardly even a strategic change in the Ostpolitik (or the Westpolitik) of the Grand Coalition.[11] (There were only small minorities on the left wings of the SPD and FDP who did want such a change.) It was not a return to the traditions of Rapallo or of Bismarckian *Schaukelpolitik* (balancing policy between East and West.) Nor did it abandon the goals of self-determination and eventually of reunification. On the contrary, it used different and, its proponents maintained, more realistic tactics to achieve them, which, it recognized, could be achieved only in the very long run, if at all.

The Brandt-Scheel Ostpolitik was not less but more committed to German than to European goals. While the CDU continued its priority for Westpolitik, because of ideology and pressure from its right wing, and maintained its claim for reunification, the new SPD-FDP coalition lowered its short-term goals in the hope of increasing security and thereby better achieving its long-term one—reunification. Brandt made this clear in his governmental declaration on October 28, 1969, which set forth the major specific changes in his new Ostpolitik: the acknowledgement of the existence of two German states and the desire for normalization through "special" relations between them, de facto but not de jure recognition.

This government starts with the premise that the questions which have arisen for the German people out of the Second World War and the national treason of the Hitler regime can only be answered in a European peace order (*Friedensordnung*). However, no one can convince us that the Germans do not have a right to self-determination just like all other peoples.

The task of practical polities in the years that lie ahead of us is to preserve the unity of the nation through overcoming the present cramped status of the relationship between the parts of Germany. . . .

Twenty years after the foundation of the Federal Republic of Germany and the DDR, we must hinder a further estrangement (*Auseinanderleben*) of the German nation, that is, we must try to come through regulated living next to each other to living with each other. . . .

Even if two states exist in Germany, they are not foreign countries for each other; their relations with each other can only be of a special nature. . . .[12]

The new Ostpolitik included seven specific moves: (1) as a clear, fixed first priority, exchange of nonuse of force declarations with the Soviet Union that would not involve Bonn's de jure recognition of the DDR, that is, of its legal permanency in international law, plus increase in Soviet-West German economic relations; (2) thereafter, a similar agreement with Poland, including the recognition by Bonn of the Oder-Neisse line; then (3) a quadripartite agreement on the status of West Berlin that would preserve (a) four-power responsibility over at least West Berlin, (b) security of the access routes for the three Western powers and for West Germans and West Berliners, and (c) existing political, economic and cultural ties between the Federal Republic and West Berlin in order to stabilize and ensure the status quo after the establishment of the Bonn-East Berlin "special relationship"; (4) a treaty with the DDR, to be obtained by Soviet pressure on East Berlin, to establish nondiscriminatory "special relations" between the "two states in Germany" (below the level of de jure recognition); (5) *menschliche Erleichterungen* (improvements of human relationships) in cultural exchange, travel, and so forth through Bonn-East Berlin negotiations at the governmental level; (6) treaties with the other Eastern European states followed by international recognition of the DDR and entry of both German states into the United Nations; and (7) at the end, participation by both German states in a European security conference. All these policies were to be linked with each other so that negotiations with Moscow, Warsaw, and East Berlin would be concluded in that order, and Moscow would agree to a Berlin settlement, whereupon Bonn would agree to a European security conference. That Bonn carried out successfully this complicated linkage was one of Brandt's greatest achievements.[13]

Initial Soviet Reactions

The Soviets were not unaware of the true motives of the new Ostpolitik, nor any less suspicious of the SPD, for they realized how far, even if how long-term, Bonn's maximum goals went. But so did Soviet goals. Moscow wanted to prevent the conversion of West German economic power into political and military power, to divert Bonn from strengthening the EEC and NATO, and above all from a European nuclear force with any West German participation. Brezhnev presumably anticipated some difficulties with Ulbricht, although perhaps not as many as he was to have. He probably felt that any increase of West German influence in the DDR could easily be controlled, if necessary, by the Red Army, which had just performed this function in Czechoslovakia.

Gomułka's May 1969 indication of his willingness, reportedly made without Brezhnev's (or Ulbricht's) previous knowledge and approval, showed that the Soviets would encounter difficulties if they remained so hostile toward Bonn. Ceauşescu, although somewhat intimidated by the Czechoslovak invasion, had already established diplomatic relations with Bonn and was increasingly diversifying his foreign trade pattern away from CMEA, particularly by increasing trade with the Federal Republic.

The Soviet Union was also scaling down its objectives, and

Bonn increasing its hopes, with respect to the European security conference. Moscow had hoped to use it to bring pressure on Bonn to accept maximum Soviet terms and to exclude Washington from it. By 1969, however, the Soviets needed the conference more, presumably in part to stabilize their European front when they were so seriously engaged against the Chinese. The West Germans and the Americans were demonstrating that the Soviets must pay a price to get it, a price that must include U.S. and Canadian participation and, for Bonn, some Soviet concessions on Berlin and East-West German relations. Thus the diverging interests of Moscow and East Berlin became clear. The USSR, bordering on China and technologically less developed, was more anxious to get Western technology than was East Berlin, which was far away from Peking and had its own technology, to which it wished to tie Moscow in order to increase its political influence there, rather than have Moscow get more West German credits and thus be more subject to West German and less to East German influence.

Bonn, Washington, and Moscow could not negotiate on Ostpolitik and the European security conference as long as Bonn and Washington opposed the conference per se and Moscow demanded maximum preconditions for it and tried to use its convening to put pressure on Bonn. But the new coalition in Bonn favored a more flexible policy: to be paid a price for participating in the conference and then to use the conference as well as the price to keep the German question at least formally open. Washington, which initially opposed the conference, opposed it less as détente intensified and as it realized that the Soviet Union would pay a significant price for it, not only (as Bonn also wanted) on Berlin but also on mutual force reduction negotiations.

The Brandt-Scheel government wanted to move rapidly on Ostpolitik, since it needed a rapid success, détente made its chances quite good, and one could not know how long these favorable circumstances would last. Nevertheless, if only because of the problem of ratification of the treaties in the Bundestag, where the new SPD-FDP coalition had only a small majority, it was clear that Bonn could not accept the maximum Soviet demands: de jure recognition of the DDR, no concessions on Berlin, and unconditional acceptance of the Soviet proposal for a European security conference.

For Moscow, speed was less important, since Brezhnev did not need rapid success. Indeed, most within the CPSU leadership who may have opposed him probably were more cautious on détente. (Shelest was ousted in 1972 probably only secondarily because he opposed détente but primarily because Brezhnev thought he had insufficiently crushed Ukrainian nationalism.) Brezhnev could hardly have wanted to bring too rapid or extreme pressure on East Berlin. There were, however, increasing signs of Soviet dissatisfaction with Ulbricht's refusal to compromise on his maximum position: de jure recognition of the DDR, the status quo minus on Berlin (the end of Bonn's presence there), no *menschliche Erleichterungen* (no intrusion of West German influence into the DDR) but, rather, more *Abgrenzung* (demarcation), that is, even fewer human contacts between them and intensification of the SED's ideological struggle against the Federal Republic and the "right-wing Social Democratic leaders."

The Soviet-West German Negotiations

Moscow soon reacted favorably to Brandt's election and policy declaration.[14] At the end of October a Warsaw Pact declaration on European security repeated the "all-European" theme of the previous Budapest declaration (that is, still implicitly rejected U.S. participation), but it no longer explicitly attacked NATO, (it preferred to ratify the European military status quo, including the Soviet military occupation of Czechoslovakia, rather than to try to change it). It also implied that Moscow would discuss what states should participate in a European security conference (it would not indefinitely oppose U.S. and Canadian participation). Moscow thus indicated that it had decided to try no longer to make either the detachment of Bonn from NATO, even if only partially, or U.S. nonparticipation in the security conference preconditions for Soviet-West German détente. Moreover, unlike the Budapest Declaration, the Prague Declaration contained no explicit polemics against Bonn whatsoever. Indeed, it did not mention Bonn at all, because Moscow and East Berlin could not agree whether Moscow-Bonn negotiations should be bilateral (which Moscow and Bonn favored) or multilateral (on which the DDR still insisted).[15] Presumably the Soviets hoped that a security conference, East-West détente, Soviet-West German détente, and continued Soviet emphasis on the "all-European" theme would gradually lower European (and U.S.) defense expenditures and NATO and EEC cohesion. However, their defensive motives were beginning to override their expansionist ones.

On November 28, Bonn signed the nonproliferation treaty, which apparently convinced Moscow that Brandt meant what he said. (Signature was for Moscow a precondition for progress in Ostpolitik.) At the beginning of December, a Brussels NATO meeting made West German-Soviet and Berlin agreements a precondition for Western participation in a European security conference, while a Moscow Warsaw Pact meeting agreed to bilateral negotiations with the Federal Republic before Bonn came to terms with East Berlin but still demanded that Bonn recognize the DDR de jure as well as all boundaries in Europe. Thus Ulbricht had to abandon his insistence on multilateral negotiations only.[16] Thereupon Ulbricht proposed to Brandt Bonn-East Berlin negotiations at heads-of-government level and enclosed a draft treaty including de jure recognition of the DDR. On January 14, 1970, Brandt rejected this but indicated willingness to compromise in return for alleviation of all the human effects of German partition. Ulbricht thereupon repeated his willingness to negotiate without the precondition of de jure recognition.[17] On January 22, Brandt proposed negotiations, with no agenda preconditions, about a nonuse of force treaty and economic and cultural cooperation but declared that the two German states were parts of one German nation (a position Ulbricht rejected) and that any treaty must take into account four-power rights in all of Germany.[18]

Thereupon negotiations for a Soviet-West German treaty began in Moscow between Gromyko and the West German ambassador. At first these got nowhere because the Soviets would agree to an exchange of nonuse of force declarations only if Bonn would recognize the finality of European boundaries and the DDR de jure, while Bonn agreed to recognize the boundaries as inviolable but not as unchangeable and to make a treaty with the DDR binding in international law but not to recognize it de jure.

Brandt, anxious to move rapidly, then sent Egon Bahr to Moscow to negotiate with Gromyko. Three rounds of negotiations followed, in January–February, March, and May. Bahr said later that they were considerably longer than he had expected and that the first breakthrough was in a talk with Kosygin on February 13.[19] (That same evening Scheel was most hospitably received by high Soviet diplomats when he passed through the Moscow airport.)[20] Only at the end of May did Moscow implicitly agree to drop its claim to intervention rights in the Federal Republic under the UN charter and to accept a unilateral Bonn declaration on German unity.[21] However, a trip by Scheel to Moscow was delayed by FDP fears that it might hurt them in the June 14 state elections and by the Springer press's publication of Bahr's negotiating position. This ignited a violent controversy in Bonn, helped make the CDU/CSU refuse to send a representative with Scheel to Moscow, and put Brandt at the disadvantage. Bonn's concessions became public with no assurance that the Berlin negotiations, then stalled, would end favorably.[22] It also made it impossible for Moscow to make major concessions to Scheel, as he had hoped.[23]

It may well be, however, that the Soviets were concerned about the CDU/CSU attacks on the negotiations, for Ulbricht's tone in June and July toward Bonn was less harsh.[24] When Scheel finally arrived in Moscow on July 27, Gromyko flatly refused to make any reference in the treaty to reunification or self-determination. He did, however, agree to accept a West German letter to this effect, but only as a one-sided document, as he put it, not as a part of the negotiations.[25] He also agreed to insert in the preamble a statement that Soviet-West German relations will be based on the UN Charter, which refers to self-determination and which Bonn could cite to demonstrate that the treaty did not preclude this for Germans. Scheel had wanted these concessions in part because of CDU/CSU criticism, and perhaps Gromyko made them in part for that reason.

The Erfurt and Kassel Meetings

While Gromyko and Bahr were negotiating in Moscow, and in considerable part because they were, the first two meetings occurred, at heads of government level, between Bonn and East Berlin: between Brandt and Stoph (then East German premier) at Erfurt, in the DDR, on March 19,[26] and at Kassel, in the Federal Republic, on May 21.[27] The meetings, although they seemed to lead to complete deadlock, may best be viewed as a significant, if secondary, sideshow to the Moscow negotiations and were a necessary prelude to the working-level Bonn-East Berlin negotiations that followed.

After an October 1969 Warsaw Pact declaration omitted the precondition of de jure recognition, on February 12, 1970, Stoph agreed to a meeting without preconditions. There ensued a controversy over the meeting place. The DDR maintained not only that it should be in East Berlin but that Brandt not travel first to West Berlin and cross over from there to East Berlin. Brandt refused because this would symbolize acceptance of the DDR's rejection of any ties between the Federal Republic and West Berlin. Then, after he had completed the first round of his Moscow negotiations with Bahr, Gromyko spent February 23–27 in East Berlin, and the communiqué omitted any reference to de jure recognition of the DDR (Moscow implicitly accepted Bahr's argument that the four-power rights precluded it). Gromyko also apparently suggested Erfurt as a compromise. Preparations for the meeting began on March 2 and on March 12 the DDR accepted Erfurt.[28]

The March 19 Erfurt meeting symbolized Bonn's de facto recognition of the DDR. It began with a large spontaneous demonstration by East German onlookers for Brandt, and it was primarily intended by both participants to influence Moscow.

The demonstration, carried on West German television, proved to most West Germans that the East Germans wanted closer ties with West Germany, and it furthered Brandt's charismatic image in both German states. The formal speeches repeated previous positions. Stoph rejected more East-West German contacts and refused to negotiate until Brandt agreed to recognize the DDR de jure and paid an indemnity of DM 100 billion for the "economic war" that the Federal Republic had allegedly waged against the DDR before the wall went up, probably intended to make up for the loss of tariff-free East-West German trade that de jure recognition would imply. Brandt rejected de jure recognition of the DDR and insisted that there must be progress in the Berlin negotiations and East-West German détente.

On March 26, four-power Berlin negotiations began but made no progress during the rest of 1970. The subsequent May 21 Brandt-Stoph meeting at Kassel also showed little change in either's position. (Its beginning was marred by right- and left-wing demonstrations.) Stoph again repeated his unyielding position. Brandt made a specific twenty-point proposal that, although totally rejected by Stoph, foreshadowed most of the agreement on Berlin and the East-West German basic treaty. It included nonuse of force declarations, territorial integrity of both German states, abandonment of the Hallstein Doctrine, retention of four-power responsibility for all of Germany, respect for the ties between the Federal Republic and West Berlin, increase in East-West German travel, including much more in border areas, family reunions, more cultural exchange, retention of special tariff-free economic relationship, membership of both German states in the UN, and permanent representatives (not ambassadors) of each to the other. The twenty points also set forth the new Bonn coalition's view on "the future and the holding together of the nation" as a result of "the special situation of Germany and the Germans who live in two states but despite that see themselves as members of one nation," a position that, not surprisingly, was not in the final agreements but was not rejected by them either. The discussions were then suspended by the DDR because it still hoped to get Bonn to recognize it de jure and by the Federal Republic because it believed, with reason, that Moscow would not support East Berlin in this respect.

The meetings failed because Bonn wanted substantive but not formal and East Berlin wanted formal but not substantive normalization. Nevertheless, they brought East Berlin closer to equality and recognition and Bonn got its negotiating position on the table plus the prospect of institutionalizing the negotiation process on a confidential working-level basis.[29]

The Moscow Negotiations

Bahr's negotiating position was not as good as it might have been. The negotiations were in Moscow—the Soviets were on their home ground. He did not have detailed written instructions, indeed, perhaps he could not have had any so rapidly, for Brandt's and his strategy was still disputed and often not understood within the new Bonn coalition. He also seldom gained time by referring disputed questions back to Bonn. In contrast, the Soviets, aware that Brandt wanted a rapid success, tried to show that they felt under no time pressure.

Bahr convinced Gromyko that de jure West German recognition of the DDR or of the boundary between West and East Germany and of the Oder-Neisse line were incompatible with four-power responsibilities—that they could come only in a German peace treaty and also that they could not be ratified by the Bundestag. Gromyko soon indicated that the Soviet Union had no intention of surrendering its four-power responsibilities. He refused to negotiate with the West Germans about Berlin, but Bonn made clear, first privately and then publicly, that the Bundestag would not ratify the Soviet-German treaty before a staisfactory Berlin agreement. The Bahr-Gromyko draft (the so-called "Bahr paper"), which included a draft treaty and a declaration of intentions, was slightly modified during the Scheel-Gromyko negotiations to give more verbal support for the so-called "German option" (Bonn's intention to pursue the peaceful reunification of Germany). Brandt and Kosygin signed the treaty in Moscow on August 12, 1970.

The treaty and its accompanying documents, the identical Soviet and West German "declarations of intent" and the West German negotiating directive and letter with respect to reunification, may best be analyzed in eight categories, four with respect to the treaty and four with respect to the other two documents.

1. *The nonuse of force declaration* was the center of the treaty. International lawyers may argue whether its reference to Article 2 of the UN Charter (nonuse or threat of use of force) legally bound the Soviet Union not to attempt to or threaten to use the intervention rights in Germany that Moscow had claimed it had been given in Articles 53 and 107 of the Charter. In any case, Gromyko declared at the end of the negotiations that there were "no exceptions" to nonuse of force.

2. *The recognition of the territorial status quo* was expressed in the formula (in which the world "recognition" did not appear) that the treaty proceeded from "the existing real situation" (*"von der in diesem Raum bestehenden wirklichen Lage"/"iz sushchesvuushchego v etom raione deistvitel'nogo polozheniya"*), that peace in Europe can only be maintained when no one "encroaches" on (*"antastet"/"posyagat"*) the present boundaries and that the boundaries of all states in Europe are inviolable (*"unverletzlich"/"niezraniony"*), "including the Oder-Neisse line, which forms the western boundary of the Polish People's Republic, and the boundary between the Federal Republic of Germany and the German Democratic Republic." (The Soviets thus finally gave up their demand that the boundaries be declared "unalterable" (*"unveränderbar"/"neizmennii"* or *"nezyblemii"*. Both states also declared that they did not have and would not have any territorial claims against any other state.

3. Existing treaty obligations, which in letters to the three Western powers Bonn defined as the four-power responsibilities for Germany and Berlin and Bonn's adherence to NATO, the West European Union, (WEU), and EEC, were excepted from the treaty.

4. Both sides agreed to work toward détente and to increase their economic, technological and cultural cooperation.

The other points were contained in simultaneous, identical)

declarations of intents and in Bonn's negotiating directive and letter on reunification.

5. Bonn declared that the Bundestag would only ratify the treaty if a Berlin agreement that would "safeguard the close ties between the Federal Republic and West Berlin and free access to West Berlin" was reached. (It hoped thereby to make CDU/CSU approval of the treaty more likely.) Bonn thus insisted on what Gromyko had refused to discuss: a link between agreement and Bundestag ratification of the Soviet-West German treaty.

6. Bonn agreed that the treaty was a part of a "united whole" that would also include treaties between the Federal Republic and Poland, Czechoslovakia, and the DDR. This could be interpreted as West German recognition of Soviet hegemony over them but also as obliging Moscow to aid in their negotiation.

The West German treaty with Poland would include Bonn's recognition of the Oder-Neisse line, but the formulation about the treaty with Czechoslovakia, that it would settle the questions "connected with the invalidity of the Munich agreement," implied that the Soviets no longer made Bonn's declaring it invalid *ex tunc* a precondition for the other treaties.

7. Bonn agreed to de facto recognition of the DDR, the abandonment of the Hallstein Doctrine, and the entry of both German states into the UN, "in the process of détente in Europe," that is, after a West German-East German treaty. It did not, however, "recognize" the DDR and could therefore continue to insist on a "special relationship" with it, short of de jure recognition; and in a letter to Gromyko, whose receipt he acknowledged and whose contents he did not contest, Scheel declared that the treaty did not conflict with Bonn's policy "to work for a state of peace in Europe in which the German nation will recover its unity in free self-determination."

8. Both agreed to support preparations for a European security conference. This was a West German concession to the Soviets.

Which gained more by the treaty, Moscow or Bonn? First, the treaty can only be judged within the context of the agreements that followed it: the Berlin agreement, the treaties with Poland and Czechoslovakia, and the West German-East German treaty. Second, it is too early to tell. In the Soviet-West German treaty itself the Soviet Union came closer to achieving its objectives than the Federal Republic did. True, as Brandt said, the treaty gave away nothing that Hitler had not lost long before; it enabled Bonn to proceed to other negotiations that turned out better for West German interests; and it strengthened Bonn's international position. But if Bonn had not been so anxious to conclude the treaty rapidly it might well have gotten more out of it.

Yet this is not the main point. The treaty began to implement the Brandt-Scheel Ostpolitik. It marked the overture, not the finale, to a series of negotiations. East Berlin's clear if implicit hostility to it soon showed that the treaty was the first instance when the Soviet Union abandoned its hitherto total support of the DDR in favor of agreement with Bonn. (The Soviet press did not reprint East Berlin's claims that the treaty required Bonn and other countries to recognize the DDR de jure.) This foreshadowed more favorable prospects for Bonn in the forthcoming negotiations on Berlin and with East Germany.

The treaty made clear that the Soviet Union preferred four-power responsibility over West German de jure recognition of the DDR. Moscow de facto accepted while publicly rejecting, a link between Bundestag ratification of the treaty and a Berlin agreement and thereby threatened the DDR's maximum Berlin position. In a four-hour conversation when Brandt went to Moscow to sign the treaty, Brezhnev pressed for rapid ratification by the Bundestag and for Bonn's participation in a European security conference, but Brandt made clear that both depended upon some progress in the Berlin negotiations and in East-West German détente. Moreover, the negotiations between West Germany and the East threatened to foil the DDR's policy of *Abgrenzung* against Bonn, force East Berlin to negotiate a treaty with Bonn, deprive it of de jure recognition, and increase West German and West Berlin travel to it and therefore threaten its destabilization, deprive it of its favorite target, "West German neonazism and militarism," and presage increased dependence by Moscow on Bonn, and therefore less on East Berlin, for technology and credits.[30]

The West German-Polish Treaty

The most difficult analytical problem about the 1969–1970 prelude to the West German-Polish treaty[31] is to judge to what extent the change in the Polish attitude toward Bonn arose from Polish as well as from Soviet motives. The latter played a major role in Polish policy: Since 1945, Warsaw has had to conform to all major Soviet foreign policy initiatives. But there were also other, genuinely Polish motives in the 1969 shift in Warsaw's attitude toward Bonn. They were not perceived by Warsaw to be contrary to Soviet policy—whether they were so perceived by Moscow is less clear—but rather as following it and also influencing it for Polish purposes.

The change in Polish policy was in part a revival of the 1956–1958 trends that led to the Rapacki Plan. Warsaw had seven political goals: (1) to maintain its alliance with the Soviet Union, *inter alia,* in order (2) to help limit rising West German power as well as to maintain communism and the communist model of modernization in power in Poland, (3) to guard against any Soviet-West German arrangement over Poland's head, and thereby, and also by moving toward an all-European security system, (4) gradually to transform its relationship with Moscow from a satellite to a "junior partner." The fifth Polish motive was economic: to get large-scale inputs of West German technology and credits, particularly since by the end of the 1960s Polish economic growth had slowed down. Sixth, Warsaw realized that Moscow was moving toward détente with Bonn and that it would be impossible, and against Poland's interests, to oppose this, as Ulbricht was doing, by continued hostility to West Germany. Seventh, Polish public opinion, notably in the Church and among the young Party intelligentsia, favored improving relations with Bonn.

West German public opinion increasingly favored agreement with Poland even if it meant formal recognition of the Oder-Neisse line. Among the liberal and left opinion-forming West German intelligentsia, reconciliation with Poland had come to be a moral duty second only to reconciliation with Israel. Polish literature, music, and art had become increasingly well known and admired in the Federal Republic, and many personal contacts had been established, including with noncommunist Polish Catholics and liberals. The West German Protestant and Catholic churches strongly supported normalization or relations with Poland. The political influence of the expellees, still adamantly opposed to recognition of the Oder-Neisse line, had continued to decline. The Polish market attracted West German industry. Those in favor of coming to terms with Moscow, no matter what they thought about Poland, increasingly realized that this would be impossible without the recognition of the Oder-Neisse line.

Professor Ulrich Scheuner well expressed the growing West German consensus:

It is . . . clear that the whole power of the Soviet Union and the East European states stands behind the Oder boundary and that there is no prospect of this changing. . . .

An agreement with Poland would also be a move of self-clarification and -reflection. To abandon historical claims which can no longer be fulfilled can be an act of liberation for a state and a people. . . .

But one should guard against illusions and too great hopes. The step which Bonn now intends to take will be basically a unilateral act of farewell and of one's own separation from the past. It will not be accompanied by significant concessions by the other side. . . .[32]

Finally, and most important, the new SPD-FDP coalition was committed to the recognition of the Oder-Neisse line. As to the CDU/CSU, although it did not formally reject recognition, and although its more liberal wing favored it, its majority continued to oppose its.

Negotiations went on in Warsaw intermittently through 1970. They were slow in part because Moscow insisted it first conclude a treaty with Bonn. Warsaw rejected Bonn's initial proposal that the Oder-Neisse problem be included in a nonuse of force agreement and insisted that the boundary be specifically recognized. Bonn agreed to this in April, because it had agreed to it before the third and last round of the Gromyko-Bahr discussions. Bonn successfully refused to agree to support the boundary in any eventual German peace negotiations, for this would have meant to agree to what it had refused in Moscow, that the boundaries were unchangeable (rather than inviolable) and that therefore German reunification was foreclosed forever. There remained the issue of the emigration to the Federal Republic of ethnic Germans in Poland, essential for Bonn but which Warsaw wanted to limit severely in order not to lose skilled labor. Finally in the Scheel-Jędrychowski November negotiations, the West German and Polish Red Cross organizations were empowered to negotiate the issue. (It was in fact not settled until the Schmidt-Gierek meeting in Helsinki in July 1975.)

Brandt signed the treaty in Warsaw on December 7. To worldwide acclaim but to the distaste of many West Germans, he symbolized the reconcilation with Poland by spontaneously kneeling before the monument to the Jews killed by the Germans in the 1943 Warsaw ghetto rising.

Warsaw gained much more from the treaty than Bonn—practically all its aims. Yet Bonn's key concession, recognition of the Oder-Neisse line, had already been conceded in the Soviet-West German treaty. It was a precondition for normalization of Bonn's relations with the East. Bonn was in an increasingly unrealistic and isolated position on the issues. Morally and politically, therefore, Bonn gained by making the concession just as Warsaw did by obtaining it.

The Berlin Agreement

The spring 1969 Berlin minicrisis had ended abruptly, simultaneously with, and probably in part because of, the Sino-Soviet Ussuri border incident. The Western powers on August 6 and 7 proposed to the Soviets an exchange of views on Berlin, to which the Soviets replied, encouragingly, on September 12, *before* the Brandt-Scheel government came to power. On December 16, the Western powers proposed a three-point agenda for negotiations alternately in East and West Berlin: improvement of traffic to and from West Berlin, restoration of traffic and postal and telephone communications between West and East Berlin, and ending economic discrimination against West Berlin in the Soviet Union and Eastern Europe. The Soviets countered that the negotiations should concern "activities" in West Berlin contrary to the city's status. On February 27, 1970, the West proposed that negotiations be at the former Allied Control Council (in West Berlin), which still houses the four-power Air Safety Center. They began on March 26.

As they went on, policy disagreements between the Soviet Union and the DDR became increasingly serious. Coordination among the four Western powers and with the Federal Republic was remarkably good, and the 1958–1962 tensions were not repeated. Bonn had much more influence on its allies than East Berlin did on Moscow. This time it was not Adenauer but Ulbricht whose policy was destroyed by his senior ally's move toward détente.[33]

Initially the negotiations made little progress but, not surprisingly, they speeded up after the August signing of the West German-Soviet treaty. The first drafts were exchanged on September 23, 1970. On October 7, a four-power expert group was set up that soon developed an agreed agenda and structure for the agreement: a four-power agreement, a detailed implementing agreement to be negotiated between Bonn and East Berlin, and a final four-power protocol. Thereupon the real negotiations began.

The three Western powers, particularly the United States, wanted to avoid another Berlin crisis as a result of the increased East German influence over the access routes that would result from upgrading or de facto Western (and West German) recognition of the DDR, which the West saw as possible, albeit not inevitable. Furthermore, not only were they at more of a disadvantage in West Berlin than elsewhere, but past experience showed how easily a Berlin crisis could interrupt détente. Brandt urged negotiations, a logical consequence of his "small steps" policy. The West wanted a Soviet guarantee for Western access that would make as certain as possible that Moscow would not allow East Berlin to precipitate a new Berlin crisis. Bonn and

West Berlin shared these motives but were more concerned about preserving West Berlin's access and viability than about a Berlin crisis interfering with détente. For both, détente threatened psychological destabilization in West Berlin because it deprived the city of its front-line (*Frontstadt*) role without giving it a new one. Therefore for them détente had to include a Berlin agreement.

Brandt had also made a Berlin agreement a precondition for Soviet-West German détente in March 1970 at Kassel. The Bonn cabinet's directives to Scheel thereafter, before the final West German-Soviet negotiations occured, reiterated this linkage (*Junktim*). After the treaty was signed in August, pressure by the Free Democrats in Bonn, reacting in part to CDU criticism of the treaty, further cemented Bonn's insistence that the Bundestag would not ratify the Soviet (and Polish) treaties until a Berlin agreement was signed. When in summer 1971 the Soviets began to make some concessions on Berlin, the Western powers' interests in the negotiations intensified. When the West and the West Germans entered into the Berlin negotiations, they did not assume that they would succeed but that they would fail. However, they, particularly Brandt, wanted to test the Soviets, since they felt that there was little to lose and perhaps something to gain.

The Soviet and East German positions on the Berlin negotiations increasingly diverged. Both would probably have preferred to continue harassment of West Berlin in order to move toward the "status quo minus" there: the end of its ties with the Federal Republic and thereby of access from West Germany through West Berlin to East Berlin and East Germany. But the Soviets had to see Berlin in the context of their confrontation with the Chinese and their desire to strengthen détente in Europe and with the United States. Finally, once the Soviet-West German treaty had been signed and Brezhnev's prestige was thereby committed to it, he was anxious to have the Bundestag ratify it. Therefore, although the Soviets continued publicly to reject any linkage between its ratification and a Berlin agreement, they were forced to accept it.

The East German minimal position was far less flexible than that of the Soviets, for East Berlin gave much less priority to the global considerations that influenced Soviet policy in Europe and much more to its fears of domestic destabilization as a result of an influx of visitors and publications from West Berlin and the Federal Republic. Soviet and East German differences became implicitly clear in March 1969, when Moscow, probably contrary to East Berlin's wishes, called off the Berlin minicrisis. They reached their height during the final stage of the Berlin negotiations with the resignation of Walter Ulbricht as SED first secretary.

The Berlin negotiations began in earnest in early 1971.[34] Several events made this possible: the signature on August 12, 1970, of the Soviet-West German treaty; the announcement of October 29, 1970, of the beginning of confidential Bonn-East Berlin negotiations; the indefinite postponement by the four powers of the disputed issue of whether or not the agreement should concern East as well as West Berlin; Brezhnev's overcoming, apparently, shortly before the April 1971 Twenty-fourth CPSU Congress, some opposition to détente with Bonn;[35] NATO's December 4, 1970, declaration making a Berlin agreement a precondition for a European security conference;[36] the April 1971 visit of a U.S. ping-pong team to China, which must have made Moscow feel that a Sino-American rapprochement was underway;[37] and, most of all, the successful West German and then Western linkage of the Bundestag ratification of Bonn's treaties with Moscow and Warsaw with the successful completion of the Berlin agreement and the convening of a European security conference, which forced Moscow to compromise on Berlin over the DDR's head and against its own view of its interests.

The Western draft of February 5, 1971, and the Soviet draft of March 26, whose details later became known in the West, although they have not as yet been published, showed that both sides had made considerable concessions. The Soviet draft accepted the Western presence in West Berlin, the economic ties of West Berlin with the Federal Republic, improvement of access to West Berlin, and partial foreign representation of West Berlin by the Federal Republic. The Western draft conceded that the Federal Republic should no longer carry on "official constitutional acts" in West Berlin (election of the federal president, meetings of the federal cabinet, and plenary meetings of the Bundestag and Bundesrat), which had precipitated Berlin crises before, and that East Germany should play some role in controls over access.

The differences, however, remained great. They centered on the role of the DDR. The Soviet draft clearly implied Soviet involvement in the control of much reduced West German activities in West Berlin. It provided that only the West Berlin authorities could negotiate with the DDR (it implied the "separate political entity" theory for West Berlin), for East German (not Soviet) control over access to West Berlin, and for a Soviet consulate general in West Berlin. Essentially, moreover, Moscow proposed that negotiations on access and travel between West Berlin and East Berlin be conducted by the West Berlin authorities and by the West Germans with the DDR for access from West Germany to West Berlin.[38] However, the Soviet draft did propose the ambiguous compromise formula that was finally adopted with respect to the area covered, neither "Berlin" nor "West Berlin" but simply "the relevant area."

The Fall of Ulbricht

One of the obstacles that slowed down and for a time threatened to prevent a Berlin agreement was Ulbricht's attempt to force Bonn to grant East Berlin de jure recognition and negotiate a Berlin agreement with East Berlin (not at the four-power level) that would give the DDR to the city and cut the ties between Bonn and West Berlin.

Bonn had made clear that it would agree to neither. The Soviet-West German and Soviet-Polish treaties included neither. Moscow (and Warsaw) made it increasingly clear in late 1970 and early 1971 that they would no longer support these maximum East German positions and were determined to normalize relations with Bonn. As Soviet pressure on East Berlin increased, while Ulbricht remained adamant, in early 1971 some of his associates, particularly Honecker, began to move toward the Soviet position.

Ulbricht saw the Soviet-West German treaty as a threat to East German interests, for it did not include his maximum demands. On August 15, the DDR declared, in a passage that *Pravda* did not reprint, that the treaty obligations "require that normal diplomatic relations be established." On August 18, *Pravda* made clear that East Berlin must moderate its policy toward Bonn: "Those who for decades have been accustomed to considering the Federal Republic of Germany as an instrument of the aggressive blocs are finding it difficult to adjust to the fact that just like any other foreign state West Germany has its own state interests and wishes to pursue a policy which considers the real situation and the real existing possibilities."[39]

On October 29, 1970, probably as a result of Soviet pressure, Stoph informed Brandt that East Berlin was prepared to resume discussions with Bonn, without, as he had previously demanded, Bonn first recognizing the DDR de jure. But on November 8, Ulbricht proposed Bonn-East Berlin negotiations on Berlin access provided that all activities in Berlin "by other states, which negates the interests of the GDR and other socialist states, be suspended...," that is, he was again trying to get the Berlin issue into inter-German rather than four-power negotiations.[40] Ulbricht did not attend the Hungarian Party congress in late November and the DDR began harassing traffic from the West to Berlin. The day that this began, Brezhnev delcared in Erivan that a Berlin settlement was "of serious importance" and must take into account "the wishes of the West Berlin population" and the (unspecified) "legitimate" rights of the German Democratic Republic. Gromyko and his German expert, Falin, suddenly arrived in East Berlin. Ulbricht declared that more consultation of the fraternal parties was desirable (that Moscow should follow his wishes).

Moscow refused to give way; and, probably as a result of Soviet pressure, East-West German talks, which had been stalled, were resumed on November 28, 1970. East Berlin wanted to negotiate a "transit agreement" with Bonn (to get Bonn to negotiate a Berlin agreement with it, as the first Soviet draft in the Berlin negotiations had indicated). Bonn refused, declaring that this was a four-power matter, and proposed a general discussion of East-West German traffic. The next month the West Berlin Senate rejected a DDR proposal for the resumption of pass negotiations for the same reason. No more progress was made until the Berlin agreement was signed in September.[41]

On that same November 28, Friedrich Ebert, an SED Politburo member, did not include Ulbricht's maximum demands in a discussion of the issues, nor did Brezhnev in a November 30 speech. The December 2, 1970, Warsaw Pact communiqué did not mention them and referred to "the needs of the population of West Berlin" as well as the "sovereign rights of the DDR," Ulbricht reiterated his two demands on December 10 and 17, but his latter speech was published only on January 14 and the Soviet press again omitted his references to them. However, he apparently still had Soviet support for the DDR's exclusive right to control civilian traffic between the Federal Republic and West Berlin.

The Polish seacoast riots and the replacement of Gomuɫka by Gierek in mid-December made Moscow briefly lower its pressure on East Berlin.[42] But soon indications began to appear that there were differences in the SED leadership. On December 17, DDR Foreign Minister Otto Winzer made a conciliatory speech, very similar to Soviet pronouncements, in which he referred to the necessity of "good neighborly relations with all European states including the Federal Republic." Such divergences in East Berlin may have reflected divergences in Moscow.[43] A series of exceptional events in November and December 1970 indicated that there was some opposition there to Brezhnev's policy of détente with Bonn. In mid-November a Soviet embassy official in Prague told some Czechoslovak neo-Stalinists that the forthcoming Twenty-fourth CPSU Congress would do away with the last remnants of Khrushchevism. In late December, the Ukrainian press announced the discovery of a mass grave of wartime victims allegedly killed by Nazis living in the Federal Republic. These articles were reprinted in East Berlin but not in Moscow.

In February 1971, reports based on interviews with Soviet officials that criticized Brandt for having been responsible for the Polish riots and refusing to negotiate with the DDR on Berlin began to circulate in the Western press. The Soviets immediately denied these charges, but their appearance was likely a signal of dissension in Moscow on the German problem.[44] When one remembers that the Ukrainian party chief, Shelest, was reportedly, along with Ulbricht and Gomuka, among the strongest advocates of the 1968 invasion of Czechoslovakia and that he was removed by Brezhnev in 1972, one may conclude that there may have been some contact between Ulbricht and Brezhnev's opponents.

In late January 1971, the DDR again began minor harassment of transit traffic to West Berlin and at the Fifteenth SED Plenum Ulbricht repeated his demand for de jure recognition and attacked the Federal Republic. He also, probably to the annoyance of the Soviets, declared that the SED was developing its own advanced "developed social system of socialism" (das entwickelte gesellschaftliche System des Sozialismus), which aided in the transition to communism. On February 4, Stoph hinted that there could be an agreement between the West Berlin Senate and the DDR. Honecker, his ranking associate, however, just stressed the necessity of the "tight indissoluble alliance with the Soviet Union as the only guarantee for a successful policy of peaceful coexistance with states of a different social system, including the Federal Republic." The plenum adopted draft resolutions for the forthcoming SED Eighth Congress, which declared inter alia that "the process of demarcation [Abgrenzung] between the socialist DDR and the imperialist Federal Republic has reached a stage from which there is no going back in order to fit the only normal diplomatic relations, on the basis of international law.[45]

Ulbricht then spent five weeks in the Soviet Union, from February 5 to March 15, during which Soviet policy began to turn away from him. On February 13, Pravda endorsed the Moscow and Warsaw treaties; and although it implied that their ratification should not be linked with a Berlin agreement, it did not specifically reject such linkage. Nor did a Warsaw Pact foreign ministers meeting in Bucharest on February 18–19 explicitly reject linkage between ratification and a European security conference. The Soviet change was rapidly reflected in a February 24 letter from Stoph to West Berlin Governing Mayor Schütz proposing negotiations about West Berliners visiting East Berlin and the DDR, which implied that the DDR had agreed that the four-power Berlin negotiations, not East-West German ones, would be decisive with respect to the status of the city.[46]

Ulbricht's fall was probably decided upon during or shortly after the CPSU Twenty-fourth Congress, which met in Moscow at the end of March 1971. From January onward Honecker began to be referred to more often in *Neues Deutschland* and he said little or nothing about the Federal Republic. At the congress Brezhnev and Gromyko gave priority to ratification of the Soviet-West German treaty. Ulbricht, although the senior first secretary present, spoke second, after the North Vietnamese delegate, did not mention his two maximum aims, and stressed the necessity of the ratification of the treaties. However, Brezhnev can hardly have enjoyed Ulbricht's ostentatious mention in his speech that he was one of the few there who had personally known Lenin. Nor, probably, had he appreciated Ulbricht's previous attempts to portray the DDR as a model of socialism (in a developed country) for Eastern and Western Europe and his trying to get ideological capital out of the DDR's high level of economic development. In a signal of his displeasure with Moscow, and perhaps as a hint that he might try to get Chinese support. Ulbricht was the only first secretary aside from Ceauşescu who did not attack the Chinese by name. Thereafter *Pravda* began to feature Honecker rather than Ulbricht. Honecker (not Ulbricht) made speeches in the provinces after the congress. The East German press featured Honecker (not Ulbricht) and named him before Stoph, although he had been named after Stoph when the SED delegations had arrived for the congress. After Honecker returned to East Berlin, he did attack the Chinese by name. Before that, on April 12, Ulbricht and Honecker met Brezhnev in Moscow.

When Ulbricht returned to East Berlin on March 14, he was met only by Politburo member Norden, State Security Minister Mielke, and the Soviet embassy's minister-counsellor, not by Ambassador Abrassimov. The announcement of his return referred to him only as "Walter Ulbricht" (without a title). On April 20, Honecker, not Ulbricht, led the SED delegation to the Hungarian Tenth Party Congress. On April 21, on the twenty-fifth anniversary of the SED, Ulbricht did not attack the Federal Republic and called only for all states who had not yet done so to recognize the DDR under international law but did not specifically mention the Federal Republic. The Soviet message on the occasion of the anniversary mentioned only Pieck and Grotewohl, but not Ulbricht, as founders of the SED and was addressed only to "Loyal Comrades." (Five years before it had been addressed to Ulbricht.) At the May Day parade Ulbricht was publicly referred to only as "chairman of the state council," not as "first secretary." At a May 3 SED Central Committee Plenum Ulbricht announced that he was retiring because of ill health, and Honecker replaced him as first secretary. (He remained head of state.)

Ulbricht was old and ailing, but his fall was in my view primarily the result of Soviet pressure. When Moscow finally decided that it had to choose between compromise with Bonn and support of Ulbricht, it chose Bonn and removed Ulbricht. Moscow's choice demonstrated something hardly lost on Honecker and other Communist leaders: Brezhnev had sacrificed an ally to détente with Washington and Bonn.

Honecker abandoned Ulbricht's technocratic domestic model and claims for its international validity for a more egalitarian, consumer-oriented one and stressed the primacy of alliance with the Soviet Union. He ceased opposing Soviet policies on Bonn and West Berlin. Four days after Ulbricht's "retirement," on May 7, Soviet Ambassador Abrasimov said that the Berlin negotiations were progressing well. Ulbricht, conversely, was clearly if esoterically criticized.[47]

Shortly after Ulbricht's fall, the Berlin negotiations picked up speed. Moscow agreed to take responsibility for transit traffic to

West Berlin.[48] Less than a month after Honecker replaced Ulbricht, on May 28, 1971, the negotiations produced a joint draft document, which became the basis for the final negotiations.[49] The four powers signed the agreement on August 23, 1971.

It is likely, although not demonstrable, that the July 1971 announcement of Kissinger's visit to Peking influenced the Soviets to make concessions to the West, including in the Berlin negotiations. At the least, the coincidence in time is striking. An August 2 Crimean meeting of Warsaw Pact first secretaries condemned Peking and endorsed Moscow's efforts to get the Moscow and Warsaw treaties ratified and a Berlin agreement signed.

The Berlin agreement may be analyzed in five categories: (1) status, (2) access, (3) ties between West Berlin and the Federal Republic and (4) between West Berlin and the DDR, and (5) West Berlin representation abroad. There was agreement to disagree on the first issue, but to agree on the de facto situation in Berlin. The West got the status quo plus in West Berlin on the second, fourth, and fifth; and Moscow and East Berlin got the status quo minus on the third.

Only agreement to disagree could be reached on the legal status of Berlin, for the Western powers maintained that the agreement should cover the whole city while the Soviets insisted that it should cover only the Western sectors. The agreement therefore referred only, as the Soviets had proposed, to all of Berlin as "the relevant area," to West Berlin as "the Western sectors," and to East Berlin as "areas bordering on these sectors." The de facto status of West Berlin was confirmed, including "quadripartite rights and responsibilities," "wartime and post-war agreements of and decisions of the four powers," and "individual and joint rights and responsibilities," which "remain unchanged." Thereby the Soviet Union confirmed the legal presence of the three Western powers in the Western sectors and their access to them, and thus abandoned its 1958 claim that they were "no longer in force," and agreed that "the situation which has developed in the area . . . shall not be changed unilaterally."

The provisions on access to West Berlin for the West were improved. For the first time they included West Germans and West Berliners. The agreement provided that transit traffic should be "unimpeded," "facilitated . . . in the most simple and expeditious manner," and "receive preferential treatment," including sealed transportation of civilian goods only with East German verification of documents, and the same for through trains and buses from the Federal Republic to West Berlin and vice versa. West and East German authorities were instructed to negotiate detailed implementation.

The provisions on the ties between West Berlin and the Federal Republic were substantially those proposed in the initial Western draft. The Western powers delcared that the ties will be "maintained and developed" but that West Berlin continue not "a constituent part of the Federal Republic of Germany" and not to be governed by it. "Constitutional or official acts" of the federal president, the federal government (the chancellor and ministers), the federal assembly (to elect the federal president), the Bundestag, Bundesrat, and their committees and party caucuses (*Fraktionen*) were no longer to occur in West Berlin. (However, this did not affect the activities of West German agencies in West Berlin, the membership of West Berlin representatives in the Bundestag, and the de facto automatic promulgation of West German laws.) That the Western powers thus prohibited previously held official acts of the Federal Republic in West Berlin was a significant concession by them and by the Federal Republic. But they made the declaration "in the exercise of their rights and responsibilities," that is, without formally conceding to the Soviets the right to interfere but—the most important point—for the first time within the context of a quadripartite agreement, that is, implying that the Soviets had a part to play in maintaining it. True, the concession was logical once Bonn and the three Western powers were committed, as the new Ostpolitik and Western endorsement of it had done, to Bonn's de facto recognition of the DDR. The Soviet gain and the West's loss was that this was a quadripartite agreement on the status quo minus in West Berlin while implicitly recognizing the status quo in East Berlin, by the absence of any Soviet or quadripartite agreement to change it.

As to travel from West Berlin to "areas bordering on these sectors" (East Berlin) and to "those areas of the German Democratic Republic which do not border on these sectors" (the DDR less East Berlin), the Soviets "after consultation and agreement" with the DDR agreed that West Berliners could visit these "areas" on the same basis as other persons, additional crossing points would be opened, and communication and transport would be improved. Details were to be negotiated "by the competent German authorities" (as it turned out, by the West Berlin Senate and the DDR). This also improved West Berlin's situation.

Finally, as to West Berlin's representation abroad, the Soviets came much closer to accepting what they and their allies had so long refused to do, the "Berlin clause" (*Berlinklausel*): that Bonn would represent West Berliners abroad except for questions of status and security. West German treaties could be applied to West Berlin when their texts so provided, Bonn could provide consular representation for permanent residents of West Berlin (that they would carry West German passports), and West Berlin could participate in West German international exchanges, exhibitions, and meetings, including those held in West Berlin. (As later events were to show, the Soviets have usually interpreted the exact phraseology—that those developments "may occur"—in a very restrictive fashion.) The Soviets also were authorized to set up a consulate general, accredited to the three Western commandants, and commercial offices in West Berlin.

Shortly thereafter, on September 16–18, Brandt visited Brezhnev at Oreanda in the Crimea. The joint communiqué referred to the forthcoming entry of the two German states into the United Nations and the preparation of the European security conference with the participation of the United States and Canada and referred favorably to mutual force reduction negotiations, in which both Bonn and Washington were very interested. After repeating his concern about rapid ratification by the Bundestag of the treaties with the Soviet Union and Poland, Brezhnev declared that Moscow would not allow the Berlin agreement to come into effect until after ratification had occured.[50] The next month Moscow formally informed Bonn of this reverse linkage (*Gegenjunktim.*)[51]

The Berlin agreement was a victory for the West and specifically for Bonn. True, it symbolically favored the East German and Soviet position that East Berlin is a part of and the capital of the DDR and Bonn's symbolic presence in West Berlin was decreased. But the Western gains far offset these: much more secure access, transit, and travel to and from West Berlin and from West Berlin and West Germany to East Berlin and East Germany, thus defusing the area where Bonn and the West were most vulnerable to Soviet and East German pressure. Bonn successfully linked a satisfactory Berlin agreement with the Soviet-West German treaty and compensated by its gains in Berlin for the Soviet gains in the treaty.

The East German-West German Negotiations

The Berlin agreement had set out the framework for détente between Bonn and East Berlin, but its avoidance of the key issues and the continuing political and ideological confrontation between East and West Germany made its implementation difficult. Honecker, while formally endorsing it, stressed "demarcation" (*Abgrenzung*), that is, minimal contacts and the intensification of ideological struggle with the Federal Republic.

He declared, but Brezhnev did not reiterate, that the agreement confirmed the DDR's "sovereignty." He tried hard to limit the agreement on representation of West Berlin by Bonn and the impact in the DDR of increased West German and West Berlin visitors. He wanted to use the agreement to get Bonn to recognize the DDR de jure and to cease blocking the DDR's admission into international organizations and its diplomatic recognition by all other states before a West-East German treaty was concluded. Bonn, in contrast, wanted the DDR to allow maximum increased travel and contact for West Germans and West Berliners with East Germans. Moreover, to symbolize the right of all Germans to self-determination (reunification), Bonn wanted East Berlin to accept four-power responsibility for all of Germany, the concept of two German states in one German nation, and the appointment of plenipotentiaries (*Bevollmächtigte*), not ambassadors, to represent each to the other.[52]

Moscow's main aim was to get the Soviet-West German treaty ratified by the Bundestag. The Soviets therefore pressured East Berlin to reach a transit agreement with Bonn and pressured Bonn (by reverse linkage) to ratify the treaty as a precondition to Moscow's consenting to put the Berlin agreement into effect.

East-West German negotiations began on September 6, 1971, Bonn's position was by then stronger than East Berlin's: Brandt had convinced the Soviets that the Bundestag would not ratify the Moscow and Warsaw treaties and Bonn would not agree to a European security conference until the East-West German implementations of the Berlin agreement were signed. East Berlin had been forced by the Soviets to endorse a Berlin agreement of which several aspects—Soviet guarantee of Western access and Soviet agreement that Bonn-West Berlin ties should be "maintained and developed" and that West Berliners could visit East Berlin and the DDR—were contrary to East German policies and prevented East Berlin from using access harassment to pressure Bonn, blocked it ending West German presence in West Berlin, and threatened West German "infiltration" into the DDR.[53]

After a brief dispute on the German translation of the Berlin agreement, the DDR tried to negotiate with Bonn only about transit from the Federal Republic to West Berlin and only with West Berlin about transit from the city to the Federal Republic in order to demonstrate that West Berlin was a "separate political entity." However, the three Western powers had made clear at the time of the agreement, without Soviet objection, that Bonn was exclusively responsible for these negotiations. Washington indicated that it would not sign the final quadripartite Berlin protocol unless West-East German agreement was reached and in the Crimea Brandt made clear that rapid ratification of the Soviet-West German treaty was impossible because of their East German position, Even so, Scheel failed to persuade Groymko to put the Berlin agreement into effect upon the conclusion of the East-West German treaty. Moscow still insisted that it would not do so until the Bundestag ratified the Moscow and Warsaw treaties. Thereupon, under Soviet pressure, the DDR agreed to negotiate only with Bonn on transit to West Berlin and only with West Berlin on visits by West Berliners to East Berlin and the DDR. On September 30, a West German-East German agreement on improved postal and telecommunications service was signed, with Bonn representing West Berlin as well. Negotiations then began on the other issues between Egon Bahr for Bonn and Michael Kohl for East Berlin and between Ulrich Müller and Günter Kohrt for West Berlin and the DDR respectively. After Brezhnev made clear in East Berlin on October 30 that he wanted negotiations concluded rapidly, a transit agreement was initialed by Bahr and Kohl and one on visits, travel, and exchange of small enclaves in Berlin by Müller and Kohrt on December 11.[54]

These agreements substantially followed the quadripartite one. East Berlin succeeded in treating West Germans and West Berliners somewhat differently, favorable in some respects and unfavorable in others, and in negotiating with West Berlin over visits of West Berliners to East Berlin; it thus symbolically emphasized its claim that East Berlin is a part of and the capital of the DDR. It also gained the right to limit the numbers of West Berliners visiting East Berlin at any one time. As to West Germans, the DDR succeeded in restricting them to specific transit routes to and from West Berlin and in forbidding them to distribute printed matter while in transit. However, since the agreement implemented the quadripartite agreement's assurances of improved access and increased travel and by it the DDR recognized that Bonn could negotiate for West Berlin on most issues, it was positive for Bonn and West Berlin and fell far short of what East Berlin had wanted.

West German Trade with the East during the Brandt-Scheel Coalition

Although none of the treaties specifically referred to a particular higher level of trade between the Federal Republic and the

Eastern states, it is clear from the rise in trade figures in the early 1970s (see appendix table) that this was an implicit part of the treaties. There continued to be ample economic incentives for West German exporting firms for this trade. West German imports of Soviet energy rose especially rapidly. West Germany became more and more a creditor country toward the East. Bonn carefully calibrated its trade with East Germany for political purposes. For example, it sunk sharply in 1973, probably in part because of East Berlin's obstructionism in implementing the treaties. Trade remained one of Bonn's major foreign policy weapons toward the East.[55]

Bundestag Ratification of the Treaties

As soon as the Berlin traffic agreement was signed, Brandt submitted the Moscow and Warsaw treaties to the Bundestag and Bundesrat for ratification. From the beginning of the Brandt-Scheel Ostpolitik the CDU/CSU had kept up a barrage of criticism of it, aided by the slowness of the Berlin negotiations and of the arrival of ethnic Germans from Poland, However, the treaties remained basically popular in West German public opinion. The CDU/CSU opposed ratification on the grounds that they did not specifically provide for self-determination of the German people, holding the frontier issue open until a peace treaty, more freedom of movement and communication between the Federal Republic and the DDR, Soviet recognition of the European Economic Community, and Soviet renunciation of its claimed right of intervention in the Federal Republic. The CDU/CSU also maintained that the treaties upgraded the DDR, that their ratification should be preceded by the promulgation of the Berlin agreement, and that in general Moscow gained more from them than Bonn. The CSU was adamantly opposed to them. The majority of the CDU was also opposed, but less strongly so. A liberal minority in the CDU favored ratification. Thus in order to hold the CDU together, and to maintain its alliance with the CSU, the easiest course was not to vote for ratification unless the treaties were amended.

Ratification also became entangled with the decision by the

CDU leader Dr. Rainer Barzel to try to overthrow the Brandt-Scheel government. Although the new Ostpolitik was popular, it had contributed to the SPD-FDP coalition losing a few of its votes in the Bundestag. The bad economic situation had also lessened its popularity, but this seemed likely to imrrove. Brandt therefore tried to reestablish bipartisan unity on the issue with the CDU/CSU. The Soviet Union realized that if ratification failed, so would the Berlin agreement, and then the three Western powers and Bonn would not agree to a European security conference. Moscow therefore made more concessions to Brandt and in effect jumped into the struggle in Bonn for ratification—and for the SPD-FDP coalition.

The CDU was divided. Barzel (once he failed to overthrow Brandt) realized how much the three Western powers wanted the treaties ratified so that the Berlin agreement would be promulgated. He therefore shared Brandt's desire for ratification, which, he knew, the CDU/CSU could likely prevent. He could not straddle the issue much longer, and by rejecting the treaties and thereby the Berlin agreement, the CDU/CSU would lose popularity and probably the next Bundestag election.

Schröder had turned against the treaty, largely out of rivalry with Barzel. Kiesinger and Strauss opposed it in principle and hoped to use it to overthrow Brandt via FDP losses in state elections. (Ironically, Strauss had supported Barzel over Schröder for party chariman in late 1971 because he thought the former would be more opposed to Ostpolitik. Thereafter, however, Barzel, realizing that public opinoon was moving in favor of it, became less opposed to it, while Schröder became more so.)

The September 3, 1971, signing of the Berlin agreement was a major blow to the CDU/CSU's opposition to ratification, because since Moscow had declared that it would not consent to the agreement's promulgation until the treaties were ratified, nonratification would delay if not prevent all the travel concessions for West German and West Berliners that the agreement provided for and would provoke a crisis in Bonn's alliance relationships. The CDU/CSU thereupon reduced its conditions for ratification to three: specific reference in the treaty to self-determination, provisions for greater contacts between the peoples of the two German states, and formal Soviet recognition of the EEC.

Meantime, the Soviets were trying very hard, by a combination of carrots and sticks, and reportedly in part at the SPD's request, to ensure ratification. Brezhnev and Gromyko threatened that its failure would mean the end of the Soviet-West German détente, of the Berlin agreement, and of the East German-West German negotiations. Suslov threatened a trade war. Brezhnev declared that the CDU/CSU's demand for renegotiating the treaty was entirely illusory. The Soviet press denounced CDU/CSU policy. On the other hand, Gromyko publicly submitted to the Supreme Soviet's foreign affairs committee the text of the unilateral West German letter on German unity at the time the treaty was signed. Beezhnev gave what amounted to de facto recognition of the EEC. The Soviets initialed a long-delayed trade treaty with West Germany that included West Berlin (which until then Moscow had refused to do) and indicated their desire for more trade with the Federal Republic and willingness to allow more ethnic Germans to leave the Soviet Union.

The Soviets also helped in the agreement between Bahr and Kohl on a traffic and transit treaty between East and West Germany, which, although officially signed on May 26, after the Bundestag ratified the treaties, was agreed upon in late April and initialed on May 12. Already in February the DDR, presumably under Soviet pressure, had changed its tune toward Bonn. On February 23, it unilaterally put into effect for Easter and Whitsunday the Berlin agreements travel concessions for West Berliners, although the agreement was not yet in force. On March 10, Honecker spoke of the political polarization in Bonn on the treaties, whose ratification would lead to both German states peacefully living together (*friedliches Nebeneinander,* meaning "good neighborly relations"—Brandt's phrase); the treaty declared that both sides would work for "normal, good neighborly relations"). Upon its initialing, East Berlin declared that after it came into force (that is, as was agreed, after the Moscow and Warsaw treaties were ratified by the Bundestag) travel of West Germans to the DDR and, for urgent family reasons, of East Germans to the Federal Republic would be facilitated.[56] In mid-April, Honecker declared that after the Moscow and Warsaw treaties had been ratified East Berlin would begin negotiations for overall normalization of relations with Bonn and spoke of "togetherness" (*Miteinander*—another Brandt phrase) as the eventual goal.

Brandt and Barzel simultaneously began to try to draft a preamble to the treaty that the Bundestag would adopt with it as it had with the 1963 Franco-German treaty. Initially Barzel had rejected this but later he agreed, to try to get out of the dilemma of wanting to vote neither for or against ratification. Brandt was under pressure to get the treaties ratified in late May before Nixon visited Moscow and a NATO meeting took place in Bonn, and he felt so unsure of his majority that he wanted a bipartisan policy on this issue. However, he refused Barzel's demand to see the minutes of the treaty negotiations, whereupon a partial version of the early part of them was published.[57] This further envenomed the domestic West German debate.

It seemed at first that the Soviet Union was prepared in principle to accept a preamble. Then, however, the CDU/CSU demanded that it be a constituent part of the treaty. By early May a declaration was worked out by joint working groups of the coalition and the opposition. Thereupon, the senior joint working group met with the new Soviet ambassador, Falin, a clear indication of how deeply Moscow had become involved in internal West German policies. Falin's acceptance of the draft was initially overruled by Moscow, which rejected the draft's declaration that the treaties created no legal basis for the existing borders and its reaffirmation of four-power responsibility for Germany and Berlin. Although Moscow reversed itself shortly thereafter, the initial rejection so strengthened the CDU/CSU opponents of ratification that the vote was postponed for a week to give Barzel time to regroup. On April 23, the CDU decisively won the Baden-Württemberg state elections, fought largely on Ostpolitik. This confirmed Barzel in the view that he could use the issue to overthrow Brandt. It also meant that the treaties still had to be ratified by an absolute majority of the Bundestag since it assured continued CDU/CSU control of the Bundesrat, which had rejected the treaties in their first reading. (Had the SPD won the election, it would have controlled the Bundesrat; and then only a simple majority in the Bundestag would have been needed for ratification.) Meanwhile, Falin was leaving no stone unturned in cultivating Bundestag members opposed to the treaty.

Brandt's majority in the Bundestag, originally twelve, had so eroded that Barzel calculated that he had a good chance of winning the constitutionally necessary "constructive vote of non-confidence," that is, no confidence in Brandt plus an absolute majority for Barzel as his replacement. He was also pressured to do so by two of his rivals, Helmut Kohl and Strauss, who reportedly not only opposed the treaties but believed that if Barzel failed to overthrow Strauss he would be deposed, to their advantage. (Kohl later did replace him, in part for that reason.) Barzel missed overthrowing Brandt on April 27 by two votes because the (unknown) two CDU members who did not vote for him counterbalanced the three FDP members who did. The next day, however, there was a tie vote at 247 on a budgetary issue. Brandt's position clearly remained shaky.

Thereafter, Barzel finally got the CDU to endorse the joint preamble and therefore by implication the treaty, but its Bundestag representatives were left free in their votes. But the CSU decided to vote against the treaties, and Barzel, faced with what could be a majority of the combined CDU/CSU vote going against him, agreed with Strauss that the CDU and CSU should abstain.

Thus on May 17, the treaty was ratified by the Bundestag with a sufficient majority so that the Bundesrat could no longer block it. Thereupon, on June 3, the four powers put the Berlin agreement into effect. Thus the normalization of relations with Moscow and Warsaw and a Berlin agreement were achieved, although by a close margin. If Barzel had overthrown Brandt, it would have postponed ratification of the treaties with unforeseeable results for East-West détente.[58]

The East German–West German Basic Treaty

It had not initially been clear whether there would be a series of agreements between Bonn and East Berlin or one overall treaty. Brandt decided for the latter, which he believed would more effectively normalize relations. Bonn could no longer pressure East Berlin, via the Soviets, by withholding ratification of the treaties with Moscow and Warsaw. It did, however, have two still unplayed cards. It could continue to prevent the DDR from joining the United Nations and other international agencies and obtaining diplomatic recognition by the Western powers and those other countries over which Bonn still had enough economic influence. It could also drag its feet on the European security conference, in which Brezhnev was so interested but the United States was much less so.

However, the French, after initially opposing any multilateral European negotiations, were prepared to make only a Berlin agreement but not an East-West treaty a precondition for multilateral preparations for a European security conference. NATO adopted this minimal position in early June 1971.[59] And Bonn was under pressure to conclude a treaty with East Berlin since it was becoming increasingly difficult for it to restrain third states from recognizing the DDR.

Formal negotiations for the East-West German Basic Treaty (*Grundvertrag*) began between Bahr and Kohl on June 15. By August, they were stalled on the issue of de jure versus "special" relations. However, by the end of October, the East Germans were no longer referring to exchange of ambassadors or de jure recognition; they had abandoned their previous position. This change was the result of West German and U.S. pressure, via the Soviet Union, and despite recognition of the DDR by Finland and India. The United States made clear to Moscow that it would veto the DDR's entry into the UN unless East Berlin formally recognized the four-power responsibilities for all of Germany. Kissinger, in Moscow on September 10–14, agreed with Brezhnev on parallel preparatory talks for CSCE and MBFR. Bonn established diplomatic relations with Peking and thereby made sure that China would not veto a DDR application for UN admission that confirmed the four-power responsibilities. After Bahr and Gromyko discussed the issue in Moscow on October 8–10, Moscow began talks with the three Western powers on the admission to the UN of the two German states.

Bonn and East Berlin then came under time pressure. Bundestag elections were to be held on Nobember 19. (Brandt had arranged for it to be dissolved in the hope, which was fulfilled, of getting a bigger majority.) Preliminary CSCE talks were scheduled to begin in Helsinki on November 22. Bonn and Moscow wanted an East-West German treaty signed before both, to help the SPD in the election and to have the issue out of the way before the CSCE began. Finally, in early November, compromises were reached between Bonn and East Berlin on the "national issue" and among the four powers on the formulation of their responsibilities. The treaty was initialed by Bahr and Kohl on November 8 and ratified by the Bundestag. The CDU/CSU, with the exception of Leisler Kiep and a few others, voted against it.

The treaty normalized East German–West German relations on the basis of the status quo. Bonn and East Berlin agreed to disagree and to proceed from "the historical facts." Thus the treaty confirmed the existence of the "national question" and the four-power responsibilities, but it did not contain Bonn's formulation of "one German nation" nor did it specifically refer to the DDR's sovereignty. Normalization was agreed upon except for the question of citizenship. There, because the Federal Republic's Basic Law automatically grants West German citizenship to any German (*inter alia* to any citizen of the DDR who enters the Federal Republic) and the DDR refuses to recognize this, they also agreed to disagree. Both states agreed to apply simultaneously for admission to the UN. The DDR agreed that West Germany could represent West Berlin vis-à-vis itself except for previous arrangements between the DDR and the West Berlin Senate and that West Berlin could be included in future agreements between them. Each state recognized the other's equality, boundaries, and territorial integrity and declared that neither could represent the other internationally;

the treaty abrogated the Federal Republic's claim to the right of sole representation (*Alleinvertretungsrecht*) for all Germans.

The DDR agreed to extensive visits of West Germans living near the border to similar East German areas, to open more border crossings, and to make family reunions easier, thereby helping Bonn's hope to "maintain the substance of the nation."

The major point of dispute was the West German insistence that the Federal Republic must have "special relations" with the DDR and the DDR's insistence that the relations be those between independent stakes—involve full de jure diplomatic recognition under international law, an issue carefully skirted in the Soviet-West German treaty. The final compromise was that the two states would exchange "permanent representatives" (not ambassadors), that the agreement to disagree should refer specifically *inter alia* to "the national question" (to Bonn's insistence that Germany was one nation and East Berlin's rejection of this), that the tariff-free trade between West and East Germany (the main specific evidence of the "special relations") should continue (that the DDR remained a "silent member" of the EEC), that West Germany would reiterate in a letter to the DDR its commitment to reunification through self-determination, and that Bonn and East Berlin would specifically reaffirm that the Basic Treaty did not affect the four-power rights and responsibilities vis-à-vis Germany as a whole.[60]

It took nearly two years more, until March 1974, for Bonn and East Berlin to agree on a compromise on their "permanent representations": Each representation would be accredited to the other's chief of state; Bonn's representation in East Berlin would deal with the DDR ministry of foreign affairs, according to East Berlin's view that the relations were those evolving from recognition in international law; but East Berlin's representation in Bonn would deal with the federal chancery, according to Bonn's view that the relations were "special."

Thus, finally, Brandt reached one of the main goals of his Ostpolitik: normalization of relations with the DDR via de facto but not de jure recognition, in order to obtain improvement of human relations across the borders and thereby to "maintain the substance of the nation." But Moscow and East Berlin also achieved a principal goal of their Westpolitik: Bonn's recognition, and after it the world's, of the DDR and of the Oder-Neisse line—that is, of the territorial status quo and, indirectly and via the forthcoming European security conference, of Soviet hegemony in Eastern Europe.[61]

West German–Chinese Diplomatic Relations

Peking violently opposed the new West German Ostpolitik, which, it felt, favored the Soviet Union and prevented Bonn from allying with the Chinese against Moscow. Because of the sharp worsening of Sino-Soviet relations and the Sino-American rapprochement in 1969–1970, Peking tried to improve its relations with Western Europe, including favoring NATO, the Common Market, and Western European and West German nuclear rearmament. Such West German opponents of the Brandt-Scheel Ostpolitik as Franz Josef Strauss and the Hesse CDU leader Alfred Dregger visited Peking and advocated a pro-Chinese anti-Soviet policy. Brandt and Schmidt, however, plus the FDP and the moderate CDU leaders, remained convinced that China was too weak and far away to be an effective counterweight to Moscow and that Bonn therefore could not do what Washington successfully did—put pressure on Moscow by improving relations with Peking.

However, the Sino-American rapprochement did remove the major barrier to the establishment of West German-Chinese relations, which occurred in 1972 (including the "Berlin clause"). West German-Chinese trade continued to increase and Bonn became Peking's major Western European trade partner. Finally, although Bonn made no move to play off Peking against Moscow, the alternative did exist; and one may assume that this also moderated Soviet policy toward the Federal Republic.[62]

The West German–Czechoslovak Treaty

After the West-East German treaty was signed, there remained only the negotiations with Prague. (It had long been clear that

once they were concluded, Budapest and Sofia would immediately establish relations with the Federal Republic.) Although
these negotiations were politically and legally very complex,
they probably would have been concluded, as the treaty with
Poland was, before the West-East German treaty, had not the
1968 Soviet invasion of Czechoslovakia excluded the possibility,
which had existed under Dubček, of Prague immediately following Warsaw's example. (However, Czechoslovak-West German
trade continued to increase.)

The legal problems arose from the Czechoslovak demand that
Bonn acknowledge "the invalidity of the Munich agreement *ab
initio* (*ex tunc*) with all the resulting consequences." Whether
the Munich agreement was legally valid when it was signed was
legally extremely complex and disputed. Moreover, Bonn's acceptance of Prague's formulation would have meant, or so the
Sudeten German expellees in the Federal Republic argued, that
they then could legally claim reparations from Bonn for their
confiscated property, because Bonn would have given away
their legal claim to reparations from Prague by accepting the
Czechoslovak view that they were Czechoslovak citizens until
1945 (since the Munich agreement, as a result of which they became German citizens, would be considered invalid from the beginning) and that for the same reason they would be subject to
war crimes prosecution by Czechoslovakia. These Sudeten German arguments were in large part political in purpose: They
were intended to block any treaty with Prague that Prague
could conceivably sign. The Sudeten Germans also demanded
that any treaty include their "right to the homeland" (*Heimatrecht*), that is, to return to Czechoslovakia, recover their property or be indemnified for it, and in effect rule themselves. But
there was sufficient legal basis for their arguments so that Bonn
was unwilling to agree to the *ab initio* formulation. Moreover,
the United Kingdom had never used this formulation. Finally,
Prague demanded large reparations from the Federal Republic.

Bonn was prepared to recognize that the Munich agreement
had become invalid as a result of Hitler's 1939 invasion of
Czechoslovakia. Indeed, West German Chancellor Erhard had

declared in 1964 that Hitler had torn up the agreement, which no longer has any territorial meaning. Chancellor Kiesinger had said in 1966 that it was no longer valid. A West German trade mission had been established in Prague in 1967.

When West German-Czechoslovak talks began in Prague in March 1971, however, Prague still insisted that the Munich agreement be declared invalid *ab initio* "with all ensuing consequences." Prague abandoned the latter phrase in autumn 1971 but continued to insist on invalidity *ab initio*. Only when the Basic Treaty was about to be signed did Moscow signal (by omitting *ab initio* from a Soviet-Hungarian communiqué) that Prague would compromise. Even then, formal negotiations did not begin until May 7, 1973. The treaty was initialed in Bonn on June 20 by the two foreign ministers, who planned to have it signed in the beginning of August.

Then, however, there arose another issue, concerning the interpretation of the Berlin agreement: *Rechtshilfe* (legal assistance), that is, whether the federal government could represent West Berlin with respect to "juridical" (firms, government agencies, courts, and so forth) as well as "natural" persons. Presumably at East German and Soviet urging, after Warsaw had first raised the issue, and because the only significant negotiation then underway was with Prague, the Czechoslovak government insisted that it would not agree to Bonn's attempt to insert into the treaty a specific provision that the Federal Republic had the right to represent both juridical and natural persons. In part because of SPD and FDP pressure for rapid conclusion of the negotiations, Scheel reached a pragmatic but not generally binding compromise on this issue (negotiations from case to case through judicial channels) in negotiations in Moscow with Gromyko in November. The treaty was signed in Prague by Brandt and Czechoslovak Prime Minister Strougal on December 11, 1973. The Bundestag ratified it, with the CDU/CSU unanimously voting against it.

Although in appearance a compromise, the treaty reflected more Czechoslovak than West German concessions. On the key issue of the Munich agreement it simply said that both "deem the Munich agreement of September 29, 1938, void as stated in this treaty with respect to their mutual relations." Thereby Prague could, if it wished, still maintain that it was void *ab initio*. But Bonn could just as well maintain the contrary, and indeed more so, for Article 2 of the treaty specifically excluded the legal consequences that Bonn had feared by providing that it did not affect legal status, nationality, war crimes liability (except for crimes carrying the death penalty), or reparations claims. The issue of representation of West Berlin juridical persons by Bonn was formally sidestepped by simply repeating the phraseology of the Berlin agreement ("in accordance with established procedures,"), but Article 2 of the treaty was specifically extended to West Berlin. It also provided for mutual renunciation of use of force, recognition of territorial boundaries, repatriation, if they desired, of ethnic Czechoslovak and Germans, and increased travel. (Little or no progress was made thereafter on these last two points.) On balance, then, Bonn profited more than Prague from the treaty, the more so because immediately after its signature, Bonn resumed diplomatic relations with Budapest and Sofia.[63]

The Years since the German Treaties
This study does not cover in detail the development of Ostpolitik after the signing in 1973 of the West German-Czechoslovak treaty.[1] However, because the Brandt-Scheel Ostpolitik was always intended to be long range and the treaties to be its beginning, not its end, a brief epilogue is necessary in order to draw some conclusions about Ostpolitik to date.

The main problem for Ostpolitik since the signing of the treaties has been West Berlin. The Berlin agreement provided that West Berlin is not a "constituent part" of the Federal Republic and prohibited "constitutional or official acts" by certain officials and agencies thereof (president, government, election of the president, Bundestag, including committees and party groups (*Fraktionen*) as well as "other state bodies"). In another passage, however, the agreement provided that existing "ties" (*"svyazi"*) may be "maintained and developed." (The West Germans translated "ties" as *Bindungen* while the East Germans insisted on *Verbindungen,* a less strong term that can mean only "means of communication.") Finally, the agreement provided that West Berlin "may" be included in international agreements signed by the Federal Republic, provided that this is specified in each case. The Federal Republic and the three Western powers interpreted this as de facto Soviet acceptance of the "Berlin clause," that the inclusion of West Berlin should be automatic, a position the Soviets have consistently refused to accept.

The subsequent East-West controversies about Berlin revolved around these two points. Bonn tried to strengthen West Berlin's ties with the Federal Republic. Moscow tried to prevent this. The major issues were four. The first was the establishment in 1975 of the Federal German Employment Environmental Agency in West Berlin. This occurred primarily because FDP Foreign Minister Genscher wanted to appear to strike an FDP blow for West Berlin. As a result the DDR began minor harassment of West German traffic to and from West Berlin. Eventually, the agency's location was implicitly accepted by East Berlin and Moscow.

The second was the controversy about West German construction of a major atomic power plant at Kalingrad (formerly Königsberg). Bonn insisted that some power from it go to West Berlin. The DDR opposed this. In early 1978, the project remained postponed.

The third was the inclusion of West Berlin in treaties negotiated between Bonn and Moscow on scientific-technological-economic cooperation, cultural exchanges, and legal aid. Again, in early 1978, no agreement had been reached.

The fourth was the question of whether representatives from West Berlin, either elected or appointed by the municipal parliament, should sit in the directly elected European parliament, scheduled for 1978. Moscow insisted that they should not, the Federal Republic and the three Western powers that they should.

One final point must be made about Ostpolitik and Berlin. Because Ostpolitik defused the city as an East-West crisis area, Bonn could no longer use Berlin crises to put pressure on the Soviet Union or East Germany or to remain so central in American, British, or French foreign policy.[2] On the other hand, Ostpolitik, and détente in general, pushed East Berlin toward intensifying its policy of demarcation (*Abgrenzung*) vis-à-vis Bonn. The DDR, therefore, did not after 1969 harass West Berlin at the same level as it had in the past, and indeed Moscow would not allow it to. It did, however, from time to time carry on minor obstructive activities there in order to put pressure on Bonn and to ensure *Abgrenzung*, thus imperiling détente.

There were also some positive developments. Trade between the Federal Republic and the CMEA countries increased greatly, as did their trade deficits vis-à-vis Bonn. In July 1972, a long-term Soviet-West German treaty including West Berlin was signed. When Brezhnev visited Bonn in May 1973, a ten-year technological-economic agreement was signed. By 1973, the Federal Republic had become the Soviet Union's largest Western trading partner and trade was 51 percent greater than in 1971. The trend continued thereafter. There remained, however, economic as well as political obstacles. The main one was Bonn's reluctance to grant Moscow long-term, low-interest credits. Even so, despite the 1973 recession, Soviet and Eastern

European trade with West Germany continued to increase. However, West German exports were consistently higher than imports.

The May 1974 replacement of Brandt by Helmut Schmidt as federal chancellor resulted in less priority to Ostpolitik. In part this was because Schmidt was less forthcoming in negotiations with the East and gave higher priority to relations with the non-communist developed world. There were other causes. After the treaties were signed, Ostpolitik could only be long range. Many issues were transferred to CSCE and MBFR negotiations. Moreover, in the mid-1970s, East-West détente came under increasing attack in the Federal Republic, in the rest of Western Europe, and in the United States. Finally, by 1975, West Germany was moving toward the right and Schmidt was therefore the more inclined not to give the CDU/CSU electoral ammunition by pressing Ostpolitik.

Even so, some progress was made. Prolonged negotiations between Bonn and Warsaw on credits and the emigration of ethnic Germans led in 1976 to an agreement whereby a greatly increased outflow of ethnic Germans was compensated for by very low interest long-term West German credits, that is, a large West German grant-in-aid. This agreement was ratified by the Bundestag with the support of some CDU/CSU members and at the last moment by the Bundesrat when its CDU/CSU majority voted for it.

In 1976, signs of elite and mass discontent appeared in the DDR. On the elite level they were sparked by the deprivation of citizenship of Wolf Biermann, the balladeer, while he was visiting West Germany; the house arrest of the dissident Communist intellectual Robert Havemann; and later by the deportation to West Berlin of many prominent dissident intellectuals and signs of dissidence within the SED. On the mass level they were most apparent in the applications for emigration to West Germany of probably more than one hundred thousand DDR citizens, the declining fear of the regime, and the frequent popular citation, vis-à-vis the regime, of the Helsinki CSCE Final Act to justify emigration and other liberalizing measures. While the Helsinki Final Act and the June 1976 East Berlin European communist conference were largely responsible for these developments, Ostpolitik also played a major role. Because of it, in 1975 up to eight million West Germans and West Berliners had visited the DDR far more than before the treaties and the Berlin agreement. Ostpolitik also brought West German television correspondents to East Berlin. Up to 80 percent of the DDR's citizens could and did watch their reports on West German television. By the end of 1976, the DDR had suppressed public expressions of discontent. But these events did demonstrate some progress toward Ostpolitik's key aim, "the maintenance of the substance of the nation" (*die Erhaltung der Substanz der Nation*).[3]

Some Provisional Conclusions

West German foreign policy has been a process of coming to terms with dynamic reality: first with defeat and partition and later with rising West German power and East-West détente. Its task was greater than that of the Weimar Republic, for defeat was much worse, Germany was partitioned, the Soviet Union was far stronger, and atomic weapons froze postwar boundaries.

The historic new aspect of West German foreign policy and the great achievement of Konrad Adenauer was the abandonment of a middle, balancing position for a Western orientation based on Franco-German reconciliation and the unity of Western Europe. Although, one may well say, Bonn had no other rational alternative, many Germans, notably Kurt Schumacher, thought that it did; and Germany had not always acted rationally before.

Adenauer, always basically disinterested in the East, thus took up again in 1945 the foreign policy he had failed to push through in 1922–1923. His cynical manipulation of the expellees and others who wanted a forward Eastern policy gave him the leeway he needed to push through the Western orientation.

Adenauer was able to pursue his single-minded Western orientation until 1955. Thereafter, especially after th 1961 construction of the Berlin Wall, West German foreign policy faced more complex problems: the rise of Soviet military power and how to manage simultaneously the growth of West German economic power, East-West détente, and the consolidation of East Germany and the Soviet hold over it and the northern tier of Eastern European states.

Adenauer and his successors shared three principal objectives; to continue his Western orientation, to avoid the diplomatic isolation of West Germany on the issue of détente, and thereby to avoid being relegated by renewed Soviet-American *double hégémonie* to second-class status in Europe. Adenauer and the CDU/CSU, however, opposed the SPD-FDP new Ostpolitik, of using détente to improve relations with the East and the de facto status quo, to prevent further cementing of the partition of Germany and gradually to improve conditions of life in East Germany. The CDU/CSU position has been that recognition of the status quo gives away something for which nothing of importance has been or will be gained in return.

Provisional judgments on contemporary history are by definition risky, subjective, and premature. Although a foreign historian may be more objective in judging a country's foreign policy, he is usually also less informed and always in danger of judging them from his own national perspective. (And for Americans who, like me, went through World War II, judgments on German history are particularly subjective.)

Yet to paraphrase Mendés-France, *écrire l'histoire c'est choisir.* The new German Ostpolitik, in my judgment, has furthered, to date (early 1978), the interests of the Federal Republic, the West, and world peace and stability. It has neither isolated nor destabilized the Federal Republic.[4] On the contrary, without it Bonn would have been increasingly out of step with the West and subject to growing domestic political strains. Through it Bonn got increased maneuverability and coordination with the United States and with its EEC partners, as was demonstrated during the CSCE and MFR negotiations. Soviet political pressure on it, and particularly on West Berlin, was largely defused, at least for the time being. It helped to keep the "substance of the nation" alive in the DDR. It favored West German exports to the East.

It aided détente even at a time of Western malaise about it. Although Ostpolitik remained an issue between the SPD and the CDU/CSU, and indeed between the CDU and the CSU, it was not a decisive one. On Ostpolitik Kohl and Schmidt were more pragmatic and less far apart than Kiesinger and Brandt. By early 1978, the SPD had lost hope for rapid, systemic change in the DDR through Ostpolitik and the CDU had realized that there was no alternative to Ostpolitik and détente.

A brief summary of the perceptions of the other states interested in Ostpolitik will throw further light on its effect.

The Soviet Union

In mid-1977, Moscow probably regarded Ostpolitik (its own Westpolitik) as successful. It had gained de facto recognition of the DDR and, by implication, of Soviet hegemony in Eastern Europe. It aided East-West détente and thereby helped keep Europe quiet while Moscow was struggling with Peking. It helped check major increases in West German military power. It greatly increased the inflow of West German technology and credits. On the negative side, West German power continued to increase. Its polity was not destabilized. Its relations with the United States improved. Finally, the economic profit to the Soviet Union, although considerable, was less than it had expected.

Eastern Europe

The balance probably also seemed positive to the Eastern European leaders. Détente was consolidated. For Yugoslavia and Rumania this made Soviet invasion or dangerous pressure less likely. West German credits and technology streamed in. Finally, although West German economic influence seemed to increase, the Eastern European states, like the Soviet Union, prevented it from being translated into decisive political or cultural impact.

The United States and Western Europe

The Western powers also saw the balance as positive. Ostpolitik contributed to détente and stability in Central Europe. It put the German question on ice. It defused the Berlin problem, where the United States and Western Europe were the most vulnerable. It did not destabilize the West German polity. It helped to improve the Federal Republic's relations with the West. Ostpolitik as a means of progress toward German reunification, like Adenauer's previous rhetorical reunification policy, did not worsen Bonn's relations with its EEC partners or with the United States, but improved them. This was probably primarily because reunification seemed very far away indeed. That it also might have contributed, at least in the short run, to stabilizing Eastern Europe was for the West of secondary interest; but as of early 1978, it had not: Eastern Europe was less stable than in 1973.

The DDR

The balance sheet was mixed for East Germany. On the credit side, the DDR achieved de jure international recognition and de facto recognition from Bonn. The East German economy remained strong. Honecker consolidated his position. Soviet-East German relations remained close. On the debit side, Moscow had had Ulbricht removed in order to reach an agreement with the West and thus showed that Moscow was willing to sacrifice East German interests for its own. Moreover, the 1976 intellectual unrest made the East German political elite only too aware of the potentially destabilizing results of such aspects of Ostpolitik as the massive visits of West Germans to the DDR.

Because Ostpolitik is part of détente, a judgment about its degree of success is inevitably based in part on one's view of East-West détente itself. The Soviets define détent as lessening the risk of nuclear war *and* helping change the status quo in favor of socialism by continuing the "ideological struggle" (for example, by arms aid to southern African black guerrillas) with less risk of successful "imperialist counterrevolution." Many in the West, in contrast, have at least until recently defined détente as lessening the risk of nuclear war plus beginning to build "a stable structure of peace."

The Soviets initially considered their Westpolitik to be a means toward stabilizing the DDR and if possible splitting and destabilizing Western Europe and gradually removing the United States from it. As time went on, they gave priority to the former and realized that they could hope to achieve little with respect to the latter.

Not all in the West have understood what the Soviets realized and feared: by increasing East-West contacts détente tends to destabilize itself. Pierre Hassner put it very perceptively:

In this new milieu of ambiguity, situations may thaw without being solved, isolation may be relinquished in favor of asymmetrical penetration or imbalance rather than reconciliation. There may always be enough social ferment to prevent stabilization through adaptation, enough communication and convergence to prevent stabilization through isolation, enough separation and divergence to prevent stabilization through integration. Perhaps a state of agitated immobility, rather than revolution or integration, is characteristic of the post-Cold War system as it seems to be of the post-industrial society, diplomatic activism being the equivalent of social unrest and both being the expression of the gap between a declining legitimacy and a persisting structure. The essential attribute of this state is neither force nor cooperation but the constant influence of societies upon one another within the framework of a competition whose goals are less and less tangible, whose means are less and less direct, whose consequences are less and less calculable, precisely because they involve activities rather than strategies and because these activities affect what societies *are* as much as what they *do*.

The real race, thus, may be less to increase one's direct power than to decrease one's comparative vulnerability. Military strength and diplomatic maneuver must be seen as part of this more complex and diffuse process, which may call for the manipulation not only of the opponent's weaknesses but of one's own, the encouragement of dissatisfaction and dissent in other societies or the control of contagious explosions within one's own society, whether such forces involve speculative dollars, immigrant workers or emigrant pens . . .[5]

. . . What characterizes all negotiations in the age of hot peace is the importance of the time dimension and therefore of uncertainty and betting: rarely had diplomacy (as also the use of force) so been based on implicit bets about its effect on long-term processes. . .about which no one can know to what point troops and treaties can manipulate, reverse, influence, control, or limit them. . . .

Hot peace does not necessarily break the equilibrium between alliances and societies, but it tends to make each more vulnerable to the other. From the moment when the existence and legitimacy of the structure are confirmed, the real competition, intentional or involuntary, begins. . . .[6]

Finally, as events in the Middle East, Vietnam, Angola, Zaire, and the Horn of Africa have shown, the inherent instability of the underdeveloped world, plus Soviet competition there with China as well with the West, may contribute to worsening East-West détente in Europe. So, of course, can weapons buildup, failure, or delay in SALT, MBFR, or CSCE follow-up negotiations. Yet as of this writing Ostpolitik has not been seriously impeded or delayed by such developments.

By mid-1977, then, the immediate objectives of the new Ostpolitik had largely been attained. It had fulfilled neither the fears of its bitter opponents nor the expectations of its enthusiastic supporters. It was probably the optimal, if certainly far from the ideal, adjustment of the Federal Republic to its decisive limits and its long-range prospects in the east.

But in terms of day-to-day struggle Ostpolitik was only beginning. Soviet military power continued to rise in Europe, although potentially counterbalanced by such new Western technologies as precision-guided munitions (PGMs) and cruise missiles. The Middle Eastern war and the resultant quadrupling of oil prices restored U.S. economic primacy in OECD and made the Federal Republic more dependent on U.S. goodwill. Because Ostpolitik had been successful, and had defused the major potential crisis area for the United States in Europe, West Berlin, Bonn's leverage in Washington became less. East-West relations continued to be strained, most recently by Soviet successes in south Africa and by general Western disillusionment with détente. The new Carter administration in Washington, in moves reminiscent of Kennedy's, precipitated strains in Bonn-Washington relations on the issues of nuclear nonproliferation—the West German-Brazilian nuclear agreement—and arms control—the Soviet effort to prevent deployment of and West German access to cruise missile technology. The possibility of Communist participation in the governments of France and Italy further weakened the chances of progress in Western European unification and strengthened the possibility of U.S.-West German "bigemony," a prospect favored by neither Bonn nor Washington and one that would hardly help Ostpolitik or European or Atlantic unity.

Thus East-West competition, including by and in the two Germanies, continues. Optimists view détente favorably, as "limited competitive coexistence," pessimists unfavorably, as "competitive decadence." Ostpolitik will remain a part of East-West competition, of its limitation and its continuation.

In the recent past, with which this study has dealt, Ostpolitik was a major motor of détente. In the future it will probably reflect it more than push it forward. Its continuing development, like that of the détente of which it is a part, will be determined by the capabilities, resolution, and leadership of the two competing sides. The result will be for future historians to chronicle.

Appendix

Appendix

West Germany, Export-Import in DM (million)

	USSR		DDR		Bulgaria		CSSR		Hungary	
	Imp.	Exp.	Imp.	Exp.	Imp.	Exp.	Imp.	Exp.	Imp.	Exp.
1955	151	112	581	521	17	21	118	63	87	146
1956	224	289	653	699	33	28	194	160	143	98
1957	409	250	817	846	37	61	205	231	106	103
1958	386	303	858	800	57	58	207	257	128	121
1959	443	383	892	1072	65	171	236	252	178	151
1960	673	778	1123	960	83	123	259	274	187	222
1961	796	823	941	873	96	72	249	309	189	204
1962	861	826	914	853	107	98	263	299	195	198
1963	835	614	1022	860	117	94	260	234	231	252
1964	937	774	1027	1151	121	156	288	332	247	296
1965	1001	586	1260	1206	165	221	336	403	288	308
1966	1153	541	1345	1625	171	433	347	503	321	371
1967	1100	792	1264	1483	178	340	361	525	276	421
1968	1175	1094	1440	1342	212	303	461	707	311	339
1969	1306	1582	1656	2272	207	247	689	823	403	354
1970	1254	1547	1996	2416	237	240	727	1058	490	522
1971	1277	1608	2319	2499	226	256	855	1289	520	710
1972	1390	2300	2400	2960	240	310	870	1230	660	850
1973	1993	3114	1270	1387	279	416	991	1486	830	1056
1974	3269	4774	N.A.	N.A.	234	766	1035	1782	908	1766

Source: *Statistizche Jahrbücher für die Bundesrepublik Deutschland,*
1959–1976.

Poland		Rumania		Yugoslavia		Albania		
Imp.	Exp.	Imp.	Exp.	Imp.	Exp.	Imp.	Exp.	
118	116	45	56	149	233	N.A.	N.A.	1955
241	299	60	50	204	197	N.A.	N.A.	1956
198	275	99	71	244	326	N.A.	N.A.	1957
298	331	123	94	200	340	0.1	0.4	1958
341	294	105	69	198	417	0.5	0.6	1959
320	304	176	150	234	544	0.3	0.9	1960
339	283	211	232	258	571	0.2	0.7	1961
327	263	247	328	325	432	0.3	2.3	1962
321	261	225	292	359	427	0.7	2.8	1963
363	314	245	331	367	533	0.3	3.4	1964
436	366	290	462	473	557	0.4	6.4	1965
482	376	298	558	541	757	2.1	3.4	1966
440	492	351	961	483	1166	0.5	4.1	1967
478	593	416	741	622	1360	3.4	6.9	1968
532	612	464	729	904	1666	2.6	7.3	1969
744	658	580	722	977	2323	4.5	12.1	1970
731	737	747	679	1138	2527	3.9	11.8	1971
990	1450	800	960	1421	2465	2.4	12.8	1972
1219	2634	850	1180	1631	2985	4.2	5.5	1973
1426	3615	964	1836	1606	4526	9.3	33.8	1974

Notes to Chapter 1

1. Martin Broszat, *200 Jahre deutsche Polenpolitik* (Munich: Ehrenwirth, 1963), pp. 17-25; Gerhard Ritter, *Das deutsche Problem* (Munich: Oldenbourg, 1962), p. 29; Elizabeth Wiskemann, *Germany's Eastern Neighbors* (London: Oxford, 1956), pp. 7-33.

2. Walter Laqueur, *Russia and Germany* (Boston: Little, Brown, 1965), pp. 27-60.

3. Helmut Böhme, *Deutschlands Weg zur Grossmacht, Studien zum Verhältnis von Wirtschaft und Staat während der Reichsgründungszeit, 1845-1881* (Cologne: Kiepenheuer and Witsch, 1966) and *Prolegomena zu einer Sozial- und Wirtschaftsgeschichte Deutschlands in 19. und 20. Jahrhundert* (Frankfurt/M.: Suhrkamp ppk., 1968); Otto Pflanze, "Another Crisis Among German Historians?," *Journal of Modern History*, vol. 40, no. 1 (March 1968), pp. 118-129; articles by Fritz Stern, Gerald D. Feldman, Henry Ashby Turner, Jr., and Ernst Nolte, *American Historical Review*, vol. 75, no. 1 (Oct. 1969), pp. 37-79; Jurgen Kocka, "Theoretical Approaches to Social and Economic History of Modern Germany; Some Recent Trends, Concepts and Problems in Western and Eastern Germany," *Journal of Modern History*, vol. 47, no. 1 (March 1975), pp. 101-119.

4. Fritz Fischer, *Griff nach der Weltmacht,* 3rd rev. ed. (Düsseldorf: Droste, 1964); Fritz T. Epstein, "Die deutsche Ostpolitik im Ersten Weltkrieg," *Jahrbücher für die Geschichte Osteuropas,* vol. 10 (1962), pp. 381-394; John A. Moses, *The Politics of Illusion: The Fischer Controversy in German Historiography* (London: George Prior, 1975), pp. 120-124.

5. Henry Cord Meyer, *Mitteleuropa in German Thought and Action* (The Hague: Nijhoff, 1955).

6. Fischer, *Griff nach der Weltmacht,* op. cit.; Immanuel Geiss, *Der polnische Grenzstreifen, 1914-1918* (Lübeck: Matthiesen, 1960); Broszat, *200 Jahre deutsche Polenpolitik,* op. cit., pp. 130-154; Werner Conze, *Polnische Nation und Deutsche Politik im Ersten Weltkrieg* (Cologne: Böhlau, 1958); Gerald Freund, *Unholy Alliance: Russian-German Relations from the Treaty of Brest-Litovsk to the Treaty of Berlin* (London: Chatto and Mindus, 1957), pp. 1-34.

7. Joseph Rothschild, *Piłsudski's Coup d'Etat* (New York: Columbia Univ. Press, 1966), pp. 292-295 and *East Central Eu-*

rope between the Two World Wars (Seattle: Univ. of Washington Press, 1974).

8. Martin Walsdorff, *Westorientierung und Ostpolitik. Stresemanns Russlandpolitik in der Locarno-Ära* (Bremen: Schünemann, 1971); Gaines Post, Jr., *The Civil-Military Fabric of Weimar Foreign Policy* (Princeton, N.J.: Princeton Univ. Press, 1973); Karl Dietrich Erdmann, "Das Problem der Ost- oder Westorientierung in der Locarno-Politik Stresemanns," *Geschichte in Wissenschaft und Unterricht*, vol. 6 (1955), pp. 133–162.

For German-Polish relations in the Weimar period, see Harald von Riekhoff, *German-Polish Relations, 1918–1933* (Baltimore: Johns Hopkins Univ. Press, 1971); Volkmar Kellermann, *Schwarzer Adler Weisser Adler. Die Polenpolitik der Weimarer Republik* (Cologne: Markus, 1970); Josef Korbel, *Poland between East and West: Soviet and German Diplomacy toward Poland, 1919–1933* (Princeton, N. J.: Princeton Univ. Press, 1963); Roman Debicki, *Foreign Policy of Poland, 1919-1939* (New York: Praeger, 1962); Zygmunt J. Gasiorowski, "Stresemann and Poland before Locarno," *Journal of Central European Affairs*, vol. 18, no. 1 (Apr. 1958), pp. 25–47 and "Stresemann and Poland after Locarno," ibid., vol. 18, no. 3 (Oct. 1958), pp. 292–317; Helmut Lippelt, "Politische Sanierung'—Zur deutschen Politik gegenüber Polen, 1925/26," *Vierteljahreshefte für Zeitgeschichte*, vol. 19, no. 4 (Oct. 1971), pp. 323–373; Rothschild, *Piłsudski's Coup d'Etat*, op. cit.

For Soviet-German relations, see Kurt Rosenbaum, *Community of Fate: German-Soviet Diplomatic Relations, 1922–1928* (Syracuse, N. Y.: Syracuse Univ. Press, 1965) (the most detailed but with little analysis); Harvey L. Dyck, *Weimar Germany and Soviet Russia* (London: Chatto and Windus, 1966) (a brilliant analysis; see pp. 13–19 for a penetrating summary of the pre-1926 period).

9. In my view the best characterization of Stresemann is in von Riekhoff, *German-Polish Relations*, op. cit., pp. 264–269. Cf. Post, *The Civil-Military Fabric of Weimar Foreign Policy*, op. cit., pp. 73–82; Walsdorff, *Westorientierung und Ostpolitik*, op. cit., pp. 19–29 and *Bibliographie Gustav Stresemann* (Düsseldorf: Droste, 1972).

10. Walsdorff, *Westorientierung und Ostpolitik*, op. cit., pp. 22–46; von Riekhoff, *German-Polish Relations*, op. cit., pp. 311–316.

11. C. A. Macartney, *October Fifteenth: A History of Modern Hungary, 1929–1945*, 2 vols., 2nd ed., (Edinburgh: Edinburgh Univ. Press, 1961).

12. Nissan Oren, *Bulgarian Communism: The Road to Power, 1933–1944* (New York: Columbia Univ. Press, 1971).

13. Piotr Wandycz, *France and her Eastern Allies, 1919–1925* (Minneapolis: Univ. of Minnesota Press, 1962); Jacob S. Hoptner, *Yugoslavia in Crisis, 1934–1941* (New York: Columbia Univ. Press, 1962); Werner Markert, ed., *Osteuropa-Handbuch Jugoslawien* (Cologne and Graz: Böhlau, 1954).

14. Zygmunt J. Gasiorowski, "Beneš and Locarno: Some Unpublished Documents," *Review of Politics*, vol. 20, no. 2 (Apr. 1958), pp. 209–224; Gerhard L. Weinberg, "Secret Hitler-Beneš Negotiations in 1936–1937," *Journal of Central European Affairs*, vol. 19, no. 4 (Jan. 1960), pp. 366–374 and *The Foreign Policy of Hitler's Germany* (Chicago and London: Univ. of Chicago Press, 1970), pp. 107–110; J. W. Brügel, "German Diplomacy and the Sudeten Question Before 1938," *International Affairs* (London), vol. 37, no. 3 (July 1961), pp. 323–331 and *Tschechen und Deutsche, 1939–1946* (Munich: Nymphenburg, 1974), pp. 198–224, 348–377; Paul E. Zinner, "Czechoslovakia: The Diplomacy of Edward Beneš," in Gordon A. Craig and Felix Gilbert, eds., *The Diplomats 1919–1939*, vol. 1 (Princeton, N. J.: Princeton Univ. Press, 1953), pp. 100–122.

15. Post, *The Civil-Military Fabric of Weimar Foreign Policy*, op. cit., pp. 110–119; see pp. 88–89, n. 3, and pp. 110–111, n. 51 for bibliographic references.

16. Hermann Graml, "Rapallo in der westdeutschen Forschtum," *Vierteljahrshefte für Zeitgeschichte*, vol. 18, no. 4 (Oct. 1970), pp. 366–391, and his criticism of the less critical interpretations of Rapallo by Paul Kluke, "Deutschland und Russland zwischen den Weltkriegen," *Historische Zeitschrift*, vol. 171, no. 3 (May 1951), pp. 519–522; Theodor Schieder, *Die Probleme des Rapallo-Vertrage. Eine Studie über die Deutsche-russischen Beziehungen, 1922–1926* (Cologne: Westdeutscher Verlag, 1956) and "Die Entstehung des Rapallo-Vertrags," *His-*

torische Zeitschrift, vol. 204, no. 3 (June 1967), pp. 545-609; Karl Dietrich Erdmann, "Deutschland, Rapallo und der Westen," *Vierteljahrshefte für Zeitgeschichte*, vol. 11, no. 2 (Apr. 1963), pp. 105-165; von Reikhoff, *German-Polish Relations*, op. cit., p. 53 and n. 1.

17. Walsdorff, *West-orientierung und Ostpolitik*, op. cit., pp. 139-155; von Riekhoff, *German-Polish Relations*, op. cit., pp. 91-130; Dyck, *Weimar Germany and Soviet Russia*, op. cit., pp. 14-19, 32-38, 64-65.

18. Rothschild, *Piłsudski's Coup d'Etat*, op. cit., pp. 23-24.

19. Von Riekhoff, *German-Polish Relations*, op. cit., pp. 108-386; cf. Kellerman, *Schwarzer Adler Weisser Adler*, op. cit., pp. 93-107.

20. See n. 16, sup.

21. Brügel, *Tschechen und Deutsche*, op. cit., and its revision, *Czechoslovakia Before Munich* (Cambridge, England: Cambridge Univ. Press, 1973) and *Ludwig Czech, Arbeiterführer und Staatsman* (Vienna: Verlag der Wiener Volksbuchhandlung, 1960); Jörg K. Hoensch, "Zum sudetendeutsch-tschechischen Verhältnis in der Ersten Republik" (rather pro-Sudetendeutsch, but with useful bibliography), in Eugen Lemberg and Gotthold Rhode, eds., *Das deutsch-tschechische Verhältnis seit 1918* (Stuttgart: Kohlhammer, 1969), pp. 21-48. See also n. 19, sup.

22. Dyck, *Weimar Germany and Soviet Russia*, op. cit., pp. 66-255.

23. Karl Dietrich Erdmann, *Adenauer in der Rheinlandpolitik nach dem Ersten Weltkrieg* (Stuttgart: Klett, 1966); Hans Maier "Konrad Adenauer," in Rudolf Morsey and Konrad Repgen, eds., *Adenauer-Studien*, vol. 1 (Mainz: Matthias-Grünewald Verlag, 1971), pp. 1-19; Rudolf Morsey, *Die Deutsche Zentrumspartei, 1917-1923* (Düsseldorf: Droste, 1966); Hans Georg Lehmann, "Adenauer und der rheinische Separatismus 1918/9," ibid., vol. 3 (1974), pp. 213-225; Heinrich Köhler, *Autonomie-Bewegung oder Separatismus* (Berlin: Colloquium, 1974).

24. Weinberg, *The Foreign Policy of Hitler's Germany*, op. cit.; Hans-Adolf Jacobsen, *Nationalsozialistische Aussenpolitik, 1933-1938* (Frankfurt/M.: Metzner, 1968).

25. Alexander Dallin, *German Rule in Russia, 1941-1945: A*

Study of Occupation Policies (London: Macmillan, 1957), pp. 7, 8; Ernst Nolte, *Three Faces of Fascism* (New York: Holt, Rinehart and Winston, 1966); Martin Broszat, *Der Nationalsozialismus*, 2nd ed. (Stuttgart: Deutsche Verlagsanstalt, 1960); Eberhard Jäckel, *Hitlers Weltanschauung* (Middletown, Conn.: Wesleyan Univ. Press, 1972); Axel Kuhn, *Hitler's aussenpolitisches Programm* (Stuttgart: Klett, 1970); Jacobsen, *Nationalsozialistische Aussenpolitik* op. cit., pp. 1–15; especially Weinberg, *The Foreign Policy of Hitler's Germany,* op. cit., pp. 1–24. See also Gerhard Ritter, *Das Deutsche Problem. Grundfragen deutschen Staatslebens gestern und heute* (Munich: Oldenbourg, 1966), pp. 190–199; and Andreas Hillgruber, "Die 'Endlösung' and das deutsche Ostimperium als des rassenideologischen Programms des Nationalsozialismus," *Vierteljahrshefte für zeitgeschichte,* vol. 20, no. 2 (April 1972), pp. 133–153; Paul Kluke, "Nationalsozialistische Europaideologie," ibid., vol. 3, no. 3 (July 1955), pp. 240-275.

26. George N. Stein, "Russo-German Military Collaboration: The Last Phase, 1933," *Political Science Quarterly,* vol. 77, no. 1 (March 1962), pp. 54-71; Weinberg, *The Foreign Policy of Hitler's Germany,* op. cit., pp. 74-75.

27. Weinberg, *The Foreign Policy of Hitler's Germany,* op. cit., pp. 75, 180-184, 220-223, 310-312.

28. Ibid., pp. 57-74; Hans Roos, *Polen und Europa: Studien zur polnischen Aussenpolitik 1931-1939* (Tübingen: Rohr, 1957), pp. 54 ff. (before AA files were available); Broszat, *200 Jahre deutsche Polenpolitik,* op. cit., pp. 182-197.

29. Weinberg, *The Foreign Policy of Hitler's Germany,* op. cit., pp. 60, 62, and, for full bibliography, p. 57, n. 1.

30. Ibid., pp. 62-74; Zygmunt J. Gasiorowski, "The German-Polish Non-Agression Pact of 1934," *Journal of Central European Affairs,* vol. 15, no. 1 (Apr. 1955), pp. 3-29; Korbel, *Poland between East and West,* op. cit., pp. 275-286.

31. Weinberg, *The Foreign Policy of Hitler's Germany,* op. cit., pp. 184-194, 302-310.

32. W. Jürgen Gehl, *Austria, Germany and the Anschluss, 1931-1938* (London: Oxford Univ. Press, 1963); Weinberg, *The Foreign Policy of Hitler's Germany,* op. cit., pp. 87-107, 232-238, 264-271, 312-321.

33. Brügel, *Tschechen und Deutsche, 1918-1938* and its revi-

sion, *Czechoslovakia Before Munich*, op. cit. and *Tschechen und Deutsche*, op. cit; Weinberg, *The Foreign Policy of Hitler's Germany*, op. cit., pp. 107-110, 224-226, 312; Boris Čelovský, *Das Münchner Abkommen 1938* (Stuttgart: Deutsche Verlagsanstalt, 1958). See also Helmuth K. G. Rönnefarth, *Die Sudetenkrise in der internationalen Politik*, 2 vols. (Wiesbaden: Steiner, 1961) (pro-Sudeten); Elizabeth Wiskemann, *Czechs and Germans* (London: Oxford Univ. Press), pp. 118-271 and *Germany's Eastern Neighbours* (London: Oxford Univ. Press, 1956), pp. 48-53; Wenzel Jaksch, *Europe's Road to Potsdam* (New York: Praeger, 1964), pp. 284-357; George F. Kennan, *Memoirs, 1925-1950* (Boston: Little Brown, 1967), pp. 87-104 and *From Prague to Munich* (Princeton, N. J.: Princeton Univ. Press, 1968).

34. C. A. Macartney and A. W. Palmer, *Independent Eastern Europe* (New York, St. Martins and London: Macmillan, 1962), pp. 289 and 315 ff.; MacAlister Brown, "The Third Reich's Mobilization of the German Fifth Column in Eastern Europe," *Journal of Central European Affairs* vol. 19, no. 2 (July 1959), pp. 128-148; L. de Jong, *The German Fifth Column in the Second World War*, trans., (Chicago: Univ. of Chicago Press, 1956); Antonin Basch, *The Danube Basin and the German Economic Sphere* (New York: Columbia Univ. Press, 1943).

35. Andreas Hillgruber, "England's Place in Hitler's Plans for World Dominion," *Journal of Contemporary History*, vol. 9, no. 1 (Jan. 1974), pp. 5-22.

36. Andreas Hillgruber, *Hitler's Strategie, Politik und Kriegsführung 1940/1941* (Frankfurt/M.: Bernard and Graefe, 1965).

37. Dallin, *German Rule in Russia*, op. cit.

38. Vojtech Mastny, *The Czechs Under Nazi Rule* (New York: Columbia Univ. Press, 1971); Detlef Brandes, *Die Tschechen unter deutschen Protektorat*, vol. 1 (Munich: Oldenbourg, 1968); Weinberg, *The Foreign Policy of Hitler's Germany*, op. cit., pp. 110-116.

39. Jörg L. Hoensch, *Die Slowakei und Hitlers Ostpolitik* (Cologne and Graz: Böhlau, 1965) and *Der ungarisch Revisionismus und die Zerschlagung der Tschechoslowakei* (Tübingen: Mohr, 1967); Josef Anderle, "The Establishment of Slovak Autonomy in 1938," in Miloslav Rechcigl, Jr., ed., *Czechoslovakia Past and Present*, vol. 1 (The Hague: Mouton, 1968), pp. 76-97; Yesha-

yahu Jelinek, *The Parish Republic: Hlinka's Slovak People's Party 1939-1945* (New York: Columbia Univ. Press, 1975).

40. Macartney, *October Fifteenth: A History of Modern Hungary,* op. cit.; Andreas Hillbruber, "Deutschland und Ungarn 1933-1944," *Wehrwissenschaftlicher Rundschau,* vol. 9, no. 11 (Nov. 1959), pp. 651-676 and "Das deutsch-ungarische Verhältnis im letzten Kriegsjahr," ibid., vol. 10, no. 2 (Feb. 1960), pp. 78-104. See also John Pelenyi, "The Secret Plan for a Hungarian Government in the West at the Outbreak of World War II," *Journal of Modern History,* vol. 36 (1964), pp. 170-177; C. A. Macartney, "Ungarns Weg aus dem Zweiten Krieg," *Vierteljahreshefte für Zeitgeschichte,* vol. 14, no. 1 (Jan. 1966), pp. 79-103; Martin Broszat, "Deutschland—Ungarn—Rumänien. Entwicklung und Grundfaktoren nationalsozialistischer Hegemonial- und Bündnispolitik 1938-1941," *Historische Zeitschrift,* vol. 206, no. 1 (Feb. 1968), pp. 45-95.

41. Henry L. Roberts, *Rumania: Political Problems of an Agrarian State* (New Haven, Conn.: Yale Univ. Press, 1951); Hillgruber, *Hitler, König Carol und Marschall Antonescu* (Wiesbaden: Steiner, 1965); Stephen A. Fischer-Galati, *Twentieth Century Rumania* (New York: and London: Columbia Univ. Press, 1970); Weinberg, *The Foreign Policy of Hitler's Germany,* op. cit., pp. 230-231, 323-325.

42. Rothschild, *East Central Europe between the Two World Wars,* op. cit.; Oren, *Bulgarian Communism,* op. cit.; Weinberg, *The Foreign Policy of Hitler's Germany,* op. cit., pp. 326-327.

43. Macartney and Palmer, *Independent Eastern Europe,* op. cit.; Markert, ed., *Osteuropa-Handbuch Jugoslawien,* op. cit., pp. 67-121; Rothschild, *East Central Europe between the Two World Wars,* op. cit.; Jacob B. Hoptner, *Yugoslavia in Crisis 1934-1941* (New York and London: Columbia Univ. Press, 1962); Ladislaus Hory and Martin Broszat, *Der Kroatische Ustascha-Staat 1941-1945,* Schriftenreihe der *Vierteljahrshefte für Zeitgeschichte,* no. 8 (Stuttgart: Deutsche Verlags-Anstalt, 1964); Stephen Clissold, *Whirlwind, an Account of Marshal Tito's Rise to Power* (London: Cresset, 1949); Walter R. Roberts, *Tito, Mihailovic and the Allies, 1941-1945* (New Brunswick, N. J.: Rutgers Univ. Press, 1973); Weinberg, *The Foreign Policy of Hitler's Germany,* op. cit., pp. 228-229, 325-326.

44. Hermann Graml, "Resistance Thinking on Foreign Policy,"

in Hermann Graml, Hans Mommsen, Hans-Joachim Reichhardt, Ernest Wolf, and F. L. Carsten, eds., *The German Resistance to Hitler* (Berkeley and Los Angeles: Univ. of California Press, 1970), pp. 1–54; Hans Mommsen, "Social Views and Constitutional Plans of the Resistance," ibid., pp. 55–147.

45. There is no satisfactory full-scale history of the KPD. Ossip K. Flechtheim's *Die Kommunistische Partei Deutschlands in der Weimarer Republik* (Offenbach a. M.: Bollwerk-Verlag Karl Drott, 1948) is an inadequate, relatively brief survey from a left-wing socialist (USPD) viewpoint. Ruth Fischer's *Stalin and German Communism* (Cambridge, Mass.: Harvard Univ. Press, 1948) is a detailed, prejudiced, largely autobiographical, and often unreliable survey by a former leader of the KPD left wing. For shorter accounts, see Franz Borkenau, *European Communism* (London: Faber and Faber, 1953) and *The Communist International* (London: Faber and Faber, 1938); Hugh Seton-Watson, *From Lenin to Khrushchev* (New York: Praeger, 1960), pp. 99–106; especially Carola Stern, *Ulbricht* (New York: Praeger, 1965) and "Tradition and History of the German Communist Party (KPD)," in William E. Griffith, ed., *Communism in Europe*, vol. 2 (Cambridge, Mass.: MIT Press, 1966), pp. 43–61; Hermann Weber, "Einleitung" to a reprinting of Flechtheim, *Die KPD in der Weimarer Republik* (Frankfurt/M.: Europäische Verlagsanstalt, 1969), pp. 5–68. Weber is the leading historian of the KPD.

More important are detailed studies of specific periods. See Richard Löwenthal, "The Bolshevisation of the Spartacus League," in David Footman, ed., *St. Antony's Papers, No. 9: International Communism* (Carbondale, Ill.: Southern Illinois Univ. Press, 1960); Siegfried Bahne, "Zwischen 'Luxenburgismus' und 'Stalinismus': Die ultralinke Opposition in der KPD," *Vierteljahreshefte für Zeitgeschichte,* vol. 9, no. 4 (Oct. 1961), pp. 359–383 and "Die Kommunistische Partei Deutschlands," in Erich Matthias and Rudolf Morskey, eds., *Das Ende der Parteien 1933* (Düsseldorf: Droste, 1960), pp. 655–739; Werner T. Angress, *Stillborn Revolution: The Communist Bid for Power in Germany, 1921–1923* (Princeton, N. J.: Princeton Univ. Press, 1963); Hermann Weber, *Die Wandlung des deutschen Kommunismus. Die Stalinisierung der KPD in der Weimarer Republik,* 2 vols. (Frankfurt/M.: Europäischer Verlagsanstalt, 1969) (excellent bibliography); Horst Duhnke, *Die KPD von 1933 bis 1945* (Cologne: Kiepenheuer and Witsch, 1972). For Ulbricht, see Stern, *Ulbricht*, op. cit.; Hermann Weber, "Die Wandlungen Walter Ulbrichts," *SBZ-Archiv*, vol. 9, no. 14 (July 25, 1958), pp. 210-214, *Ulbricht fälscht Geschichte* (Cologne: Neuer Deutscher, 1964), and *Von Rosa Luxemburg zu Walter Ulbricht*, 3rd ed. (Hannover: Verlag für Literatur und Zeitgeschehen, 1962). For documentation, see Hermann Weber, *Der Deutsche Kommunismus: Dokumente* (Cologne and Berlin: Kiepenheuer and Witsch, 1963). For bibliography, see Enzo Colotti, *Die Kommunistische Partei Deutschlands 1918-1933: Ein bibliographischer Beitrag* (Milan: Feltrinelli, 1961); Weber, *Die Wandlung des deutschen Kommunismus*, op. cit., and "Einleitung," op. cit. For the Russo-German secret negotiations, see H. W. Koch, "The Spectre of a Separate Peace in the East: Russo-German Peace Feelers, 1942-44," *Journal of Contemporary History*, vol. 10, no. 3 (July 1975), pp. 531-549.

46. K. L. Seleznev at a GlavPURKKA meeting, Sept. 11, 1945, in his "Zur Hilfe Georgi Dimitroffs für die Propaganda der Politorgane der Roten Armee in der faschistischen Wehrmacht," *Bibliothek für Zeitgeschichte* (Stuttgart), vol. 14, no. 5 (1971), pp. 790-804, tr. from quotations in Alexander Fischer, *Sowjetische Deutschlandpolitik im Zweiten Weltkrieg 1941-1945* (Stuttgart: Deutsche Verlags-Anstalt, 1945), p. 157, on which I have primarily relied. For British and American wartime postwar planning, see Tony Sharp, *The Wartime Alliance and the Zonal Division of Germany* (Oxford: Clarendon, 1975).

Notes to Chapter 2

1. For review articles on this controversy, see Irwin Unger, "The 'New Left' and American History: Some Recent Trends in United States Historiography," *American Historical Review*, vol. 72, no. 4 (July 1967), pp. 1237-1263; Charles S. Maier, "Revisionism and the Interpretation of Cold War Origins," *Perspectives in American History*, vol. 4 (1970), pp. 313-347; J. L. Richardson, "Cold-War Revisionism: A Critique," *World Politics.* vol. 24 (July 1972), pp. 579-612. In my view the best recent treatments are John Lewis Gaddis, *The United States and the Origins of the Cold War, 1941-1947* (New York: Columbia Univ. Press, 1972); Lynn Etheridge Davis, *The Cold War Begins,*

Soviet-American Conflict over Eastern Europe (Princeton, N.J.: Princeton Univ. Press, 1974). Prof. Vojtech Mastny's forthcoming *Russia's Road to the Cold War: Stalin's War Aims, 1941-1945*, to be published by Columbia University Press, will undoubtedly be in the same category. See also Daniel Yergin, *Shattered Peace* (Boston: Houghton Mifflin, 1977) (moderately revisionist). For the Marshall Plan see John Gimbel, *The Origins of the Marshall Plan* (Stanford, Cal.: Stanford Univ. Press, 1976) and the critical review by Max Beloff in *The Times Literary Supplement*, November 26, 1976.

2. Cf. Adam Ulam, *Expansion and Coexistence* (New York: Praeger, 1968), pp. 437 ff.; Waldemar Besson, *Die Aussenpolitik der Bundesrepublik; Erfahrungen und Massstäbe* (Munich: Piper, 1970), p. 33; Eberhard Schulz, "Die sowjetische Deutschlandpolitik," *Osteurope Handbuch Sowjetunion*, vol. 2, *Aussenpolitik* (Cologne: Böhlau, 1977), pp. 229-291. (I am grateful to Dr. Schulz for allowing me to read this in page proofs.)

3. Cf. Leo Bauer, "Die Partei hat immer recht," *Aus Politik und Zeitgeschichte*, supplement to *Das Parlament*, July 4, 1956, p. 410.

4. Henry Krisch, *German Politics under Soviet Occupation* (New York: Columbia Univ. Press, 1974); Hans Herzfeld, *Berlin in der Westpolitik, 1945-1970* (Berlin: Gruyter, 1973), pp. 80-88.

5. Richard Löwenthal, "Vom kalten Krieg zur Ostpolitik," in Richard Löwenthal, ed., *Die Zweite Republik: 25 Jahre Bundesrepublik Deutschland—Eine Bilanz* (Stuttgart: Seewald, 1974).

6. Ibid., pp. 610-611.

7. The best general works are Fritz René Alleman, *Bonn ist nicht Weimar* (Cologne: Kiepeneuer and Witsch, 1956) and *Zwischen Stabilität und Krise* (Munich: Piper, 1963); Fred Luchsinger, *Bericht über Bonn: Deutsche Politik 1955-1965* (Zurich: Fretz and Wasmuth, 1966). See also Alfred Grosser, *The Federal Republic of Germany; a Concise History* (New York: Praeger, 1964); Karl W. Deutsch and Lewis J. Edinger, *Germany Rejoins the Powers* (Stanford, Cal.: Stanford Univ. Press, 1959); Hans Speier and W. Phillips Davison, *West German Leadership and Foreign Policy* (Evanston, Ill.: Row, Peterson, 1957).

For West German foreign policy see Besson, *Aussenpolitik* (op. cit.); Wolfram F. Hanrieder, *West German Foreign Policy 1949-*

1963; International Pressure and Domestic Response (Stanford
Cal.: Stanford Univ. Press, 1967) and *The Stable Crisis* (New
York: Harper & Row, 1970); Ferenc A. Vali, *The Quest for a
United Germany* (Baltimore: Johns Hopkins Univ. Press, 1967);
Werner Feld, *Reunification and West German-Soviet Relations*
(The Hague: Nijhoff, 1963); Wilhelm Cornides, *Die Weltmächte
und Deutschland 1945-1955*, 3rd rev. ed. (Tübingen: Leins and
Stuttgart: Metzler, 1965); Charles R. Planck, *The Changing Sta-
tus of German Reunification in Western Diplomacy, 1955-1966*
(Baltimore: Johns Hopkins Univ. Press, 1967); James L. Rich-
ardson, *Germany and the Atlantic Alliance; the Interaction of
Strategy and Politics* (Cambridge, Mass.: Harvard Univ. Press,
1966); Karl Kaiser, *German Foreign Policy in Transition* (London and New York: Oxford Univ. Press, 1968); Pierre Hassner,
"Change and Security in Europe," Adelphi Papers, Nos. 45
(Feb. 1968) and 49 (July 1968), (London: Institute for Strategic Studies, 1968).

For the early post war period see Hans-Peter Schwarz, *Vom
Reich zur Bundesrepublik* (Neuwied and Berlin: Luchterhand,
1966); Arnulf Baring, *Aussenpolitik in Adenauers Kanzlerdemokratie* (Munich: Oldenbourg, 1969) and *Sehr verehrter Herr
Bundeskanzler* (extensively commented letters between von
Brentano and Adenauer) (Hamburg: Hoffman and Campe,
1974), which uses the important unpublished study by Hans
Buchheim, based (uniquely) on the Bundeskanzleramt archives,
Adenauers Alternative. See also Hans Buchheim, "Die westdeutsche Aussenpolitik in der Ära Adenauer," *Politische Vierteljahresschrift*, vol. 9, no. 1 (March 1968), pp. 45-55.

For the 1954-1963 period see Klaus Gotto, "Adenauers
Deutschland- und Ostpolitik 1954-1963" in Rudolph Morsey
and Konrad Repgen, *Adenauer Studien*, vol. 3 (Mainz: Mathias
Gruenewald, 1971-1976), pp. 3-91; Werner Weidenfeld, "Der
Einfluss der Ostpolitik de Gaulles auf die Ostpolitik Adenauers,"
ibid., pp. 116-128; the Krone diary and the Globke Plan text,
ibid., pp. 129-212; Josef Joffe, "Society and Foreign Policy in
the Federal Republic: 1949-1962," (unpublished Ph.D. dissertation, Harvard University, 1975), cited hereafter as "Joffe."
The Yearbook series, Wilhelm Cornides et al., eds., *Die Internationale Politik* (Munich: Oldenbourg) issued by the Deutsche
Gesellschaft für auswärtige Politik in Bonn, is essential, espe-

cially the contributions by the late Wilhelm Cornides, as well as the yearly volumes published by Oxford University Press for the Royal Institute of International Affairs (Chatham House) in London, *Survey of International Affairs.* For further bibliography see Gotto, "Adenauers Deutschland- und Ostpolitik," op. cit.; p. 3, ns. 1–3 and passim.

8. See Chapter 1, sup.

9. Baring, *Aussenpolitik in Adenauers Kanzlerdemokratie,* op. cit., p. 1.

10. Löwenthal, ed., *Die Zweite Republik,* op. cit., pp. 609–611.

11. Gotto, "Adenauers Deutschland– und Ostpolitik," op. cit., p. 9.

12. Baring, *Aussenpolitik in Adenauers Kanzlerdemokratie,* op. cit.

13. Ibid., p. 98.

14. Konrad Adenauer, *Erinnerungen,* 4 vols. (Stuttgart: Deutsche Verlags-Anstalt, 1965–1969); Rüdiger Altmann, *Das Erbe Adenauer* (Stuttgart: Seewald, 1960); Gordon A. Craig, "The Statecraft of Konrad Adenauer," in *From Bismarck to Adenauer: Aspects of German Statecraft* (Baltimore: Johns Hopkins Univ. Press, 1958), pp. 124–148; Henry Kissinger, *The Troubled Partnership* (New York: McGraw-Hill, 1965), pp. 66–68; Besson, *Aussenpolitik,* op. cit., pp. 34–39, 56–61; Arnold J. Heidenheimer, *Adenauer and the CDU; the Rise of the Leader and the Integration of the Party* (The Hague: Nijhoff, 1960); Schwarz, *Vom Reich zur Bundesrepublik,* op. cit., and "Das aussenpolitischen Grundlagen des westdeutschen Staates" in Löwenthal, ed., *Die zweite Republik*, op. cit., pp. 27–63; Baring, *Aussenpolitik in Adenauers Kanzlerdemokratie,* op. cit. (in my view the best characterization of Adenauer) and *Sehr verehrter Herr Bundeskanzler*, op. cit.; and the most recent large-scale reconsideration, Dieter Blumenwitz et al., eds., *Konrad Adenauer und seine Zeit,* 2 vols. (Stuttgart: Deutsche Verlags-Anstalt, 1976).

15. For example, in the ideas of Rudolf Nadolny and Jacob Wirth: See the advocacy of it in Paul Sethe, *Zwischen Bonn und Moskau* (Frankfurt/M.: Scheffler, 1956); especially in Karl Georg Pfleiderer, *Politik für Deutschland* (Stuttgart: Deutsche Verlags-Anstalt, 1961).

16. Werner Conze, Erich Kosthorst, and Elfreide Nebgen, *Jakob Kaiser* (Stuttgart: Kohlhammer, 1967); Besson, *Aussenpolitik,* op. cit., pp. 34–39.

17. See the best biography, Carola Stern, *Willy Brandt,* (Reinbeck bei Hamburg: Rowohlt, 1975), pp. 1–46.

18. Lewis J. Edinger, *Kurt Schumacher* (Stanford, Cal.: Stanford Univ. Press, 1965); Douglas A. Chalmers, *The Social Democratic Party of Germany* (New Haven, Conn.: Yale Univ. Press, 1964); Schwarz, *Vom Reich zur Bundesrepublik,* op. cit.; Willy Brandt and Richard Löwenthal, *Ernst Reuter* (Munich: Kindler, 1957); Abraham Ashkenasi, *Reformpartei und Aussenpolitik. Die Aussenpolitik der SPD Berlin-Bonn* (Cologne and Opladen: Westdeutscher Verlag, 1968); Besson, *Aussenpolitik,* op. cit., pp. 62–68; Helga Haftendorn, *Abrüstungs- und Entspannungspolitik zwischen Sicherheitsbefriedigung und Friedenssicherung. Zur Aussenpolitik der BRD 1955-1973* (Düsseldorf: Bertelsmann, 1974), pp. 37–40.

19. Eugen Lemberg and Friedrich Edding, eds., *Die Vertriebenen in Westdeutschland; ihre Eingliederung und ihr Einfluss auf Gesellschaft, Wirtschaft, Politik und Geistesleben,* 3 vols. (Kiel: Hirt, 1959); Geza C. Paikert, *The German Exodus; a Selective Study on the Post-World War II Expulsion of German Populations and its Effects* (The Hague; Nijhoff, 1962); Elizabeth Wiskemann, *Germany's Eastern Neighbours* (London: Oxford, 1956); Radomír Luža, *The Transfer of the Sudeten Germans, A Study of Czech-German Relations, 1933-1962* (New York: New York Univ. Press, 1964); Bertram Lattimore, Jr., *The Assimilation of German Expellees into the West German Polity and Society since 1945. A Case Study of Eutin, Schleswig-Holstein* (The Hague: Nijhoff, 1974).

20. Walter Phillips Davison, *The Berlin Blockade; A Study in Cold War Politics* (Princeton, N. J.: Princeton Univ. Press, 1958); Brandt and Löwenthal, *Ernst Reuter,* op. cit.; Alois Riklin, *Das Berlinproblem* (Cologne: Verlag Wissenschaft und Politik, 1964); Robert M. Slusser, *The Berlin Crisis of 1961: Soviet-American Relations and the Struggle for Power in the Kremlin, June–November 1961* (Baltimore and London: Johns Hopkins Univ. Press, 1973); Dieter Mahncke, *Berlin im geteilten Deutschland* (Munich: Oldenbourg, 1973).

21. Documentation: Deutsche Gesellschaft für Auswärtige Politik, *Dokumente zur Berlin-Frage 1944-1966* (Munich: Oldenbourg, 1967), p. 67 ff.

22. Pfleiderer, *Politik für Deutschland,* op. cit.; Baring, *Aussenpolitik in Adenauers Kanzlerdemokratie,* op. cit., pp. 310-311. For FDP Ostpolitik, see Hans-Dietrich Genscher, "Adenauer die Ost- und Deutschlandpolitik der Freien Demokraten," in Blumenwitz, ed., *Konrad Adenauer und seine Zeit,* op. cit., vol. 1, pp. 108-116.

23. Löwenthal, ed., *Die zweite Republik,* op. cit., pp. 612-617; Thilo Vogelsang, *Das geteilte Deutschland* (Munich: Deutscher Taschenbuch Verlag, 1966). pp. 135-140; Besson, *Aussenpolitik,* op. cit., pp. 122-129; Thomas W. Wolfe, *Soviet Power and Europe, 1945-1970* (Baltimore: Johns Hopkins Univ. Press, 1970) pp. 28-31; and (the most recent authoritative analysis), Andreas Hillgruber, "Adenauer und die Stalin-Note vom 10. Marz 1952," in Blumenwitz, ed., *Konrad Adenauer und seine Zeit,* vol. 2, pp. 111-130.

I do not regard the changes in Soviet foreign policy presaged in Stalin's last years as having affected the German question decisively. See Marshall Shulman, *Stalin's Foreign Policy Reappraised* (Cambridge: Harvard Univ. Press, 1963).

24. Wilhelm Cornides in Cornides et al., eds., *Die Internationale Politik 1955,* op. cit., pp. 779-782 and *Survey of International Affairs 1954,* op. cit., pp. 7-11. For analyses of the Adenauer-Dulles relationship, see Eleanor Dulles, "Adenauer und Dulles," in Blumenwitz, ed., *Konrad Adenauer und seine Zeit,* op. cit., vol. 1, pp. 377-389, and Dieter Oberndörfer, "John Foster Dulles und Konrad Adenauer," ibid., vol. 2, pp. 299-348, and for an authoritative West German account of Adenauer's relations with Washington, Kurt Birrenbach, "Adenauer und die Vereinigten Staaten in der Periode seiner Kanzlerschaft," ibid., pp. 477-509.

25. Stanley Hoffmann, *Gulliver's Troubles* (New York: McGraw-Hill, 1968), p. 400.

26. Hans Wolfgang Kuhn in Cornides et al., eds., *Die Internationale Politik 1956/7,* op. cit., pp. 381 ff.

27. H. P. Schwarz in Morsey and Repgen, *Adenauer Studien,* op. cit., vol. 1, pp. 90 ff.

253

28. Heinz Brandt, *The Search for a Third Way* (Garden City, N.Y.: Doubleday, 1970.)

29. Arnulf Baring, *Uprising in East Germany: June 17, 1953* (New York: Cornell Univ. Press, 1972); Löwenthal, ed., *Die Zweite Republik,* op. cit., pp. 619-623; Victor Baras, "Beria's Fall and Ulbricht's Survival," *Soviet Studies,* vol. 27, no. 3 (July 1975), pp. 381-395.

30. Löwenthal, ed., *Die Zweite Republik,* op. cit., pp. 619-623; Ulam, *Expansion and Coexistence,* op. cit., pp. 551-552. Documentation: Auswärtiges Amt der Bundesrepublik Deutschland, *Die Auswärtige Politik der Bundesrepublik Deutschland,* (Cologne: Verlag Wissenschaft und Politik, 1972), pp. 256 ff.

31. Cornides et al., eds., *Die Internationale Politik 1955,* op. cit., pp. 172-177, 343-348, 349-360; *Survey of International Affairs 1954,* op. cit., pp. 129-148; Planck, *The Changing Status of German Reunification,* op. cit., pp. 6 ff.; Arnulf Baring, "Die westdeutsche Aussenpolitik in der Ära Adenauer," *Politische Vierteljahresschrift,* vol. 9, no. 1 (March 1968), p. 50; Wilhelm Cornides, "Das Problem der europaischen Sicherheit auf der Berliner Viermächtekonferenz 1954," *Europa Archiv,* vol. 9 nos. 8-9 (Apr. 20-May 5, 1954), pp. 6489 ff.; Walter Bodigheimer, "Die Verhandlungen über das Sicherheitsproblem auf der Berliner Konferenz von 1954, ibid., pp. 6496-6513; Hermann Volle and Ernst Wallrapp, "Die Österreichverhandlungen auf der Berliner Konferenz von 1954," ibid., pp. 6514-6524. Documentation: ibid., pp. 6525-6537 and *Die Viererkonferenz in Berlin 1954. Reden und Dokumente* (Bonn: Bundespresseamt, n.d.); Löwenthal, ed., *Die Zweite Republik,* op. cit., pp. 623-624; cf. Klaus Mehnert in *Osteuropa,* vol. 4, no. 2 (Apr. 1954), pp. 104-111. For subsequent developments see Wolf Gunther Contius in ibid., vol. 4, no. 5 (Oct. 1954), pp. 379-383; vol. 5, no. 1 (Feb. 1955), pp. 38-41; vol. 5, no. 3 (June 1955), pp. 185-189.

32. Gotto, "Adenauers Deutschland- und Ostpolitik," op. cit., pp. 11-12. Documentation: *Die Auswärtige Politik,* op. cit., pp. 292 ff.; Boris Meissner, ed., *Moskau Bonn. Die Beziehungen zwischen der Sowjetunion und der Bundesrepublik Deutschland 1955-1973. Dokumentation* (Cologne: Verlag Wissenschaft und Politik, 1975), vol. 1, pp. 74 ff.

33. Gotto, "Adenauers Deutschland- und Ostpolitik,", op. cit., pp. 13-14; Cornides et al., eds., *Die international Politik 1955*, op. cit., pp. 365-390, 425-434, 797-856; Ulrich Scheuner, "Voraussetzungen und Verfahren der Wiedervereinigung Deutschlands," *Europa Archiv*, vol. 10, no. 16 (Aug. 20, 1955), pp. 8071-8080; Khrushchev in *Neues Deutschland*, July 28, 1955; Eberhard Gelbe-Haussen, "Die Aussenministerkonferenz von Genf," *Osteuropa*, vol. 6, no. 2 (Feb. 1956), pp. 61-68; Löwenthal, ed., *Die Zweite Republik*, op. cit., pp. 627-631.

34. *Die Auswärtige Politik*, op. cit., pp. 301 ff.; Meissner, ed., *Moskau Bonn*, op. cit., vol. 1, pp. 77 ff.

35. Adenauer, *Erinnerungen*, vol. 2, op. cit., pp. 496-556; cf. Gotto, "Adenauers Deutschland- und Ostpolitik," op, cit., pp. 14-16.

36. Wilhelm Starlinger, *Hinter Russland China* (Würzburg: Marienburg, 1957).

37. See William E. Griffith, *Sino-Soviet Relations, 1964-1965* (Cambridge, Mass.: MIT Press, 1967), p. 28 and *The Sino-Soviet Rift* (Cambridge, Mass.: MIT Press, 1964), p. 16, n. 11.

38. Notably in an unpublished manuscript by Kevin Devlin.

39. Besson, *Aussenpolitik*, op. cit., pp. 202-203, 209.

40. Baring, *Sehr verehrter Herr Bundeskanzler*, op. cit., pp. 173-179.

41. Adenauer, *Erinnerungen*, vol. 2, pp. 487-556; *Survey of International Affairs 1955-56*, op. cit., pp. 138-147; Cornides et al., eds., *Die Internationale Politik 1955*, op. cit., pp. 382 ff. and *Die internationale Politik 1956/7*, op. cit., pp. 404 ff.; Klaus Mehnert, "Der Kanzler in Moskau," *Osteuropa*, vol. 5, no. 6 (Dec. 1955), pp. 448-454; Löwenthal, ed., *Die Zweite Republic*, op. cit., pp. 629-630.

42. Robert W. Dean, *West German Trade with the East: The Political Dimension* (New York: Praeger, 1974), p. 172; W. W. Kulski, *Germany and Poland* (Syracuse N. Y.: Syracuse Univ. Press, 1976), p. 112; Angela Stent Yergin, "The Political Economy of West German-Soviet Relations 1955-1973" (unpublished Ph.D. dissertation, Harvard University, 1977).

43. See chart in Appendix; Angela Yergin, op. cit., pp. 37-128.

44. Dean, *West German Trade with the East*, op. cit., pp. 46-58, 102-110.

45. Schulz, "Die sowjetische Deutschlandpolitik," op. cit., p. 247.

46. Cornides et al., eds., *Die Internationale Politik 1956/57,* op. cit., pp. 21–31; *Survey of International Affairs 1956/57,* op. cit., pp. 253–263; Planck, *The Changing Status of German Reunification,* op. cit., pp. 22–23; Joffe, pp. 210–212; Baring, *Sehr verehrter Herr Bundeskanzler,* op. cit., pp. 180–191.

47. Zbigniew Brzezinski, *The Soviet Bloc,* 3rd ed. (Cambridge, Mass.: Harvard Univ. Press, 1971.)

48. Cornides et al., eds., *Die Internationale Politik 1956/57,* op. cit., pp. 36–46, 393; *Survey of International Affairs 1956/57,* op. cit., p. 217; Joffe, pp. 173–174; Baring, *Sehr verehrter Herr Bundeskanzler,* op. cit., pp. 193–194.

49. Baring, ibid., pp. 18–27.

50. Cornides et al., eds., *Die Internationale Politik 1956/57,* op. cit., pp. 404 ff.; Hansjakob Stehle, *Nachbar Polen,* rev. ed. (Frankfurt/M.: Fischer, 1968), pp. 334–370.

51. Löwenthal, ed., *Die Zweite Republik,* op. cit., p. 637.

52. Cornides et al., eds., *Die Internationale Politik 1956/57,* op. cit., pp. 406 ff.; Schulz, "Die sowjetische Deutschlandpolitik," op. cit., pp. 250–251.

53. Joffe, pp. 175–176, 188–197; Catherine McArdle Kelleher, *Germany and the Politics of Nuclear Weapons* (New York: Columbia Univ. Press, 1975), pp. 43–59, 64–74; Baring, *Sehr verehrter Herr Bundeskanzler,* op. cit., p. 209; Haftendorn, *Abrüstungs- und Entspannungspolitik,* op. cit., pp. 113–120.

54. Cornides et al., eds., *Die Internationale Politik 1956/57,* op. cit., pp. 3–20, 382, 397.

55. Ulam, *Expansion and Coexistence,* op. cit., p. 611.

56. The most balanced brief analysis of the Rapacki Plan is, in my view, by B. A. Osadczuk-Korab in Cornides et al., eds., *Die Internationale Politik 1958–1960,* op. cit., pp. 712–716. The most detailed ones are the favorable one by Stehle, *Nachbar Polen,* op. cit., the first edition of which was translated as *The Independent Satellite* (New York: Praeger, 1965) (see pp. 220–236) and the critical one by Charles Planck, *Sicherheit in Europa: Die Vorschläge für Rustungsbeschränkung und Abrüstung 1955–1965* (Munich: Oldenbourg, 1968), pp. 118–155. See also Joffe. pp. 210–212; Baring, *Sehr verehrter Herr Bundes-*

kanzler, op. cit., pp. 223-224; Haftendorn, *Abrüstungs- und Ent spannungspolitik,* op. cit., pp. 43-55 (regarding West German disengagement plans); Schulz, "Die sowjetische Deutschland-politik," op. cit., pp. 251-253; Besson, *Aussenpolitik,* op. cit., p. 209; Paul E. Zinner, ed., *Documents on American Relations 1958* (Council on Foreign Relations) (New York: Harper, 1959), pp. 195-202.

57. Stephen A. Fischer-Galati, *The New Rumania: From People's Democracy to Socialist Republic* (Cambridge, Mass.: MIT Press, 1967) and *Twentieth Century Rumania* (New York: Columbia Univ. Press, 1970); John Michael Montias, *Economic Development in Communist Rumania* (Cambridge, Mass.: MIT Press, 1967).

58. William E. Griffith, *Albania and the Sino-Soviet Rift* (Cambridge, Mass.: MIT Press, 1963).

59. Unpublished manuscript by Kevin Devlin.

60. Griffith, *The Sino-Soviet Rift,* op. cit.; unpublished manuscript by Kevin Devlin.

61. Baring, *Sehr verehrter Herr Bundeskanzler,* op. cit., pp. 216-222.

62. Dean, *West German Trade with the East,* op. cit., pp. 109-120; Schulz, "Die sowjetische Deutschlandpolitik," op. cit., p. 248; especially Angela Yergin, op. cit., pp. 96-128.

63. Gotto, "Adenauers Deutschland- und Ostpolitik," op. cit., pp. 34-40; Baring, *Sehr verehrter Herr Bundeskanzler,* op. cit., pp. 226-238, 302-303; Hans Buchheim, "Die Deutschland- und Aussenpolitik Konrad Adenauers," *Politische Bildung,* vol. 8, no. 2 (Apr. 1971), pp. 31-42 at pp. 36-38.

64. On the crisis see Schulz, "Die sowjetische Deutschlandpolitik," op. cit., pp. 257-265; Besson, *Aussenpolitik,* op. cit., pp. 211-319; Dennis L. Bark, *Agreement on Berlin* (Washington, D.C.: American Enterprise Institute and Stanford, Cal.: Hoover Institution, 1974); Jean Edward Smith, *The Defense of Berlin* (Baltimore; Johns Hopkins Univ. Press, 1963); Thomas W. Wolfe, *Soviet Power and Europe, 1945-1970* (Baltimore: Johns Hopkins Univ. Press, 1970), pp. 89-99 (with full bibliography, including Soviet sources); Jack M. Schick, *The Berlin Crisis 1958-1962* (Philadelphia: Univ. of Pennsylvania Press, 1971) (most detailed account of U.S. policy and four-power negotiations). For background see Dennis L. Bark, *Die Berlin-Frage*

1949-1955 (Berlin: Walter de Gruyter, 1972); Diethelm Prowe, *Weltstadt in Krisen. Berlin 1949-1958* (Berlin: Walter de Gruyter, 1973).

65. Khrushchev's opening of the crisis was clearly foreshadowed in an October 27, 1958, Ulbricht speech. See Schulz, "Die sowjetische Deutschlandpolitik," op. cit., p. 257. Documentation: Forschungsinstitut der Deutschen Gesellschaft für Auswärtige Politik, *Dokumente zur Berlin-Frage 1944-1966* (Munich: Oldenbourg, 1967), pp. 296-307; Meissner, ed., *Moskau Bonn,* op. cit., pp. 455 ff.; Zinner, ed., *Documents on American Relations 1958,* op. cit., pp. 209 ff.

66. von Scherpenberg to von Brentano, Oct. 27, 1959, tr. from Baring, *Sehr verehrter Herr Bundeskanzler,* op. cit., p. 281.

67. As paraphrased in Morsey and Repgen, *Adenauer Studien,* op. cit.; vol. 4, pp. 24-25. However, a senior Western diplomat present at the meeting denied to me that Eisenhower said anything like this. For Khrushchev's feelers to Brandt and Adenauer see Willy Brandt, *Begegnungen und Einsichten* (Hamburg: Hoffman and Campe, 1976), pp. 108-112.

68. Roger Morgan, *The United States and West Germany 1945-1973: A Study in Alliance Politics* (London: Oxford Univ. Press, 1974), pp. 78-79; Wolfgang Wagner in Morsey and Repgen, *Adenauer Studien,* op. cit., vol. 2.

69. Dean, *West German Trade with the East,* op. cit., pp. 59-70, 121-127; Schulz, "Die sowjetische Deutschlandpolitik," op. cit., pp. 263-264; especially Angela Yergin, op. cit., pp. 147-185.

70. Dean, *West German Trade with the East,* op. cit., pp. 127-140; Schulz, "Die sowjetische Deutschlandpolitik," op. cit., pp. 266-267; especially Angela Yergin, op. cit., pp. 186-238.

71. Morgan, *The United States and West Germany 1945-1973,* op. cit., pp. 90-104.

72. See particularly his November 25, 1961, interview in *Izvestia* with Khrushchev's son-in-law, Adzhubei, in *Public Papers of the Presidents of the United States, John Kennedy, January 20 to December 31, 1961* (Washington, D.C.: GPO, 1962), pp. 741-752, at p. 751, cited in Morgan, *The United States and West Germany 1945-1973,* op. cit., p. 109 q.v. See also Walther Stuetzle, *Kennedy und Adenauer in der Berlin-Krise 1961-1962* (Bonn: Verlag Neue Gesellschaft, 1973).

73. Quoted in Baring, *Sehr verehrter Herr Bundeskanzler,* op. cit., p. 328.

74. Cf. Haftendorn, *Abrüstungs- und Entspannungspolitik,* op. cit., pp. 61–65.

75. Baring, *Sehr verehrter Herr Bundeskanzler*, op. cit., pp. 300–337; Kelleher, *Germany and the Politics of Nuclear Weapons*, op. cit., pp. 162–202.

76. Ibid., p. 335.

77. Ibid., pp. 377–380.

78. Ibid., p. 331; Dean, *West German Trade with the East*, op. cit., pp. 70–71; Brandt, *Begegnungen und Einsichten*, op. cit., pp. 9–33.

79. Baring, *Sehr verehrter Herr Bundeskanzler,* op. cit., pp. 341–380; cf. Brandt, *Begegungen und Einsichten,* op. cit., pp. 33–53.

80. Gotto, "Adenauers Deutschland- und Ostpolitik," op. cit., pp. 70–75 and Vogelsang, *Das geteilte Deutschland,* op. cit., pp. 272–275.

81. Herbert Dinerstein, *The Making of a Missile Crisis: October 1962* (Baltimore: Johns Hopkins Univ. Press, 1976), pp. 186–187.

82. Robert M. Slusser, *The Berlin Crisis of 1961* (Baltimore: Johns Hopkins Univ. Press, 1973).

83. Kelleher, *Germans and the Politics of Nuclear Weapons*, op. cit., pp. 124–155; Morgan, *The United States and West Germany 1945–1973*, op. cit., pp. 82, 87.

84. Besson, *Aussenpolitik*, op. cit., pp. 246–248; Brandt, *Begegnungen und Einsichten*, op. cit., pp. 17, 43–47; Morgan, *The United States and West Germany 1945–1973*, op. cit., pp. 80–81.

85. Edward Kolodziej, *French International Policy under de Gaulle and Pompidou: The Politics of Grandeur* (Ithaca N.Y.: Cornell Univ. Press, 1974).

86. Bruno Bandulet, *Adenauer zwischen West und Ost. Alternativen der deutschen Aussenpolitik* (Munich: Weltforum, 1970).

87. Kelleher, *Germany and the Politics of Nuclear Weapons*, op. cit., pp. 207–228.

88. Documentation: Auswärtiges Amt der Bundesrepublik Deutschland, *Die Auswärtige Politik der Bundesrepublik Deutschland,* op. cit., pp. 499–500.

89. Address at the Free University of Berlin, June 26, 1963, in

Public Papers of the Presidents of the United States, John F. Kennedy, January 1 to November 22, 1963 (Washington, D.C.: GPO, 1964), pp. 526-529, at p. 527.

90. Ibid., pp. 459-464.

91. Haftendorn, *Abrüstungs- und Entspannungspolitik* op. cit., pp. 127-137; Morgan, *The United States and West Germany 1945-1973,* op. cit., pp. 132-135; Gotto, "Adenauers Deutschland- und Ostpolitik," op. cit., pp. 75-83.

Notes to Chapter 3

1. Zbigniew K. Brzezinski, *The Soviet Bloc* (Cambridge, Mass.: Harvard University Press, 1967), pp. 433 ff.; Stephen Fischer-Galati, *The New Rumania* (Cambridge, Mass.: MIT Press, 1967); John Michael Montias, *Economic Development in Communist Rumania* (Cambridge, Mass.: MIT Press, 1967); H. Gordon Skilling, *Czechoslovakia's Interrupted Revolution* (Princeton, N.J.: Princeton Univ. Press, 1976).

2. For West German public opinion trends see Elizabeth Noelle and Erich Peter Neumann, eds., *Jahrbuch der öffentlichen Meinung, 1957* (Allensbach: Verlag für Demoskopie, 1957), ibid., *1958-1964* (Allensbach and Bonn: Verlag für Demoskopie, 1965) especially p. 481; ibid., *1965-1967* (Allensbach and Bonn: Verlag für Demoskopie, 1967), especially pp. 435-463; ibid., *1968-1973* (Allensbach and Bonn: Verlag für Demoskopie, 1974), especially pp. 567-585; Erich Peter Neumann, "Wiedervereinigung in der öffentlichen Meinung," *Die Politische Meinung*, vol. 9, no. 91 (Jan. 1964), pp. 19-31; Lutz Neithammer, "Traditionen und Perspektiven der Nationalstaatlichkeit," in *Aussenpolitische Perspektiven des westdeutschen Staates*, vol. 2 (Munich: Oldenbourg, 1972), pp. 13-107, especially pp. 47-107; Klaus Erdmenger, "Zielvorstellungen für die Weltpolitik," ibid., pp. 108-126; Thomas Paul Koppel, "Sources of Change in West German Ostpolitik: The Grand Coalition, 1966-1969" (unpublished Ph.D. dissertation, University of Wisconsin, 1972), pp. 33-37, 208-392; Johannes R. Gascard, "Junge Generation und Aussenpolitik," *Europa Archiv*, vol. 27, no. 6 (March 25, 1972), pp. 219-226; Erwin Häckel, "Die Kritik der Jungen Linken an der Europäischen Gemeinschaft," ibid., no. 23 (Dec. 10, 1972), pp. 810-818.

3. Henry Kissinger, *The Troubled Partnership* (New York: McGraw-Hill, 1965), especially pp. 31–64.

4. F. L. [Fred Luchsinger] from Bonn in the *Neue Zürcher Zeitung*, August 6, 16, and 20, 1963; Dietrich Schwarzkopf and Olaf von Wrangel, *Chancen für Deutschland* (Hamburg: Hofman and Campe, 1965), pp. 114–117; Wilhelm Cornides, "Das Moskauer Moratorium und die Bundesrepublik," *Europa Archiv*, vol. 18, no. 16 (Aug. 25, 1963), pp. 583–592; Stanley Hoffmann, *Gulliver's Troubles* (New York: McGraw-Hill, 1968), pp. 452–453.

5. Ralf Dahrendorf, "Bonn after Twenty Years: Are Germany's Problems Nearer Solution?," *The World Today*, vol. 25, no. 4 (Apr. 1969), pp. 168–171, at pp. 169–170.

6. Rolf Sannwald, "Die Europäische Wirtschaftsgemeinschaft und der Osthandel," *Europa Archiv*, vol. 20, no. 4 (Feb. 25, 1965), pp. 115–126; Matthias Schmitt, Die deutsch-sowjetischen Wirtschaftsbeziehungen," ibid., vol. 22, no. 1 (Jan. 10, 1967), pp. 11–22; Jürgen Nötzold, "Das Interesse Osteuropas an Wirtschaftsbeziehungen mit dem Westen," ibid., no. 11 (June 10, 1967), pp. 383–391; Ernst Schneider, "Die Entpolitisierung des deutschen Osthandels," *Aussenpolitik*, vol. 18, no. 7 (July 1967), pp. 389–397; Kurt Birrenbach, "Lockt der rote Handel?," *Die Zeit*, April 12, 1964; Gerard Braunthal, *The Federation of German Industry in Politics* (Ithaca, N.Y.: Cornell Univ. Press, 1965), pp. 305–316; Angela Stent Yergin, "The Political Economy of West German-Soviet Relations, 1955–1973" (unpublished Ph.D. dissertation, Harvard University, 1977).

7. Willy Brandt, "Gemeinschaftsideale und nationale Interessen in der deutschen Aussenpolitik," *Europa Archiv*, vol. 19, no. 12 (June 25, 1964), pp. 419–426; Günter Gaus, *Staatserhaltende Opposition; oder, Hat die SPD kapituliert? Gespräche mit Herbert Wehner* (Reinbek bei Hamburg: Rowohlt, 1966).

8. Arnulf Baring, "Die westdeutsche Aussenpolitik in der Ära Adenauer," *Politische Vierteljahresschrift*, vol. 9, no. 1 (March 1968), pp. 51–54; Waldemar Besson, *Die Aussenpolitik der Bundesrepublik* (Munich: Piper, 1970), pp. 329–333; Klaus Erdmenger, "Zielvorstellungen für die Weltpolitik," in *Aussenpolitische Perspektiven des westdeutschen Staates*, op. cit., vol. 2, pp. 116–124.

9. Catherine Kelleher, *Germany and the Politics of Nuclear Weapons* (New York and London: Columbia Univ. Press, 1975).

10. Helga Haftendorn, *Abrüstungs- und Entspannungspolitik zwischen Sicherheitbefriedigung und Friedenssicherung. Zur Aussenpolitik der BRD 1955-1973* (Düsseldorf: Bertelsmann Universitätsverlag, 1974).

11. Besson, *Aussenpolitik*, op. cit.

12. Gerhard Schröder, "Germany Looks at Eastern Europe," *Foreign Affairs*, vol. 44, no. 1 (Oct. 1965), pp. 15-25, at p. 16 and "Grundproblemen der Aussenpolitik der Bundesrepublik Deutschland," *Europa Archiv*, vol. 17, no. 17 (Sept. 10, 1962), pp. 581-594. Cf. his speeches, *Wir brauchen eine heile Welt; Politik in und für Deutschland* (Düsseldorf: Econ, 1963). See also Karl Birnbaum, *Peace in Europe: East-West Relations 1966-1968 and the Prospects for a European Settlement* (London and New York: Oxford Univ. Press, 1970) pp. 44-45; Haftendorn, *Abrüstungs- und Entspannungspolitik*, op. cit., pp. 204-206; Koppel, "Sources of Change in West German Ostpolitik," op. cit., pp. 363-367; Boris Meissner, ed., *Die deutsche Ostpolitik 1961-1970: Kontinuität und Wandel: Dokumentation* (Cologne: Verlag Wissenschaft und Politik, 1970), pp. 17-18.

13. Philip Windsor, *Germany and the Management of Détente* (London: Chatto and Windus, 1971), pp. 56-57. See also Adenauer re the Oder-Neisse line, September 22, 1957, in *Der europäische Osten*, vol. 3, no. 11 (Nov. 1957), pp. 685 ff; re Poland, ibid., vol. 5, no. 57/58 (Aug. 31, 1959), pp. 457 ff.: *Bulletin des Presse- und Informationsamt der Bundesregierung*, September 1, 1957; Noelle and Neumann, eds., *Jahrbuch der öffentlichen Meinung, 1958-1964*, op. cit., p. 567; Gebhardt Schweigler, *National Consciousness in Divided Germany* (London and Beverly Hills Cal.: Sage, 1975), especially pp. 5-6, 11, 71, 167-171, 205-206.

14. Strauss in *Die Zeit*, April 8, 1967, "Nation mit neuen Auftrag," *Die Politische Meinung*, vol. 12, no. 120 (1967), pp. 12-20 and *Entwurf für Europa* (Stuttgart: Seewald, 1966); Kelleher, *Germany and the Politics of Nuclear Weapons*, op. cit., p. 311; Alf Mintzel, *Die CSU* (Opladen: Westdeutscher Verlag, 1975).

15. Richard Löwenthal, ed., *Die Zweite Republik: 25 Jahre Bundesrepublik Deutschland—Eine Bilanz* (Stuttgart: Seewald, 1974), p. 655.
16. Ibid., pp. 667–668.
17. Carola Stern, *Willy Brandt* (Reinbek bei Hamburg: Rowohlt, 1975); Willy Brandt, *Begegnungen und Einsichten* (Hamburg: Hoffman and Campe, 1976); cf. David Binder, *The Other German: Willy Brandt's Life and Times* (Washington, D.C.: New Republic, 1975); Viola Drath, *Willy Brandt, Prisoner of his Past* (Radnor, Penn.: Chilton, 1975).
18. Their main spokesman was Peter Bender of the Westdeutscher Rundfunk; see his *Offensive Entspannung; Möglichkeit für Deutschland*, 4th ed. (Cologne: Kiepenheuer and Witsch, 1965) and *Zehn Gründe für die Anerkennung der DDR* (Frankfurt/M.: Fischer, 1968). Some of the group around *Die Zeit* sympathized with this view. See also Karl Kaiser, *German Foreign Policy in Transition* (London and New York: Oxford Univ. Press, 1968).
19. Stern, *Willy Brandt*, op. cit., p. 83; Brandt, *Begegnungen und Einsichten*, op. cit.
20. Stern, *Willy Brandt*, op. cit., pp. 17, 101–102.
21. Koppel, "Sources of Change in West German Ostpolitik," op. cit., pp. 385–387.
22. Speech at the Evangelische Akademie at Tutzing, July 15, 1963, quoted from Meissner, ed., *Die deutsche Ostpolitik* op. cit., pp. 45–46, 48. See also Brandt, *Begegnungen und Einsichten*, op. cit., pp. 56–57.

For Bahr's general views, see the long interview with him in Dettmar Cramer, *Gefragt: Egon Bahr* (Bornheim: Dagmar Zirngibl, 1957); another in Günther Schmid, *Politik des Ausverkaufs?* (Munich: Tuduv, 1975), pp. 245–257 and the analysis in ibid., pp. 92–98; and the controversial but probably generally accurate report of an interview with him by Walter F. Hahn, "West Germany's Ostpolitik: The Grand Design of Egon Bahr," *Orbis*, vol. 16, no. 4 (Winter 1973), pp. 859–880. For Wehner's views see Schmid, *Politik des Ausverkaufs?*, op. cit., pp. 98–99.
23. Windsor, *Germany and the Management of Détente*, op. cit., pp. 62–63. The reader may wonder why the 1962 article Z. K. Brzezinski and I wrote supported isolation of the DDR. It did so because it was then the policy of Bonn and because in our view the United States should follow Bonn's policy toward the

DDR. See Zbigniew K. Brzezinski and William E. Griffith, "Peaceful Engagement in Eastern Europe," *Foreign Affairs*, vol. 39, no. 4 (July 1961), pp. 642-654.

24. Georg W. Ströbel, "Der Ausbau der polnischen Beziehungen zu Pankow," *Europa Archiv*, vol. 18, no. 4 (Feb. 25, 1963), pp. 135-144; Erwin Weit, *At the Red Summit, Interpreter behind the Iron Curtain* (New York: Macmillan, 1973).

25. Documentation: Ingo von Münch, ed., *Ostverträge II: Deutsch-polnische Verträge* (Berlin and New York: Walter de Gruyter, 1971), pp. 80-83.

26. Documentation: Auswärtiges Amt der Bundesrepublik Deutschland, *Die Auswärtige Politik der Bundesrepublik Deutschland* (Cologne: Verlag Wissenschaft und Politik, 1972), p. 504; Meissner, ed., *Die deutsche Ostpolitik*, op. cit., p. 63.

27. Documentation: *Die Auswärtige Politik*, op. cit., p. 512; Meissner, ed., *Die deutsche Ostpolitik*, op. cit., p. 74.

28. Documentation: *Die Auswärtige Politik*, op. cit., p. 516; Meissner, ed., *Die deutsche Ostpolitik*, op. cit., p. 75.

29. Ronald F. Bunn, *German Politics and the Spiegel Affair* (Baton Rouge, La.: Louisiana State Univ. Press, 1968).

30. Brandt, *Begegnungen und Einsichten*, op. cit., pp. 101-107, 112-113; Löwenthal, ed., *Die Zweite Republik*, op. cit., p. 667; Gottfried Vetter, "Innerdeutsche Kontakte. Wandel durch Annäherung oder Bestätigung der Teilung?," *Europa Archiv*, vol. 19, no. 23 (Dec. 10, 1964), pp. 875-884; "Bilanz der Passierscheinaktion 1964," *SBZ Archiv*, vol. 16, no. 1/2 (Jan. 1965), p. 1; Fred Luchsinger, *Bericht über Bonn: Deutsche Politik 1955-1965* (Zurich: Fretz and Wasmuth, 1966), pp. 335-341; F. R. Allemann, "Berlin in Search of a Purpose," *Survey*, no. 61 (Oct. 1966), pp. 129-138.

31. Löwenthal, ed., *Die zweite Republik*, op. cit., p. 668; Koppel, "Sources of Change in West German Ostpolitik," op. cit., pp. 92-96; Peter Bender, *Die Ostpolitik Willy Brandts* (Reinbek bei Hamburg: Rowohlt, 1972), p. 30. Documentation: Meissner, ed., *Die deutsche Ostpolitik*, op. cit., pp. 85-90. For DDR harassment of West Berlin access route in April 1965, see Gerhard Wettig, *Community and Conflict in the Socialist Camp. The Soviet Union, East Germany and the German Problem 1965-1972* (New York: St. Martin's, 1975), pp. 9-19.

32. Robert Dean, *West Germany's Trade with the East: The Po-

itical Dimension (New York: Praeger, 1974), pp. 72-82, 143-151, 174-186, Appendix I; Eberhard Schulz, "Die sowjetische Deutschlandpolitik," *Osteuropa Handbuch Sowjetunion*, vol. 2 *Aussenpolitik* (Cologne: Böhlau, forthcoming), pp. 269, 273; Angela Yergin, op. cit., pp. 258-283, 289-300.

33. Gerhard Wettig, "The SED-SPD Dialogue: Communist Political Strategy in Germany," *Orbis*, vol. 11, no. 2 (Summer 1967), pp. 570-581, revised in his *Community and Conflict in the Socialist Camp*, op. cit., pp. 20-32; Löwenthal, ed., *Die zweite Republik*, op. cit., pp. 672-673; Brandt, *Begegnungen und Einsichten*, op. cit., pp. 125-129. Documentation: *Europa Archiv*, vol. 21, no. 7 (April 10, 1966), pp. D176-D188. For SPD encouragement from the episode see Egon Bahr, "Nach dem abgesagten Redneraustausch SPD-SED," *Aussenpolitik*, vol. 17, no. 8 (Aug. 1966), pp. 475-479.

34. Brandt at the SPD Dortmund Congress, June 1, 1966, in Meissner, ed., *Die Deutsche Ostpolitik*, op. cit., p. 131; Erich Mende to FDP Frankfurt party congress, March 22, 1965, in ibid., p. 101; see Koppel, "Sources of Change in West German Ostpolitik," op. cit., pp. 99-101; Brandt, *Begegnungen und Einsichten*, op. cit., pp. 124-125. For the Abrassimov-Brandt meetings see ibid., pp. 114-122.

35. Text of their memorandum, with comments on it by expellees and other West German public opinion figures, in Reinhard Henkys, *Deutschland und die östlichen Nachbarn* (Stuttgart and Berlin: Kreuz, 1966). See also T. W. (Theodor Wieser) from Bonn in the *Neue Zürcher Zeitung*, October 19 and 30, 1965. The text is also in *Europa Archiv*, vol. 21, no. 1 (Jan. 10, 1966), pp. D1-D10. See also an article by the committee's chairman, Professor Ludwig Raiser of Tübingen, "Deutsche Ostpolitik im Lichte der Denkschrift der evangelischen Kirche," ibid., vol. 21, no. 6 (March 25, 1966), pp. 195-208.

36. Text of the letters between the Polish and West German Catholic hierarchies: *Europa Archiv*, vol. 21, no. 1 (Jan. 10, 1966), pp. D11-D19.

37. Eberhard Schulz, *An Ulbricht führt kein Weg Mehr vorbei* (Hamburg: Hoffman und Campe, 1967); Wolfgang Wagner, "Auf der Suche nach einem neuen Weg. Die Zukunft Europas und die deutsche Frage," *Europa Archiv*, vol. 21, no. 18 (Sept. 25, 1966), pp. 645-654.

38. Koppel, "Sources of Change in West German Ostpolitik," op. cit., pp. 33-37, 208-356.
39. Text: *Europa Archiv*, vol. 21, no. 7 (Apr. 10, 1966), pp. D171 ff.; answering notes, ibid., no. 11 (June 10, 1966), pp. D277 ff.; both also in *Moderne Welt*, vol. 7, no. 4 (1966), pp. 393-440; analysis: Herbert Krüger, "Die deutsche Friedensnote," ibid., pp. 349-367; Theo Sommer, "Eine Note macht noch keine Politik," *Die Zeit*, April 5, 1966; Kurt Becker, "Das Fazit einer Bonner Aktion," ibid., August 12, 1966; Dietrich Schwarzkopf, "Die Idee des Gewaltverzichts. Ein Element der neuen Ostpolitik der Bundesrepublik," *Europa Archiv*, vol. 22, no. 24 (Dec. 25, 1967), pp. 893-900; Charles R. Planck, *Sicherheit in Europa: Die Vorschläge für Rüstungsbeschränkung und Abrüstung 1955-1965* (Munich: Oldenbourg, 1968); Löwenthal, ed., *Die Zweite Republik*, op. cit., pp. 670-671. See also Haftendorn, *Abrüstungs- und Entspannungspolitik*, op. cit., pp. 193-204, 206-215; Schulz, "Die sowjetische Deutschlandpolitik," op. cit. Documentation: Meissner, ed., *Die deutsche Ostpolitik*, op. cit., pp. 120-128; *Die Auswärtige Politik*, op. cit., pp. 559-563; Hans-Adolf Jacobsen, ed., *Misstrauische Nachbarn: Deutsche Ostpolitik 1919/1970* (Düsseldorf: Droste Verlag, 1970), pp. 383-389; Soviet response: Boris Meissner, ed., *Moskau Bonn: Die Beziehungen zwischen der Sowjetunion und der Bundesrepublik Deutschland 1955-1973. Dokumentation*, vol. 2 (Cologne: Verlag Wissenschaft und Politik, 1975), pp. 1050-1059.
40. Schulz, "Die sowjetische Deutschlandpolitik," op. cit., pp. 267 ff.
41. Löwenthal, ed., *Die zweite Republik,* op. cit., p. 668. Documentation: Meissner, ed., *Moskau Bonn*, vol. 2, op. cit., pp. 971-980, 982-983; *Die Auswärtige Politik*, op. cit., pp. 515-516.
42. Schulz, "Die sowjetische Deutschlandpolitik," op. cit., pp. 269-271.
43. Thomas W. Wolfe, *Soviet Power and Europe, 1945-1970* (Baltimore: Johns Hopkins Univ. Press, 1970), pp. 282-288.

Notes to Chapter 4
1. Uwe Nerlich, " Die nuclearen Dilemmas der Bundesrepublik Deutschland," *Europa Archiv*, vol. 20, no. 17 (Sept. 10, 1965), pp. 637-652; Wilhelm Cornides, "Prioritäten des Friedens in Europa. Ein Diskussionsbeitrag über den Zusammenhang von

Abrüstung und Deutschland-Frage," ibid., no. 4, (Dec. 25, 1965), pp. 907–918.

2. The main contribution to the speech was made by Zbigniew K. Brzezinski, then a member of the Policy Planning Council of the Department of State.

3. F. L. [Fred Luchsinger], "Deutsche Ungewissheiten," *Neue Zürcher Zeitung*, August 21, 1966.

4. Richard Löwenthal, ed., *Die Zweite Republik: 25 Jahr Bundesrepublik Deutschland Eine Bilanz* (Stuttgart: Seewald, 1974), p. 671; Karl E. Birnbaum, *Peace in Europe* (London: Oxford Univ. Press, 1970), pp. 9–14, 18–27; Pierre Hassner, "Change and Security in Europe, Part I: The Background," Adelphi Paper no. 45 (London: Institute for Strategic Studies, Feb. 1968); Thomas Paul Koppel, "Sources of Change in West German Ostpolitik: The Grand Coalition, 1966–1969" (unpublished Ph.D. dissertation, University of Wisconsin, 1972), pp. 105–122.

5. Willy Brandt, *Begegnungen und Einsichten* (Hamburg: Hoffmann and Campe, 1976), pp. 172–176.

6. See especially Koppel, "Sources of Change in West German Ostpolitik," op. cit., pp. 122–206; Brandt, *Begegnungen und Einsichten*, op. cit., pp. 219–292.

7. See the authoritative anonymous article, "Modèles de sécurité européene," *Politique étrangère*, vol. 32, no. 6 (1967), pp. 519–541, tr. as "Sicherheitsmodelle für Europa," *Europa Archiv*, vol. 23, no. 2 (Jan. 25, 1968), pp. 51–64; Waldemar Besson, *Die Aussenpolitik der Bundesrepublik. Erfahrungen und, Massstäbe* (Munich: Piper Verlag, 1970), pp. 395–401.

8. Cf. Birnbaum, *Peace in Europe*, op. cit., pp. 40–41.

9. Rudiger Altmann, "Eine neue Strategie; Uberlegungen zur deutschen Aussenpolitik," *Der Monat*, vol. 17, no. 199 (Apr. 1965), pp. 7–13; see also in general Gerhard Wettig, *Community and Conflict in the Socialist Camp* (New York: St. Martin's, 1975) pp. 33–47.

10. Koppel, "Sources of Change in West German Ostpolitik op. cit., pp. 446–447.

11. Tr. from Peter Bender, *Die Ostpolitik Willy Brandts* (Hamburg: Rowohlt, 1972), p. 34.

12. Brandt, *Begegnungen und Einsichten*, op. cit., pp. 191–194; Birnbaum, *Peace in Europe*, op. cit., pp. 31–32; Walter

Hahn, "West Germany's Ostpolitik: The Grand Design of Egon Bahr," *Orbis*, vol. 16, no. 4 (Winter 1973), pp. 859-880.

13. Interview with Wehner, *SBZ Archiv*, vol. 18, no. 14 (July 1967), pp. 210-211; "Neue Profile der Deutschlandpolitik". ibid., vol. 18, no. 19 (Oct. 1967), pp. 291-292; Ulrich Scheuner, "Entwicklungslinien der deutschen Frage," *Europa Archiv*, vol. 24, no. 13 (July 10, 1969), pp. 453-464, at p. 458 (politically a very important article).

14. Bahr on September 4, 1967, quoted from Günther Schmid, *Politik des Ausverkaufs?* (Munich: Tuduv, 1975), p. 17; for the USSR, Brandt, *Begegnungen und Einsichten*, op. cit., pp. 222-223.

15. Eberhard Menzel, "Die Anerkennung von Staaten und die Aufnahme diplomatischer Beziehungen als rechtliches und politisches Problem. Zu den volkerrechtlichen Grundlagen einer deutschen Ostpolitik," *Moderne Welt*, vol. 8, no. 2 (1967), pp. 120-142.

16. Speech by Brandt in Vienna, June 10, 1963, in *Wiener Zeitung*, June 11, 1968; cf. R. L. from Vienna in *Neue Zürcher Zeitung*, June 12, 1968.

17. Kiesinger's December 13, 1966, governmental declaration, *Europa Archiv*, vol. 22, no. 1 (Jan. 10, 1967), pp. D15-19; Willy Brandt, "Entspannungspolitik mit langem Atem," *Aussenpolitik*, vol. 18, no. 8 (Aug. 1967), pp. 449-454, "Deutsche Aussenpolitik nach zwei Weltkriegen," *Der Monat*, vol. 19, no. 230 (Nov. 1967), pp. 7-17, interview in *Moderne Welt*, vol. 8, no. 4 (1967), pp. 354-361, "German Policy Toward the East," *Foreign Affairs*, vol. 46, no. 3 (Apr. 1968), pp. 476-486; see also Jens Hacker, *Deutsche unter sich* (Stuttgart: Seewald, 1977), pp. 33-40.

18. The March 1968 SPD Nürnberg Party Congress resolved to "respect and recognize it until the peace treaty." *New York Times*, March 21, 1968. Documentation: Boris Meissner, ed., *Die deutsche Ostpolitik 1961-1970: Kontinuität und Wandel* (Cologne: Verlag Wissenschaft und Politik, 1970), pp. 245-247.

19. Wa. [Wolfgang Wagner], "Zwischenbilanz der deutschen Ostpolitik," *Neue Zürcher Zeitung*, August 11, 1967.

20. Carola Stern, *Willy Brandt* (Reinbek bei Hamburg: Rowohlt, 1975), pp. 84-88.

21. Schmid, *Politik des Ausverkaufs?*, op. cit., pp. 17, 22.

22. Koppel, "Sources of Change in West German Ostpolitik," op. cit., pp. 133-138.

23. Schmid, *Politik des Ausverkaufs?*, op. cit., pp. 20, 21.

24. Koppel, "Sources of Change in West German Ostpolitik," op. cit., pp. 144-149, 160-176.

25. T.W. [Theodor Wieser] from Bonn in the *Neue Zürcher Zeitung*, October 12, 1967; Ströhm in *Christ und Welt*, October 13, 1967; Strobel in *Die Zeit*, October 17, 1967.

26. Peter Bender, *Zehn Gründe für die Anerkennung der DDR* (Frankfurt/M: Fischer, 1968).

27. Wilhelm Wolfgang Schutz, *Deutschland-Memorandum. Eine Denkschrift und ihre Folgen* (Frankfurt/M.: Fischer, 1968; Theo Sommer, "Schneller verdammt als gelesen. Das Schütz-Memorandum zur Deutschland-Politik," *Die Zeit*, December 12, 1967. Cf. Wilhelm Wolfgang Schütz, *Modelle zur Deutschland–Politik* (Cologne: Kiepenhauer and Witsch, 1966).

28. Text: *Europa Archiv*, vol. 23, no. 12 (June 25, 1968), pp. D273-282.

29. Text: *Memorandum deutscher Katholiken zu den polnisch-deutschen Fragen* (Mainz: Grünewald, 1968); T.W. [Theodore Wieser], "Katholische Denkschrift zur deutsch-polnischen Versöhnung," *Neue Zürcher Zeitung*, March 5, 1968.

30. "Aktive Deutschlandpolitik, Ziele, Bedingungen, Strategien. Eine Studie des Politischen Klubs," *Deutschland Archiv*, vol. 6, no. 4 (Apr. 1969), pp. 384-403. I owe this reference to Schmid, *Politik des Ausverkaufs?* op. cit., p. 29, q.v., pp. 29-33, for summary and analysis.

31. Helga Haftendorn, *Abrüstungs- und Entspannungspolitik zwischen Sicherheitsbefriedigung und Friedenssicherung. Zur Aussenpolitik der BRD 1955-1973* (Düsseldorf: Bertelsmann Universitätsverlag, 1974), pp. 161-191. Cf. Koppel, "Sources of Change in West German Ostpolitik," op. cit., pp. 178-191.

32. Robert W. Dean, *West Germany's Trade with the East: The Political Dimension* (New York: Praeger, 1974), pp. 82-93, 151-156, 186-191; Angela Stent Yergin, "The Political Economy of West German-Soviet Trade, 1955-1973." (unpublished Ph.D. dissertation, Harvard University, 1977), pp. 253-297.

33. See the excellent and detailed treatment in F. Stephen Larrabee, "The Politics of Reconciliation: Soviet Policy Towards

West Germany, 1966-1972" (unpublished Ph.D. dissertation, Columbia University, 1977). (Hereafter cited as "Larrabee.")

34. Thomas W. Wolfe, *Soviet Power and Europe, 1945-1970* (Baltimore: Johns Hopkins Univ. Press, 1970), pp. 315-324, 348-351. See also Brandt, *Begegnungen und Einsichten,* op. cit., pp. 224-227.

35. Text: *Europa Archiv,* vol. 21, no. 16 (Aug. 25, 1966), pp. D414-424, at p. D418; analysis: Fritz Ermarth, "The Warsaw Pact Summit," *RFE Research,* July 9, 1966.

36. Wolfgang Berner, "Das Karlsbader Aktionsprogramm," *Europa Archiv,* vol. 22, no. 11 (June 10, 1967), pp. 393-400; Brezhnev in *Pravda,* April 25, 1967; Larrabee, pp. 101-117; Birnbaum, *Peace in Europe,* op. cit., pp. 60-70.

37. See for example, E. Novolseltsev, "Vostochnaya politika FRG," *Mezhdunarodnaya Zhizn',* no. 7 (1968), excerpts: *Ost-Probleme,* vol 20, no. 18 (Sept. 6, 1968), pp. 410-414; see also M. S. Voslenskii, *Vostochnaya politika FRG 1949-1966* (Moscow: Nauka, 1967), cited from ibid.; analysis: Gerhard Wettig, "Moskau und die Grosse Koalition in Bonn," *Aus Politik und Zeitgeschichte,* March 6, 1968, "Tendenzen und Motivationen der gegenwärtigen sowjetischen Deutschland-Politik," Berichte des Bundesinstituts für ostwissenschaftliche und internationale Studien, no. 54 (1967), "The Soviet Policy of European Security: Behavior and Motivation," ibid. (Oct. 1968); J. F. Brown, "East Europe and the Kiesinger Offensive," *RFE Research,* February 4, 1967; for DDR-Rumanian polemics, *Neues Deutschland,* February 3, 1967, *Scinteia,* February 4, 1967 (Moscow did not publicly attack Bucharest's resumption of relations with Bonn); Richard Löwenthal, "The Sparrow in the Cage," *Problems of Communism,* vol. 17, no. 6 (Nov.-Dec. 1968), pp. 2-28.

38. See especially James Richardson, "Germany's Eastern Policy: Problems and Prospect," *The World Today,* vol. 24, no. 9 (Sept. 1968), pp. 375-386. See also Larrabee, pp. 118-120; Richard Löwenthal, "Germany's Role in East-West Relations," *The World Today,* vol. 23, no. 6 (June 1967), pp. 240-249. The best running coverage was in the *Neue Zürcher Zeitung* and the (favorable coverage) in *Die Zeit.* See also F.L. [Fred Luchsinger], "Hoffnungen und Risiken der deutschen Ostpolitik," *Neue Zürcher Zeitung,* February 2, 1967; Carl Gustav Ströhm,

"Die Rückkehr nach Osteuropa," *Christ und Welt*, February 3, 1967 "Ist die Ostpolitik gescheitert? Mehr Geduld für weitgesteckte Ziele," ibid., April 14, 1967; Rolf Zundel, "Gemischte Gefühle in Bonn," *Die Zeit*, February 14, 1967; T.W. [Theodor Wieser] from Bonn, "Zwischenbilanz der Ostpolitik Bonns," *Neue Zürcher Zeitung*, April 4, 1967; for documentation, *Europa Archiv*, vol. 22, nos. 5, 6, 8 (March 10, 15, Apr. 25, 1967), pp. D97 ff., D117 ff., D187 ff. The best general recent treatments of these and other German foreign policy problems are Hassner, "Change and Security in Europe," op. cit.; Karl Kaiser, *German Foreign Policy in Transition* (London and New York: Oxford Univ. Press, 1968).

39. Cf. Birnbaum, *Peace in Europe,* op. cit., pp. 2-3, 52-58, 70-77.

40. Documentation: *The Policy of Reununciation of Force. Documents on German and Soviet Declarations on the Renunciation of Force. 1949 to July 1968.* (Bonn: Federal Press and Information Office, July 1968). The Soviet documents were also published in *Izvestiya,* July 12-14, 1968. See Larrabee, pp. 123 ff,; for the February 7 note, Haftendorn, *Abrüstungs- und Entspannungspolitik*, op. cit., p. 459, n. 171. I owe this reference to Larrabee, p. 124, n. 77.

41. Documentation: *The Policy of Renunciation of Force.* op. cit., p. 19. Cf. Gerhard Wettig, "Der Wandel in der sowjetischen Stellung zum Potsdamer Abkommen in den Fragen der deutschen politischen Entscheidungsfreiheit (1945-1967)," *Berichte des Bundesinstituts für ostwissenschaftlichen und internationale Studien,* no. 70 (1967); Dietrich Frenzke, "Gewaltverzicht und Feindstaatenklauseln," *Europa Archiv*, vol. 25, no. 2 (Jan. 25, 1970), pp. 49-58; Larrabee, pp. 126-127; Bender, *Die Ostpolitik Willy Brandts,* op. cit., pp. 81-82; Eberhard Schulz, "Die sowjetische Deutschlandpolitik," *Osteuropa Handbuch Sowjetunion,* vol. 2, *Aussenpolitik* (Cologne: Böhlau, forthcoming), pp. 276-278.

42. Brandt, *Begegnungen und Einsichten,* op. cit., p. 227; Larrabee, pp. 130-133.

43. Larrabee, pp. 146 ff.; Documentation: Boris Meissner, ed., *Moskau Bonn: Die Beziehungen zwischen der Sowjetunion und der Bundesrepublik Deutschland 1955-1973. Dokumentation,*

vol. 2 (Cologne: Verlag Wissenschaft und Politik, 1975, pp. 1114 ff.

44. Larrabee, pp. 152-156.

45. *The Policy of Renunciation of Force*, op. cit., p. 89.

46. Text: *Department of State Bulletin*, vol. 59, no. 1516 (July 15, 1968).

47. Brandt, *Begegnungen und Einsichten* op. cit., pp. 247-250; Larrabee, pp. 153-156.

48. Documentation: Meissner, ed., *Moskau Bonn,* op. cit., vol. 2, pp. 1116-1121.

49. Larrabee, pp. 152-156.

50. See *Mirovaya Ekonomika i Mezhdunarodniye Otnosheniya,* June 1968 (for hard-line speeches by I. I. Orlik and O. N. Bykov, pp. 102-121 and for Melnikov, p. 127; ibid., August 1968, pp. 72-81 (for Inozemtsev); Brandt, *Begegnungen und Einsichten,* op. cit., pp. 252-253.

51. Dieter Mahncke, *Berlin in geteilten Deutschland* (Munich: Oldenbourg, 1973), pp. 19, 200-203. Meissner, ed., *Die Deutsche Ostpolitik,* op. cit., Doc. II/45, p. 245; Brandt, "German Policy Towards the East," op. cit., pp. 476-486, *Begegnungen und Einsichten,* op. cit., pp. 247-250; Löwenthal, ed., *Die Zweite Republik,* op. cit., p. 678.

52. Heinz Timmermann, "Im Vorfeld der neuen Ostpolitik. Der Dialog zwischen italienischen Kommunisten und deutschen Sozialdemokraten 1967/68," *Osteruopa,* vol. 21, no. 6 (June 1971), pp. 388-399; Brandt, *Begegnungen und Einsichten,* op. cit., pp. 289-292.

53. Meissner, ed., *Die deutsche Ostpolitik,* op. cit., Doc. II/45, p. 245; Brandt, "German Policy Towards the East." op. cit., Löwenthal, ed., *Die Zweite Republik,* op. cit., p. 678.

54. Heinrich Bechtoldt, "Ulbricht's Niederlage in Osteuropa," *Aussenpolitik,* vol. 18, no. 3 (March 1967), pp. 129-132.

55. Documentation: Meissner, ed., *Die deutsche Ostpolitik* op. cit., pp. 179-181; Auswärtiges Amt der Bundesrepublik Deutschland, *Die Auswärtige Politik der Bundesrepublik Deutschland* (Cologne: Verlag Wissenschaft und Politik, 1972), pp. 588-589.

56. William E. Griffith, "Eastern Europe After the Invasion of Czechoslovakia," RAND, P-3983, October 9, 1968; Lawrence

Whetten, *Germany's Ostpolitik* (London: Oxford Univ. Press, 1971), pp. 35-65; Brandt, *Begegnungen und Einsichten,* op. cit., pp. 227-231; Schulz, "Die sowjetische Deutschlandpolitik," op. cit., p. 274; "Bonn-Bucharest Relations—An Anniversary," *RFE Research,* February 5, 1968; Hansjakob Stehle in *Die Zeit,* February 14 and August 8, 1967; Harry Hamm, "Rumänien und deutsche Ostpolitik," *Frankfurter Allgemeine Zeitung,* May 30, 1967.

57. Heinz Zöger, "Reaktionen auf die Ostpolitik Bonns in den kommunistischen Ländern," Deutsche Welle, Dokumentation: April 23, 1968.

58. T.W. [Theodor Wieser], "Zwischenbilanz der Bonner Ostpolitik," *Neue Zürcher Zeitung,* October 14, 1967.

59. Griffith, "Eastern Europe after the Invasion of Czechoslovakia," op. cit., Brandt, *Begegnungen und Einsichten,* op. cit., pp. 244-247; Schmid, *Politik des Ausverkaufs?,* op. cit., pp. 34-44.

60. Peter C. Ludz, *The Changing Party Elite in East Germany* (Cambridge, Mass.: MIT Press, 1972); Werner Gumpel, "Wichtiger Handelspartner Moskaus," *SBZ-Archiv,* vol. 17, no. 1/2 (Jan. 1966), pp. 14-19; Jens Hacker, "Die 'DDR' in Warschauer Pakt," ibid., vol. 17, no. 12 (June 1966), pp. 179-182.

61. Schmid, *Politik des Ausverkaufs?,* op. cit., pp. 34-38.

62. Jens Hacker, "Beistandspakte mit Warschau und Prag," *SBZ-Archiv,* vol. 18, no. 6 (March 1967), pp. 81-82.

63. Jens Hacker, "Liquidation der Wiedervereinigung," ibid., no. 8 (Apr. 1967), pp. 114-116.

64. Gerhard Wettig, "Aktionsmuster der sowjetischen Berlin-Politik," *Aussenpolitik,* vol. 19, no. 6 (June 1968), pp. 325-339.

65. Karl C. Thalheim, "Die innerdeutschen Wirtschaftsbeziehungen—Bedeutung und Perspektiven," *Moderne Welt,* vol. 8, no. 2 (1967), pp. 156-165; Michael von Berg, "Zwanzig Jahre deutscher Interzonenhandel," *Neue Zürcher Zeitung,* October 23, 1965.

66. Stoph-Kiesinger exchange of letters: *Europa Archiv,* vol. 22, no. 20 (Oct. 25, 1967), pp. D472-478; Hartmut Jackel, "Kontakte ohne Anerkennung?", *Der Monat,* vol. 20, no. 235 (Apr. 1968), pp. 37-45; Erhard Albrecht, "Nationaler Dialog völlig

neuen Typus," *SBZ Archiv*, vol. 18, no. 5 (March 1967), pp. 68-70; Löwenthal, ed., *Die Zweite Republik*, op. cit., pp. 675-676.

67. Löwenthal, ed., *Die Zweite Republik*, op. cit., p. 669; Arnold Hottinger, "Die Hintergrunde der Einladung Ulbrichts nach Kairo," *Europa Archiv*, vol. 20, no. 4 (Feb. 25, 1965), pp. 107-114; F.L. [Fred Luchsinger], "Deutschlandpolitik im Nahen Osten," *Neue Zürcher Zeitung*, February 28, 1965; Wolfgang Wagner, "Der Ruckschlag der Bonner Politik in den arabischen Staaten," *Europa Archiv*, vol. 20, no. 10 (May 25, 1965), pp. 359-370, "Überprufung des deutschen politischen Instrumentariums. Die Hallstein-Doktrin nach Ulbrichts Besuch in Ägypten," ibid., no. 5 (March 10, 1965), pp. 157-165; Otto Frei, "Die aussenpolitischen Bemuhungen der DDR in der nicht-kommunistischen Welt," *Europa Archiv*, vol. 20, no. 22 (Nov. 25, 1965), pp. 843-852 and no. 23 (Dec. 10, 1965), pp. 897-906; "Zur Asienpolitik Ostberlins," Deutsche Welle, Dokumentation, March 13 and May 6, 1968.

68. Melvin Croan, "Bonn and Pankow," *Survey*, no. 67 (Apr. 1968), pp. 77-89; Kurt Tudyka, "The Foreign Policy of the DDR," ibid., pp. 56-69, "Die DDR in Kräftefeld des Ost-West-Konflikts," *Europa Archiv*, vol. 21, no. 1 (Jan. 10, 1966), pp. 16-27; Gottfried Vetter, "Zur Entwicklung der innerdeutschen Beziehungen," ibid., vol. 23, no. 9 (May 10, 1968), pp. 309-319; Ilse Spittman, "Soviet Union and DDR," *Survey*, no. 61 (Oct. 1966), pp. 165-176.

69. A. Ross Johnson, "A Survey of Poland's Relations with West Germany, 1956-1967," *RFE Research*, February 20, 1968; Brandt, *Begegnungen und Einsichten*, op. cit., pp. 240-243; Adam Bromke and Harald von Riekhoff, "Poland and West Germany: a Belated Détente?", *Canadian Slavonic Papers*, vol. 12, no. 2 (1970), pp. 195-210; Neal Ascherson, "Poland's Place in Europe," *The World Today*, vol. 25, no. 12 (Dec. 1969), pp. 520-529; Oliver von Gajzago, "Die Entwicklung des Polnischen Aussenhandels in den Jahren 1965 und 1966," Berichte des Bundesinstitute für ostwissenschaftliche und internationale Studien, no. 50, September 1968.

70. In a letter of September 12, 1968; *Tygodnik Powszechny*, October 2, 1968.

71. *RFE Polish Press Survey*, April 30, 1968.

72. J. F. Brown, "Hungary's Relations with the Soviet Union since the Fall of Khrushchev," *RFE Research*, August 8, 1966; a later German version in *Europa Archiv*, vol. 22, no. 15 (Aug. 10, 1967), pp. 541–550; ok. [Bogdan Osadczuk-Korab]. "Ungarn und die Ostpolitik Bonns," *Neue Zürcher Zeitung*, December 28, 1966; A.K. [Andreas Kohlschutter] from Budapest, "Blockgebundene Deutschlandpolitik Ungarns," ibid., January 25, 1967; Michel Tatu from Budapest, "La Hongrie a renoncé provisoirement à poursuivre le dialogue avec la République fédérale," *Le Monde*, March 22, 1967.

73. Tatu from Vienna in *Le Monde*, September 22, 1967; O.D. from Bonn in *Frankfurter Allgemeine Zeitung*, March 4, 1967; Bourne from Plovdiv in *The Christian Science Monitor*, September 28, 1966.

74. Ernst Majonica, *Bonn-Peking* (Stuttgart, Kohlhammer, 1971), pp. 1–117 (primarily based on access to West German diplomatic archives). Cf. *Die Aussenpolitik Chinas* (Munich: Oldenbourg, 1975), pp. 368 ff.; William E. Griffith, *The Sino-Soviet Rift* and *Sino-Soviet Relations 1964–1965* (Cambridge, Mass.: MIT Press, 1964 and 1966); Harry Hamm, "Das chinesische Deutschland," *Moderne Welt*, vol. 6, no. 3 (1965), pp. 247–256; Carola Stern, "'East Germany," in William E. Griffith, ed., *Communism in Europe*, vol. 2 (Cambridge, Mass.: MIT Press, 1966), pp. 97–154; Eberhard Schulz, *An Ulbricht führt kein Weg mehr vorbei* (Hamburg: Hoffmann and Campe, 1967), pp. 129–139.

75. F.L. [Fred Luchsinger], "Ein deutsches Dilemma," *Neue Zürcher Zeitung*, January 28, 1968.

76. Documentation: *Die Auswärtige Politik*, op. cit., p. 616; Meissner, ed., *Die deutsche Ostpolitik*, op. cit., pp. 240–241.

77. For general Yugoslav developments see Christian Meier, *Trauma deutscher Aussenpolitik* (Stuttgart: Seewald Verlag, 1968); Griffith, "Eastern Europe After the Invasion of Czechoslovakia," op. cit. The best running analysis of Yugoslav developments was by Slobodan Stankovic in *RFE Research* and Carl Gustav Ströhm in *Christ und Welt*. See for Bonn-Belgrade relations Brandt, *Begegnungen und Einsichten*, op. cit., pp. 231–240; Harry Schleicher, "Wandlungen der jugoslawischen Deutschland-Politik," *Europa Archiv*, vol. 18, no. 3 (Feb. 10,

1963), pp. 99-106; Carl Gustav Ströhm, "Schwerer Schiffbruch vor Belgrade," *Christ und Welt,* September 16, 1964; Dietrich Frenzke, "Die Bundesrepublik Deutschland in der aussenpolitischen und völkerrechtlichen Publizistik Jugoslawiens," *Moderne Welt,* vol. 7, no. 1 (1966), pp. 3-21; Dorothy Miller, "Ulbricht's First State Visit to Yugoslavia," *RFE Research,* October 3, 1966; T.W. [Theodor Wieser], "Kritischer Punkt der deutschen Ostpolitik," *Neue Zürcher Zeitung,* November 12, 1967; E. Schulz, *An Ulbricht,* op. cit., pp. 115-128; Hans Lindemann, "Belgrad und seine Widergutmachungsanspruche gegenüber beiden Teilen Deutschlands," Deutsche Welle, Dokumentation, October 9, 1967; Oliver von Gajzago, "Die Entwicklung des jugoslawischen Aussenhandels in Jahre 1966," Berichte des Bundesinstituts für ostwissenschaftliche und internationale Studien, no. 41 (1968); "Die Deutsch-jugoslawischen Beziehungen (1945 bis 1967)," Deutsche Welle, Dokumentation, December 15, 1967.

78. See the 1967 study by Radovan Richta of the Czechoslovak Academy of Sciences, *Civilization at the Crossroads* (White Plains, N.Y.: International Arts and Sciences Press, 1969).

79. Grey Hodnett and Peter Potichnyj, *The Ukraine and the Czechoslovak Crisis* (Canberra: Australian National Univ. Press, 1970).

80. Griffith, "Eastern Europe After the Invasion of Czechoslovakia," op. cit.; Brandt, *Begegnungen und Einsichten,* op. cit., V.M. [Viktor Meier] from Prague in the *Neue Zürcher Zeitung,* March 13, 1966; A.K. [Andreas Kohlschutter] from Prague in ibid., December 3, 1966; ok. [Bogdan Osadczuk-Korab] in ibid., January 12, 1967; Eberhard Schulz, "Prag und Bonn, Politische Belastungen im deutsch-tschechoslowakischen Verhältnis," *Europa Archiv,* vol. 22, no. 4 (Feb. 25, 1967), pp. 115-124, *An Ulbricht,* op. cit., pp. 98-114; Löwenthal, ed., *Die Zweite Republik,* op. cit.; Wa. [Wolfgang Wagner] from Bonn in the *Neue Zürcher Zeitung,* August 5, 1967 (the Bahr mission and the establishment of the West German trade mission); A.K. [Andreas Kohlschutter] in ibid. August 6, 1967; Wa. [Wolfgang Wagner], "Bewusste Zurückhaltung in Bonn," ibid., July 23, 1968; David Binder from Bonn, "Bonn Ready to Invalidate Munich Pact as of 1938," *New York Times,* August 17, 1968; F.L. [Fred Luchsinger], "Gefangene der deut-

schen Frage," *Neue Zürcher Zeitung*, August 18, 1968; Antonín Snejdárek, "Several Questions in Czechoslovak-German Relations in Modern History and in Recent Times," a lecture at the Deutsche Gesellschaft für Auswärtige Politik, Bonn, March 29, 1967, in *International Relations* (Prague), vol. 2., 1967, pp. 13-14; Melvin Croan, "Czechoslovakia, Ulbricht, and the German Problem," *Problems of Communism* vol. 18, no. 1 (Jan.-Feb. 1969), pp. 1-7; Larrabee, pp. 142-166. For general Czechoslovak developments see H. Gordon Skilling, *Czechoslovakia's Interrupted Revolution* (Princeton: Princeton Univ. Press, 1976); Galia Golan, *The Czechoslovak Reform Movement; Communism in Crisis, 1962-1968* (Cambridge, England: Cambridge Univ. Press, 1971), *Reform Rule in Czechoslovakia, The Dubček Era 1968-1969* (Cambridge, England; Cambridge Univ. Press, 1973), especially pp. 200-204, 224-225; Barbara Wolfe Jancar, *Czechoslovakia and the Absolute Monopoly of Power; a Study of Political Power in a Communist System* (New York: Praeger, 1971); Vladimir V. Kusin, *The Intellectual Origins of the Prague Spring, the Development of Reformist Ideas in Czechoslovakia, 1956-1967* (Cambridge, England: Cambridge Univ. Press, 1971); Birnbaum, *Peace in Europe*, op. cit., pp. 78-85; R. V. Burks, "The Decline of Communism in Czechoslovakia," RAND P-3939. For 1968 West German- ČSSR relations, cf. Whetten, *Germany's Ostpolitik*, op. cit., p. 23.
81. See T.W. [Theodor Wieser] from Bonn in the *Neue Zürcher Zeitung*, September 13 and 28, 1968; Kurt Becker in *Die Zeit*, October 15, 1968; Karl Kaiser, "Deutsche Aussenpolitik nach der tschechoslowakischen Krise von 1968," *Europa Archiv*, vol. 24, no. 10 (May 25, 1969), pp. 353-364; Wolfe, *Soviet Power and Europe*, op. cit., pp. 414-418, 425-426.
82. S. Kovalev, "Sovereignty and the Internationalist Obligations of Socialist Countries," *Pravda*, September 26, 1968.
83. As Stanley Hoffman had prophetically written in 1967, "If West Germany's aim is a gradual reunification through reassuring East Europe and the Soviet Union about its intentions, and through a gradual kind of subversion of East Germany, then its new policy is probably too subtly balanced to succeed." *Gulliver's Troubles; Or, the Setting of American Foreign Policy* (New York: McGraw-Hill, 1968), p. 434.

84. Koppel, "Sources of Change in West German Ostpolitik," op. cit., pp. 191-204.
85. Ulrich Scheuner, "Entwicklungslinien der deutschen Frage," *Europa Archiv*, vol. 24, no. 13 (July 10, 1969), pp. 453-464. See also Karl Kaiser, "Deutsche Aussenpolitik nach der tschechoslowakischen Krise von 1968," *Europa Archiv* vol. 24, no. 10 (1969), which went much further.
86. William E. Griffith, ed., *The World and the Great Power Triangles.* (Cambridge, Mass.: MIT Press, 1975), *The Soviet Empire: Expansion and Détente* (Lexington, Mass.: Lexington Books, 1976).
87. This is not a view generally held in the Federal Republic. For a rare similar West German view see Schmid, *Politik des Ausverkaufs?*, op. cit., pp. 84-85.
88. Keith Bush, "Die Dezember-Sitzung 1969 des Oberston Sowjets der UdSSR," *Osteuropa Wirtschaft,* no. 1 (1970), pp. 32-41; Gertrude Schroeder, "Soviet Technology: System vs. Progress," *Problems of Communism*, vol. 19, no. 5 (Sept.-Oct. 1970), pp. 19-30, cited from Larrabee, p. 176, q.v.
89. Schmid, *Politik des Ausverkaufs?*, op. cit., p. 84.
90. Cf. Wolfgang Wagner, "Voraussetzungen und Folgen der deutschen Ostpolitik," *Europa Archiv*, vol. 25, no. 17 (Sept. 10, 1970), pp. 627-638.
91. Re SALT, Gromyko in *Pravda*, June 28, 1968; Lawrence T. Caldwell, *Soviet Attitudes to SALT,* Adelphi Paper no. 75 (London: ISS, Feb. 1971); Thomas Wolfe, "Soviet Approaches to SALT," *Problems of Communism*, vol. 19, no. 5 (Sept.-Oct. 1970), pp. 1-10; Zamyatin in *Pravda*, January 21, 1969. For the Balkans, J. F. Brown, "Romania Today: The Strategy of Defiance," *Problems of Communism,* vol. 18, no. 2 (March-Apr. 1969), pp. 32-38; F. Stephen Larrabee, "The Rumanian Challenge to Soviet Hegemony," *Orbis*, vol. 17, no. 1 (Spring 1973), pp. 227-246, "The Balkans," *Survey*, vol. 18, no. 3 (Summer 1972), pp. 16-35; Robert R. King, "Autonomy and Détente: The Problems of Rumanian Foreign Policy," *Survey*, vol. 20, no. 2/3 (Spring-Summer 1974), pp. 46-58; F. Stephen Larrabee, "Die sowjetische Politik in Osteuropa und das Problem der Entspannung," *Europa Archiv*, vol. 28, no. 8 (Apr. 25, 1973), pp. 274-282. (All cited from Larrabee, pp. 170-171, 203-211, q.v.)

92. *Europa Archiv,* vol. 23, no. 22 (1968), pp. D552–560, cited from Larrabee, p. 182, q.v.

93. Brandt, *Begegnungen und Einsichten,* op. cit., pp. 253–256.

94. D. E. Melnikov, "The German Nation and the Future of Europe," *Mirovaya Ekonomika i Mezhdunarodniye Otnosheniya,* November 1968, pp. 39–50. See also his "History Cautions," ibid., September 1969, pp. 28–38; A. N. Kovalev, "For Relaxation of Tension and Security in Europe," *Kommunist,* May 1969, pp. 92–102.

95. Schulz, "Die sowjetische Deutschlandpolitik," op. cit., pp. 279–280.

96. Brandt, *Begegnungen und Einsichten,* op. cit., p. 256; Larrabee, P. 186.

97. Klaus Mehnert, "Der Moskauer Vertrag," *Osteuropa,* vol. 20, no. 12 (Dec. 1970), pp. 809–830 (the best analysis); Gerhard Wettig, "Die Berlin Krise 1969," ibid., vol. 19, no. 9 (Sept. 1969), pp. 685–697; Larrabee, pp. 191–200; Schulz, "Die sowjetische Deutschlandpolitik," op. cit., pp. 279–280; Brandt, *Begegnungen und Einsichten,* op. cit., pp. 296–300.

98. *Neues Deutschland,* Feb. 7, 8, 9, 1969), reprinted in *Deutschland Archiv,* vol. 2, no. 3 (1969), pp. 299–302, cited from Larrabee, p. 187, q.v.

99. For the Ulbricht letter see *Neues Deutschland,* Feb. 27, 1969, reprinted in *Deutschland Archiv,* vol. 2, no. 3 (1969), p. 307; for Tsarapkin and the letter see Binder in the *New York Times,* February 25, 1969, both cited from Larrabee, pp. 188–189, q.v.

100. Suslov declared that "the thesis according to which the SPD was the greatest danger, and because of which in a certain period the main thrust of the KPD was against it, in the last analysis led to sectarianism." (*Kommunist,* no. 5, 1969, p. 9, passed for the press, March 26, 1969.) *Neues Deutschland* (March 26, 1969), p. 4) translated this as "should have been directed against." Ulbricht on the same occasion denounced the SPD for refusing at that time to cooperate with the KPD (*Neues Deutschland,* March 27, 1969, p. 4). I owe this point and the references to Mehnert, "Der Moskauer Vertrag," op. cit., pp. 812–813. Cf. Larrabee, pp. 194–195.

101. Text: *Europa Archiv,* vol. 24, no. 7 (1969), pp. D151–153.

See Brandt, *Begegnungen und Einsichten,* op. cit., pp. 256-257; Viktor Meier, "Neue Phase in den deutsch-sowjetischen Beziehungen," *Osteuropa,* vol. 20, no. 3 (March 1970), cited from Larrabee, p. 207, q.v.; ibid., pp. 196-200; Schmid, *Politik des Ausverkaufs,* op. cit., pp. 82-83.

102. Gerhard Wettig, *Europäische Sicherheit; das europäische Staatensystem in der sowjetischen Aussenpolitik 1966-1972,* (Düsseldorf, Bertelsmann Universitätsverlag, 1972), pp. 84-96; Mehnert, "Der Moskauer Vertrag," op. cit., p. 813; Löwenthal, ed., *Die Zweite Republik,* op. cit., pp. 678-680; Christian Meier, "Der Budapester Appell der Warschauer Pakt-Staaten," *Berichte des Bundesinstituts für ostwissenschaftliche und internationale Studien,* no. 42 (Aug. 1969); Larrabee, pp. 213-216. For the natural gas deal, see Angela Yergin, op. cit., pp. 312-322.

103. Documentation: U.S. Congress, House of Representatives, "Conference on European Security," Hearings before the Subcommittee on Europe of the Committee of Foreign Affairs (Washington D.C.: GPO, 1972), pp. 144-145.

104. Documentation: Auswärtiges Amt der Bundesrepublik Deutschland, *Die Auswärtige Politik der Bundesrepublik Deutschland* (Cologne: Verlag Wissenschaft und Politik, 1972), pp. 676-677.

105. Documentation: Meissner, ed., *Moskau Bonn,* op. cit., p. 1180.

106. Larrabee, pp. 210-213; Haftendorn, *Abrüstung- und Entspannungspolitik,* op. cit., pp. 233-237; Schulz, "Die sowjetische Deutschlandpolitik," op. cit., p. 281.

107. Brandt, *Begegnungen und Einsichten,* op. cit., pp. 257-261.

108. Löwenthal, ed., *Die Zweite Republik,* op. cit., pp. 678-680; Gomulka speech; see text in *Europa Archiv,* vol. 24, no. 12 (1969), pp. D313-320; A. Ross Johnson, "A New Phase in Polish-West German Relations," *RFE Research,* June 20, July 3, August 12, 1969; Larrabee, pp. 205-207; Karl E. Birnbaum, *East and West Germany: a Modus Vivendi* (Lexington, Mass.: Lexington Books, 1973), p. 6; Bender, *Die Ostpolitik Willy Brandt,* op. cit. pp. 72-73.

109. Larrabee, pp. 216-218.

110. Stern, *Willy Brandt,* op. cit., p. 101.

111. Cf. Löwenthal, ed., *Die Zweite Republik*, op. cit., pp. 673-674; Bender, *Die Ostpolitik Willy Brandts*, op. cit., pp. 38-40; Schmid, *Politik des Ausverkaufs?*, op. cit., pp. 27-28.

Notes to Chapter 5

1. This is primarily based on a special issue on the elections of *Comparative Politics*, vol 2., no. 4 (July 1970), especially the articles by Werner Kaltefleiter and Ernst-Otto Czempiel. See also Roger Morgan, "The 1969 Election in West Germany," *The World Today*, vol. 25, no. 11 (Nov. 1969), pp. 470-477, Willy Brandt, *Begegnungen und Einsichten* (Hamburg: Hoffmann und Campe, 1976), pp. 293-297.

2. Lawrence Whetten, *Germany's Ostpolitik* (New York: Oxford Univ. Press, 1971), pp. 94 ff.

3. Günter Schmid, *Politik des Ausverkaufs?* (Munich: Tuduv, 1975), pp. 53-67. For the Grand Coalition's Ostpolitik see also Jens Hacker, *Deutsche unter sich* (Stuttgart: Seewald, 1977), pp. 41-109.

4. Peter Bender, *Die Ostpolitik Willy Brandts* (Hamburg: Rowohlt, 1972), p. 53.

5. Schmid, *Politik des Ausverkaufs?*, op. cit., pp. 73-77.

6. Cf. ibid., p. 79.

7. Karl Birnbaum, *East and West Germany: A Modus Vivendi* (Lexington, Mass.: Lexington Books, 1973), pp. 31-32, based on interviews with Bahr in late 1971.

8. Richard Löwenthal, ed., *Die zweite Republic* (Stuttgart: Seewald Verlag, 1974), pp. 680-681.

9. F. Stephen Larrabee, "The Politics of Reconciliation: Moscow and the West German Ostpolitik, 1966-1972" (unpublished Ph.D. dissertation, Columbia University, 1977). pp. 308-341, (Hereafter cited as "Larrabee.")

10. Birnbaum, *East and West Germany*, op. cit., pp. 54-56. See also Schmid, *Politik des Ausverkaufs?*, op. cit., pp. 119-127.

11. Documentation: Russian and German texts: *Osteuropa*, vol. 20, no. 12 (Dec. 1970), pp. 821-822; English texts: *Documentation Relating to the Federal Government's Policy of Détente* (Bonn: Federal Press and Information Office, 1974) (the most convenient collection of the texts of all the treaties), *The Treaty of August 12, 1970* (Bonn: Federal Press and Information Office, 1970). In my view the most illuminating analysis is

by Klaus Mehnert, "Der Moskauer Vertrag," *Osteuropa*, vol. 20, no. 12 (Dec. 1970), pp. 809-830. See also Wolfgang Wagner, "Voraussetzungen und Folgen der deutschen Ostpolitik. Der Vertrag von Moskau und seine Bedeutung für die internationale Lage," *Europa Archiv*, vol. 25, no. 17 (Sept. 10, 1970), pp. 627-638; two articles by senior West German diplomats, Paul Frank, "Sicherheitsprobleme im Lichte des Moskauer Vertrags," ibid., no. 24 (Dec. 25, 1970), pp. 867-876, Georg Ferdinand Duckwitz, "Die Wende im Osten," *Aussenpolitik*, vol. 21, no. 11 (Nov. 1970), pp. 645-660; and a critical analysis by CDU foreign policy expert Karl Carstens, "Eine Wende in der Deutschland-Politik," *Frankfurter Allgemeine Zeitung*, August 25, 1970. See also Helmut Allardt, *Moskauer Tagebuch* (Düsseldorf: Econ, 1973) (critical); Schulz, "Die sowjetische Deutschlandpolitik," pp. 282 ff.; Löwenthal, ed., *Die zweite Republic*, pp. 681-683; Birnbaum, *East and West Germany,* op. cit., pp. 30-40.

12. Tr. from text in *Europa Archiv*, vol. 24, no. 21 (Nov. 10, 1969), pp. D499-506, at p. D500.

13. Löwenthal, ed., *Die zweite Republik*, op. cit., p. 682.

14. Grigoriev in *Pravda*, October 22, 1969; Brezhnev in ibid., October 7, 1969; Kosygin in Allardt, *Moskauer Tagebuch*, p. 214, all cited from Larrabee, pp. 224-226, q.v.; S. Zonov, "Current Problems of World Politics," *Mirovaya Ekonomika i Mezhdunarodniye Otnosheniya,* January 1970, pp. 57-76; L. Khodorkovskii and L. Istayagin, "Bonn Alternatives," ibid., pp. 77-84.

15. The members "were not unanimous in their assessment of the intentions of the new Bonn coalition...," *Mlada Fronta,* November 4, 1969. See also DDR Foreign Minister Winzer arguing that it would be "wrong to regard such bilateral agreements as necessary preliminary steps ... to a security conference," *Neues Deutschland*, November 5, 1969, *Horizont*, no. 46 (1969), both cited from Larrabee, pp. 223-226, q.v. (excellent analysis). See also A. Ross Johnson, "The Warsaw Pact's Campaign for 'European Security'," Rand R-565-PR, November 1970, pp. 61-62. Documentation: U.S. Congress, House of Representatives, "Conference on European Security," Hearings before the Sub-committee on Europe of the Committee on Foreign Affairs (Washington, D.C.: GPO, 1972), pp. 146-147.

16. Löwenthal, ed., *Die zweite Republik*, op. cit., p. 682; Larra-

bee, pp. 227-228; Helga Haftendorn, *Abrüstungs und Entspannungspolitik zwischen Sicherheitbefriedigung und Friedenssicherung. Zur Aussenpolitik der BRD 1955-1973* (Düsseldorf: Bertelsmann Universitätsverlag, 1974), pp. 187-191; Catherine Kelleher, *Germany and the Politics of Nuclear Weapons* (New York: Columbia Univ. Press, 1975), p. 295 (for NPT ratification). Documentation: Meissner, *Moskau-Bonn* (Cologne Verlag Wissenschaft und Politik, 1972) vol. 2., pp. 1195-1202.

17. Birnbaum, *East and West Germany,* op. cit., pp. 37-38; Schmid, *Politik des Ausverkaufs?,* op. cit., pp. 119-127. Documentation: Meissner, ed., *Moskau Bonn,* op. cit., vol. 2, pp. 1204-1208; Bundesministerium für innerdeutsche Beziehungen, *Die Entwicklung der Beziehungen zwischen der Bundesrepublik Deutschland und der Deutschen Demokratischen Republik: Bericht und Dokumentation,* April 1973, pp. 49 ff; *Texte zur Deutschlandpolitik,* vol. 7, pp. 5 ff.

18. Löwenthal, ed., *Die zweite Republik,* op. cit., pp. 685-686; Birnbaum, *East and West Germany,* op. cit., p. 38; Bender, *Die Ostpolitik Willy Brandts,* op. cit., p. 55; Brandt, *Begegnungen und Einsichten,* op. cit., p. 488. Documentation: *Die Entwicklung der Beziehungen,* op. cit., p. 52.

19. Birnbaum, *East and West Germany,* op. cit., p. 23; Dettmar Cramer, *Gefragt: Egon Bahr* (Bornheim: Dagmar Zirngibl, 1975), pp. 55-64.

20. Allardt, *Moskauer Tagebuch,* op. cit., pp. 276-283; Larrabee, pp. 235-236.

21. Shub in *Washington Post,* May 27, 1970, Binder in *New York Times,* May 28, 1970, cited from Larrabee, p. 237.

22. Löwenthal, ed., *Die zweite Republik,* op. cit., pp. 683-685.

23. Ibid., pp. 683-684; Larrabee, pp. 238-242; "Bahr Paper," *Quick,* July 1, 1970; Bahr and Gromyko Papers, *Die Welt,* July 23, 1970; Cramer, *Gefragt,* op. cit., p. 62.

24. Larrabee, p. 255

25. Ibid., p. 240, citing from the excerpts from the protocols of the Gromyko-Bahr, Gromyko-Scheel and Gromyko-Brandt negotiations, in *Süddeutsche Zeitung,* April 19, 1972, and ibid., pp. 264-265. Documentation: Meissner, ed., *Moskau Bonn,* op. cit., vol. 2, pp. 1220-1223; *Texte zur Deutschlandpolitik,* vol. 6, pp. 90-92.

26. The fullest account, with long excerpts of the stenographic protocol, is in Brandt, *Begegnungen and Einsichten*, op. cit., pp. 484-501. Documentation: *Europa Archiv*, vol. 25, no. 9 (May 10, 1970), pp. D203-D224, *Deutschland Archiv*, vol. 3, no. 5 (May 1970), pp. 505-524. Analysis: Joachim Bölke, "Zur Erfurter Begegnung," *Europa Archiv*, vol. 25, no. 7 (Apr. 10, 1970), pp. 223-236; Gottfried Vetter, "Annäherung mit Hindernissen," ibid., vol. 25, no. 9 (May .20, 1970), pp. 301-310; F.L. [Fred Luchsinger], "Kein 'Durchbruch' in Erfurt," *Neue Zürcher Zeitung*, March 22, 1970; Rolf Zundel, "Seit Erfurt ist alles anders," *Die Zeit*, March 31, 1970; P. J. Franceschini, "La fiction abondonnée," *Le Monde,* sélection hebdomadaire, March 19-25, 1970; Ilse Spittman, "Deutscher Gipfel in Erfurt," *Deutschland Archiv*, vol. 3, no. 4 (Apr. 1970), pp. 431-439; journalistic eyewitness accounts: David Binder in *New York Times,* March 20, 1970, T.W. [Theodor Wieser] in *Neue Zürcher Zeitung*, March 21, 1970.

27. The fullest account is in Brandt, *Begegnungen und Einsichten*, op. cit., pp. 501-509. Documentation: *Deutschland Archiv*, vol. 3., no. 6 (June 1970), pp. 620-655; *Die Entwicklung der Beziehungen,* op. cit., pp. 54 ff., *Texte zur Deutschlandpolitik*, vol. 4, pp. 325 ff., vol. 5, pp. 96 ff. Analysis: Joachim Nawrocki, "Ein Offenes Ende in Kassel," ibid., pp. 668-669; E.M. [Eric Mettler], "Getrennte oder gemeinsame Ostpolitik?", *Neue Zürcher Zeitung*, May 24, 1970; Löwenthal, ed., *Die zweite Republik*, op. cit., p. 84; journalistic eyewitness accounts: T.W. [Theodor Wieser] in *Neue Zürcher Zeitung,* May 23 and 24, 1970; Carl-Christian Kaiser in *Die Zeit*, June 2, 1970. See also Löwenthal, ed., *Die zweite Republic*, op. cit., p. 84; Larrabee, pp. 258 ff.; Schmid, *Politik des Ausverkaufs?*, op. cit., pp. 133-137, 141-146.

28. Larrabee, pp. 260-262.

29. Birnbaum, *East and West Germany*, op. cit., p. 39.

30. Ibid., pp. 56-57; Larrabee, pp. 267-272; Brandt, *Begegnungen und Einsichten*, op. cit., pp. 428-455, especially regarding the Brandt-Brezhnev meeting. I differ with the unfavorable analysis in Laszlo Görgey, *Bonn's Eastern Policy, 1964-1971* (Hamden, Conn.: Archon, 1972), pp. 166-168. Documentation: *Texte zur Deutschlandpolitik,* vol. 6, pp. 93-95; Press and

Information Office of the Government of the Federal Republic of Germany, *Documentation Relating to the Federal Government's Policy of Détente* (Bonn, 1974) pp. 13-15.

31. Brandt, *Begegnungen und Einsichten*, op. cit., pp. 524-543; Löwenthal, ed., *Die zweite Republik*, op. cit., pp. 684-685; Adam Bromke and Harald von Riekhoff, "The West German-Polish Treaty," *The World Today*, vol. 27, no. 3 (March 1917), pp. 124-131; Neal Ascherson, "Poland's Place in Europe," ibid., vol 25, no. 12 (December 1969), pp. 520-529; Wolfgang Wagner, "Ein neuer Anfang zwischen Polen und Deutschen. Der Vertrag von Warschau," *Europa Archiv*, vol. 25, no. 23 (Dec. 10, 1970), pp. 837-844; ok. [Bogdan Osadczuk-Korab], "Polens aussenpolitische Taktik," *Neue Zürcher Zeitung*, December 31, 1969, "Die Anbahnung des Dialogs zwischen Warschau und Bonn," ibid., December 13, 1969. Documentation: *Europa Archiv*, vol. 26, no. 1 (Jan. 10, 1972), pp. D1-D32; Ingo von Münch, ed., *Ostverträge II: Deutsch-polnische Verträge* (Berlin and New York: Walter de Gruyter, 1971), pp. 186 ff.

32. Ulrich Scheuner, "Die Oder-Neisse-Grenze und die Normalisierung der Beziehungen zum Osten," *Europa Archiv*, vol. 25, no. 11 (June 10, 1970), pp. 377-386, at pp. 379, 384.

33. This last point is very well made by Larrabee, p. 229.

34. Documentation: *The Quadripartite Agreement on Berlin* (Bonn: Federal Press and Information Office, 1971), *Documentation Relating to the Federal Government's Policy of Détente* (Bonn: Federal Press and Information Office, 1974); also *Europa Archiv*, vol. 26, no. 19 (Oct. 10, 1971), pp. D441-D470. Analysis: Dieter Mahncke, "In Search of a *modus vivendi* for Berlin," *The World Today*, vol. 26, no. 4 (Apr. 1970), pp. 137-146, "The Berlin Agreement: Balance and Prospects," ibid., vol. 17, no. 12 (Dec. 1971), pp. 511-521, *Berlin im geteilten Deutschland* (Munich: Oldenbourg, 1973); Wolfgang Wagner, "Das Berlin-Problem als Angelpunkt eines Ausgleichs zwischen West und Ost in Europa," *Europa Archiv*, vol. 26, no. 11 (June 10, 1971), pp. 375-382; Gerhard Wettig, "Aktionsmuster der sowjetischen Berlin-Politik," *Aussenpolitik*, vol. 19, no. 6 (June 1968), pp. 325-339, "Das Berlin-Problem-Ruckblick und Gegenwart," *Aus Politik und Zeitgeschichte*, Beilage zu *Das Parlament*, no. 9 (1969), pp. 3-26, "Das Entspannungsproblem Berlin," *Osteuropa*, vol. 21, no. 1 (Jan. 1971), pp. 1-22, *Com-*

munity and Conflict in the Socialist Camp, op. cit., pp. 82–117; Gunther Doeker, Klaus Melsheimer, and Dieter Schröder, "Berlin and the Quadripartite Agreement of 1971," *American Journal of International Law*, vol. 67, no. 1 (Jan. 1973), pp. 44–62; Löwenthal, ed., *Die zweite Republik*, op. cit., pp. 686–688; Larrabee, pp. 272 ff. See also Brandt, *Begegungen und Einsichten*, op. cit., pp. 509–517.

35. Analyzed in Löwenthal, ed., *Die zweite Republik*, op. cit., p. 687.

36. Larrabee, p. 227.

37. Gerhard Wettig, "Die amerikanisch-chinesische Annäherung aus sowjetischer Perspektive," *Osteuropa*, vol. 22, no. 7 (July 1972), pp. 489–496; Larrabee, p. 298.

38. For an informed analysis of the two drafts, see Wolfgang Wagner, "Mit den Augen des Westens und Ostens," *Der Tagesspiegel*, April 28, 1971, cited in Löwenthal, ed., *Die zweite Republik*, op. cit., p. 698, 292.

39. Yu. Rzevski, "Important Stimulus," *Pravda*, August 18, 1970, quoted and translated in Larrabee, p. 271 q.v. for analysis; Gerd Hagen, "Die DDR und der Moskauer Vertrag," *Aussenpolitik*, vol. 21, no. 11 (Nov. 1970), pp. 661–667.

40. Larrabee, p. 281.

41. Löwenthal, ed., *Die zweite Republik*, op. cit., p. 689.

42. A. Ross Johnson, "Polish Perspectives, Past and Present," *Problems of Communism*, vol. 20, no. 4 (July–Aug. 1971), pp. 59–72.

43. Birnbaum, *East and West Germany*, op. cit., p. 59; Larrabee, p. 285.

44. Löwenthal, ed., *Die zweite Republik*, op. cit., p. 687; Larrabee, pp. 331–334.

45. Gregory Flynn, "European Security and the Divided Germany in the Era of Negotiations, 1969–1972" (unpublished Ph.D. dissertation, Fletcher School, 1975), p. 56.

46. Birnbaum, *East and West Germany,* op. cit., pp. 15, 60.

47. I have been unable to find any extensive published analysis of Ulbricht's fall. Perhaps the best one is by the late Heinz Lippmann (Honecker's deputy when the latter was head of the DDR youth organization, the FDJ) in his *Honecker and the New Politics of Europe*, tr. Helen Sebba (New York: Macmillan, 1972), pp. 213–225. I have drawn on unpublished papers by two of my

students, Gregory Flynn, "Der Sturz Ulbrichts: A Lesson in Soviet Bloc Diplomacy" (Fletcher School, 1972), Paul F. Walker, "Ulbricht's Ouster, May 1971–The Soviet Perspective" (MIT, 1973). For background see Gerhard Wettig, "Die Berlin-Politik der USSR und der DDR," *Aussenpolitik*, vol. 21, no. 5 (May 1970), pp. 284–296, "East Berlin and the Moscow Treaty," *Aussenpolitik* (English ed.), vol. 22, no. 3 (1971), pp. 259–269, *Community and Conflict in the Socialist Camp*, op. cit., pp. 118–135; Gerd Hagen, "Die DDR und der Moskauer Vertrag," op. cit.; Peter C. Ludz, "Von Ulbricht zu Honecker," *Osteuropäischer Rundschau*, vol. 9, no. 1 (Sept. 1971), pp. 1–7, "Continuity and Change since Ulbricht," *Problems of Communism*, vol. 21, no. 2 (March-Apr. 1972), pp. 56–67, revised in his *Die DDR zwischen Ost und West. Politische Analysen von 1961 bis 1976* (Munich: Beck, 1977), pp. 144–165; Robert Bleimann, "Ostpolitik and the GDR," *Survey*, vol. 18, no. 3 (Summer 1972), pp. 36–53; Larrabee, pp. 282–290; Schmid, *Politik des Ausverkaufs?*, op. cit., pp. 152–153, 274–176. For the contrast between Ulbricht's and Brezhnev's pronouncements concerning West Berlin and the Federal Republic, see, for example, Ulbricht in *Neues Deutschland*, June 16 and November 15, 1970, and January 14, 1971, and Brezhnev in *Pravda*, November 30, 1970, and at the CPSU Twenty-fourth Congress in *Pravda*, March 31, 1971. For the view that Moscow was not primarily responsible for Ulbricht's fall, see N. Edwina Moreton, "The Impact of Détente on Relations Between the Member States of the Warsaw Pact: Efforts to Resolve the German Problem and Their Implications for East Germany's Role in Eastern Europe, 1967–1972" (unpublished Ph.D. dissertation, Glasgow University, 1976), pp. 295–299.

48. *New York Times*, September 24, 1971, cited from Larrabee, p. 291.

49. *Die Berlin-Regelung. Das Viermächte-Abkommen über Berlin und die ergänzenden Vereinbraungen* (Bonn: Presse-und Informationsamt der Bundesregierung, Dec. 1971), pp. 259–260; Schmid, *Politik des Ausverkaufs?*, op. cit., p. 153; Hartmut Schiedermair, *Der völkerrechtliche Status Berlins nach dem Viermächte-Abkommen vom 3. September 1971* (Berlin: Springer, 1975). Documentation: *Texte zur Deutschlandpolitik*, vol. 8. pp. 371–384.

50. Brandt, *Begegnungen und Einsichten*, op. cit., pp. 459-471; Löwenthal, ed., *Die zweite Republik*, op. cit., pp. 688-689. Documentation: Meissner, ed., *Moskau Bonn*, op. cit., vol. 2, pp. 1361-1366; Federal Republic of Germany, Auswärtiges Amt, *Die Auswärtige Politik der Bundesrepublik Deutschalnd* (Cologne: Verlag Wissenschaft und Politik, 1972), pp. 820-832; *Texte zur Deutschlandpolitik*, vol. 9, pp. 110-115.

51. Löwenthal, ed., *Die zweite Republik*, op. cit., p. 287;

52. Birnbaum, *East and West Germany*, op. cit., pp. 74-75; Brandt, *Begegnungen und Einsichten*, op. cit., pp. 517-523.

53. Birnbaum, *East and West Germany*, op. cit., pp. 41-43.

54. Ibid., pp. 43-45. Documentation: *Text zur Deutschlandpolitik*, vol. 9, pp. 159-167, pp. 320 ff.: *Die Entwicklung der Beziehungen*, op. cit., pp. 104 ff.: *Documentation Relating to the Federal Government*, op. cit., pp. 55 ff.

55. Angela Stent Yergin, "The Political Economy of West German-Soviet Trade" (unpublished Ph.D. dissertation, Harvard University, 1977), pp. 369-389; Appendix, Table I; Otto Wolff von Amerongen, "Aspekte des deutschen Osthandels," *Aussenpolitik*, vol. 21, no. 3 (March 1970), pp. 143-149; Gerhard Ollig, "Economic Relations with the GDR," ibid. (English ed.), vol. 26, no. 2 (1975), pp. 185-200; Peter Hermes, "Trends of Trade with the Comecon Countries," ibid. (English ed.), vol. 26, no. 4 (1975), pp. 367-380.

56. Birnbaum, *East and West Germany*, op. cit., p. 46.

57. *Die Welt*, April 16, 1972, cited from Larrabee, p. 346.

58. Larrabee, pp. 322-362 (by far the most complete account, upon which I have primarily relied); Birnbaum, *East and West Germany*, op. cit., pp. 45-47; Christian Hacke, *Die Ost- und Deutschlandpolitik der CDU/CSU. Wege und Irrwege der Opposition seit 1969* (Cologne: Verlag Wissenschaft und Politik, 1975), pp. 1-79 (written from a left-wing CDU viewpoint: sharply critical of almost all CDU/CSU leaders except Leisler Kiep and Richard von Weizsäcker); Brandt, *Begegnungen und Einsichten*, op. cit., pp. 471-473; W. W. Kulski, *Germany and Poland: From War to Peaceful Relations* (New York: Syracuse Univ. Press, 1976), pp. 203-275; Geoffrey Pridham, "The Ostpolitik and the Opposition in West Germany," in Roger Tilford, ed., *The Ostpolitik and Political Change in West Germany* (Farnborough: Saxon and Lexington, Mass.: Lexington Books,

1975), pp. 45–48 (excellent analysis); Elizabeth Noelle and Erich Peter Neumann, eds., *Jahrbuch der offentlichen Meinung 1968–1973* (Allensbach and Bonn: Institut fur Demoskopie, 1974), p. 570 (for public support for ratification).

59. Birnbaum, *East and West Germany,* op. cit., p. 44. Documentation: *Die Entwicklung der Beziehungen,* op. cit., pp. 133 ff.: *Texte zur Deutschlandpolitik,* vol. 11, pp. 380 ff.: *Documentation Relating to the Federal Government,* op. cit., pp. 71 ff.

60. Cf. Birnbaum, *East and West Germany,* op. cit., pp. 77–85.

61. Ibid., pp. 43–47, 73–89 (on whose analysis of the Basic Treaty and the negotiations preceding it I have drawn extensively); Hacke, *Die Ost- und Deutschlandpolitik der CDU/CSU.* op. cit., pp. 96–101; Karl Kaiser, "Prospects for West Germany after the Berlin Agreement," *The World Today,* vol. 28, no. 1 (Jan. 1972), pp. 30–35; Robert Bleimann, "Détente and the GDR: The Internal Implications," *The World Today,* vol. 29, no. 6 (June 1973), pp. 257–265; Roger Morgan, "Political Prospects in Bonn," ibid., vol. 28, no. 8 (Aug. 1972), pp. 351–359; Hilary Black, "The East-West German Treaty," ibid., no. 12 (Dec. 1972), pp. 512–515; Gerhard Wettig, "Das Berlin-Problem—Rückblick und Gegenwart," op. cit., "Prämissen der Kontroverse um die Anerkennung der DDR," *Deutschland Archiv,* vol. 2, no. 3 (March 1969), pp. 257–261 (a useful review of controversial literature on the subject, including Peter Bender's *Zehn Gründe für die Anerkennung der DDR),* "Ost-Berlin im Schatten der Moskauer Deutschland-Politik," *Aussenpolitik,* vol. 20, no. 5 (May 1969), pp. 261–272, and "Die Berlin-Politik der UdSSR und der DDR," ibid., vol. 21, no. 5 (May 1970), pp. 284–296; Wolfgang Wagner, "Aussichten der Ostpolitik nach dem Abschluss der Berlin-Verhandlungen," *Europa Archiv,* vol. 27, no. 3 (Feb. 10, 1972), pp. 79–86, "Ein Modus Vivendi in Deutschland. Der Grundvertrag der beiden deutschen Staaten und seine Bedeutung für Europa," ibid., vol. 28, no. 1 (Jan. 10, 1973), pp. 1–6; Wilhelm Kewenig, "Die Bedeutung des Grundvertrags für das Verhältnis der beiden deutschen Staaten," ibid., no. 2 (Jan. 25, 1973), pp. 37–46; Eberhard Schulz, "Die DDR als Element der sowjetischen Westeuropa-Politik," ibid., vol. 27, no. 24 (Dec. 25, 1972),

pp. 835–843; Dettmar Cramer, "Die DDR und die Bonner Ost-politik," ibid., vol. 25, no. 5 (March 20, 1970), pp. 167–172; Josef Joffe, "Westverträge, Ostverträge und die Kontinuität der deutschen Aussenpolitik," ibid., vol. 28, no. 4 (Feb. 25, 1973), pp. 111–124; Manfred Rexin, "Zwanzig Jahre Aussenpolitik der DDR," *Liberal*, October 1969, pp. 725–750; Dieter Blumenwitz, "Der Grundvertrag zwischen der Bundesrepublik Deutschland und der DDR," *Politische Studien*, vol. 207, no. 1 (Jan.–Feb. 1973), pp. 3–10 (very critical); Dettmar Cramer, "Modifizierte Abgrenzung?" *Deutschland Archiv*, vol. 4, no. 10 (Oct. 1971), pp. 1009–1016, "Ostpolitik im Wettlauf mit der Zeit," ibid., vol. 5, no. 1 (Jan. 1972), pp. 2–6; Peter Bender, "The Special Relationship of the Two German States," *The World Today*, vol. 20, no. 9 (Sept. 1973), pp. 389–397; Jens Hacker, *Deutsche unter sich*, op. cit., pp. 67–109.

62. Schriften des Forschungsinstituts der Deutschen Gesel-lschaft für Auswärtige Politik, *Die Aussenpolitik Chinas* (Mu-nich: Oldenbourg, 1975), pp. 394–408; for Brandt's reassurances to Brezhnev regarding Bonn-Peking relations at Oreanda, see his *Begegnungen und Einsichten*, op. cit., pp. 469–470; for the es-tablishment of relations, ibid., pp. 549–553.

63. Wolfgang Wagner, "Der Prager Vertrag also Schlussstein der bilateralen Ostpolitik," *Europa Archiv*, vol. 29, no. 3 (Feb. 10, 1974), pp. 63–70; Robert W. Dean, "Bonn-Prague Relations: The Politics of Reconciliation," *The World Today*, vol. 29, no. 4 (Apr. 1973), pp. 149–159; James H. Wolfe, "West Germany and Czechoslovakia: The Struggle for Reconciliation," *Orbis*, vol. 14, no. 1 (Spring 1970), pp. 154–179; Brandt, *Begegnungen und Einsichten*, op. cit., pp. 543–549; Rudolf Hilf, "Die tsche-choslowakische Forderung auf Ungültigkeit des Münchner Ab-kommens ab initio," *Osteuropa*, vol. 21, no. 11 (Nov. 1971), pp. 880–884; H. Hajek and L. Niznansky, "Signing of FRG-Czechoslovak Treaty: The Thorny Road to Normalization," *Radio Free Europe Research*, December 7, 1973; Melvin Croan, "Czechoslovakia, Ulbricht, and the German Problem," *Problems of Communism*, vol. 18, no. 1 (Jan–Feb. 1969), pp. 1–7; Chris-tian Schmidt-Häuer, "Die Deutschlandpolitik der CSSR," *Mo-derne Welt*, vol. 10, no. 4 (1969), pp. 416–420. Documenta-tion: Federal Republic of Germany, Press and Information Of-

tion: Federal Republic of Germany, Press and Information Office, *Documentation Relating to the Federal Goverment's Policy of Détente* (Bonn, 1974), pp. 36-54, *Europa Archiv,* vol. 29, no. 3 (Feb. 10, 1974), pp. D57–D71.

Notes to Chapter 6
1. F. Stephen Larrabee, "Soviet-West German Relations: Normalization and Beyond," *Radio Liberty Research,* May 16, 1975; Helga Haftendorn, "Ostpolitik Revisited 1976," *The World Today,* vol. 32, no. 6 (June 1976), pp. 232-229; Melvin Croan, *East Germany: The Soviet Connection,* The Washington Papers, vol. 4, no. 36 (Beverly Hills and London: Sage, 1976); Anita Dasbach-Mallinckrodt, *Wer macht die Aussenpolitik der DDR?,* (Düsseldorf: Droste Verlag, 1972) and *Die Zeit,* November 26, 1976; Gerhard Wettig, "Die praktische Anwendung des Berlin-Abkommens durch UdSSR und DDR (1972-1976)," *Berichte den Bundesinstituts für ostwissenschaftliche und internationale Studien,* no. 31 (Aug. 1976); Klaus Schütz, "Berlin in the Age of Détente," *The World Today,* vol. 31, no. 1 (Jan. 1975), pp. 29-35; Günther van Well, "Die Teilnahme Berlins am internationalen Geschehen: ein dringender Punkt auf der Ost-West-Tagesordnung," *Europa Archiv,* vol. 31, no. 20 (Oct. 25, 1976), pp. 647-657; Jens Hacker, *Deutsche unter sich* (Stuttgart: Seewald, 1977), pp. 110-133; Hans-Peter Schwarz, "Brauchen wir ein neues deutschlandpolitisches Konzept?", *Europa Archiv,* vol. 32, no. 11 (June 10, 1977), pp. 327-338.
2. Philip Windsor, "Europe and the Superpowers" in Nils Andrén and Karl E. Birnbaum, *Beyond Détente* (Leyden: Sijthoff, 1976), pp. 37-50, at p. 46.
3. *Die Zeit,* November 28, 1976; Rudolf Bahro, *Die Alternative* (Cologne: Europäisches Verlagsanstalt, 1977); a book for whose publication in West Germany its author, a middle-level SED functionary, was arrested; and a "manifesto" allegedly (and in my view probably) written by various anonymous SED cadres and published in *Der Spiegel,* Jan. 2 and 9, 1978.
4. For a positive view of the Federal Republic's stability, with which I agree, see Hans Schuster, "Diese gelungene Republik," *Merkur,* vol. 28, no. 5 (May 1974), pp. 401-417 and "Bleibt die Bundesrepublik regierbar?", ibid., vol. 29, no. 10 (Oct. 1975), pp. 956-969; for a more negative view see Arnulf Baring,

"Zweifel," ibid., vol. 28, no. 5 (May 1974), pp. 418-431.
5. Quoted from Hassner, "Europe: Old Conflicts, New Rules,"
Orbis, vol. 17, no. 3 (Fall 1973), pp. 895-911, at p. 897.
6. Tr. from Hassner, "L'Europe de la guerre froide à la paix
chaude," *Défense nationale,* vol. 29 (March 1973), pp. 35-54,
at pp. 45-47.

Index

Index

Anti-Semitism, 3, 16
Antonescu, Ion, 22
Arab states, 151–152
Arms control, 233
  Adenauer's policies in, 66, 76,
    83–85
  Brandt's view of, 134
  détente and, 66
  Erhard's policies on, 131
  flexible Atlanticists and, 113
  Grand Coalition on, 135, 139
  Johnson's policies on, 107
  mutual balanced force reduction
    (MBFR) in, 146, 177–178,
    180, 217, 227, 230
  1955 summit conference on,
    70–71
  non-agression pacts in, 14, 91,
    104
  nonuse of force treaties in, 168–
    169, 189, 191, 195
  peace note and, 128
  post-war Soviet policy on, 31, 33,
    35
  post-World War II period and, 31
  Rapacki Plan in, 80, 82–83
  reunification and, 66, 71, 76
  SALT negotiations in, 166, 169,
    233
  second Berlin crisis and, 87, 92
  test-ban treaty in, 104–105, 107,
    109
  West German support for, 133
  see also Multilateral Nuclear
    Force (MLF); Nonproliferation
    treaty (NPT); Nuclear policy;
    Rearmament, German
Ascherson, Neal, 273n69, 284n31
Ashkenasi, Abraham, 251n18
Asia, 158
Atlantic Alliance, 44, 108–109
Atlanticism, 62, 147
Attlee, Clement, 35
Atomic weapons. See Arms control;
  Nuclear policy
Auseinanderleben, 182
Austria
  Anschluss in, 8
  Bismarck's policies in, 2, 42

German policy in, 1, 12–13
Hitler's policies in, 8, 16, 18
nationalism in, 3
Polish feelings toward, 3
resistance movement in, 23–24
Russian rivalry with, 3
World War I and, 4–5
Austrian State Treaty, 69–70

Baden, 41
Bahne, Siegfried, 246n45
Bahr, Egon, 262n22, 264n33
  East-German-West German treaty
    and, 211, 214, 217–218
  flexible leftists and, 117–120
  foreign policy views of, 175
  German security system and, 134
  Italian Communist Party and,
    148
  second Berlin crisis and, 102–
    103, 136
  Soviet-West German negotiations
    and, 187–188, 190, 193
Bahr papers, 190
Bahro, Rudolf, 290n3
Balance of payments, 109
Balkan states, 4, 18–19, 107–108
Bandulet, Bruno, 258n86
Baras, Victor, 263n29
Baring, Arnulf, 43, 249n7, 250nn9,
  12,14, 252n22, 253nn29,31,
  254n40, 255nn46,48–49,53,
  56, 256n61,63, 257nn66,72,
  258nn75,79, 260n8, 290n4
Bark, Dennis L., 256n64
Barzel, Rainer, 213, 215–216
Basch, Antonin, 244n34
Basic Law (1949), 50–51, 218
Bauer, Leo, 148, 248n3
Bavaria, 1, 41–42
Bavarian Christian Social Union.
  See Christian Social Union
  (CSU)
Bechtoldt, Heinrich, 271n54
Becker, Kurt, 265n39, 276n81
Belgium, 4
Beloff, Max, 248n1
Bender, Peter, 262n18, 263n31,
  266n11, 268n26, 270n41,

Index

Index

Index

Gaus, Günter, 260n6
Geburtsfehler theory, 84, 156
Gegenjunktim, 209
Gehl, W. Jürgen, 243n32
Gelbe-Haussen, Eberhard, 254n33
Gemeinschaft, 110–111
Geneva meetings. *See* Summit
meetings
Genscher, Hans-Dietrich, 62, 225
252n22
German Communist Party (KPD).
See Communist Party of
Germany (KPD)
German Democratic Republic
(DDR). *See* East Germany
German option, 190
German Social Democratic Party.
See Social Democratic Party
of Germany (SPD)
Ghana, 152
Gierek, Edward, 196, 202
Gilbert, Feliz, 241n13
Gimbel, John, 248n1
Globke, Hans, 77, 85–87, 97
Globke Plan, 85–87, 249n7
Gniffe, Erich, 38
Godesberg Program, 98
Golan, Halia, 276n80
Gomułka, Władysław, 78, 82–83
Czechoslovakia and, 159–160,
203
Gierek replacement of 202
Grand Coalition and, 141,
144–145, 152–154
Hungary and, 154
Polish-West German relations
and, 168
Soviet-West German relations
and, 183
trade and, 121, 140
Gördeler, Carl, 23, 25
Görgey, Laszlo, 283n30
Gotto, Klaus, 249–250n7, 253n32,
254nn33,35, 256n63, 258n80,
259n91
Grain sales, 105
Graml, Hermann, 241n16, 245–
246n44

Grand Coalition (CDU-SPD)
Budapest Declaration and,
167–169
Bulgaria and, 154–155
Cambodia's recognition of DDR
and, 169
concepts of Ostpolitik of,
133–138
Czechoslovakia and, 158–162
Eastern Europe and, 149
East Germany and, 150–152
exchange of speakers episode
and, 125–126
flexible Atlanticists and, 113–114
globalization of European politics
and, 162–163
Hungary and, 154
in retrospect, 169–171
Italian Communist Party (PCI)
and, 148–149
ministers in, 131–132
nonproliferation treaty and,
138–140
opposition to, 175
Ostpolitik of, 131–171
Poland and, 152–154
reunification of Europe and, 117
Rumania and, 149–150
Soviet policy of, 164–167
Soviet reaction to, 130, 141–147
Soviet Westpolitik in, 163–164
SPD changes in, 112
SPD-FDP coalition and, 173
Western Allies and, 132–133
Yugoslavia in, 156–158
Great Britain
arms control and, 66
colonial policy of, 5, 24
Common Market entry by, 103,
108
détente and, 132
EEC and, 175
Locarno treaties and, 11–12
post-World War I revisionist states
and, 6
Soviet relations with (*see* Soviet-
British relations)
Tehran Conference and, 27

Index

Index

Index

Index

Index

Index

Index

Index